Education plc

The privatisation of education is controversial but is it inevitable? How widespread is it? What does it mean for educational practice?

In *Education plc*, Stephen Ball provides a comprehensive, analytical and empirical account of the privatisation of education. He questions the kind of future we want for education and what role privatisation and the private sector may have in that future. Using policy sociology to describe and critically analyse changes in policy, policy technologies and policy regimes, he looks at the ethical and democratic impacts of these changes and raises the following questions:

- Is there a legitimacy for privatisation based on the convergence of interests between business and the 'third way' state?
- Is the extent and value of private participation in public education misunderstood?
- How is the selling of private company services linked to the remodelling of schools?
- Why have the technical and political issues of privatisation been considered but ethical issues almost totally neglected?
- What is happening here, beyond mere technical changes in the form of public service delivery?
- Is education policy being spoken by new voices?

Drawing upon extensive documentary research and interviews with senior executives from the leading 'education services industry' companies, the author challenges preconceptions about privatisation. He concludes that blanket defence of the public sector as it was, over and against the inroads of privatisation, is untenable and that there is no going back to a past in which the public sector as a whole worked well and worked fairly in the interests of all learners, because there was no such past.

This book breaks new ground and builds on Stephen Ball's previous work on education policy. It should appeal to those researching and studying in the fields of social policy, policy analysis, sociology of education, education research and social economics.

Stephen J. Ball is Karl Mannheim Professor of Sociology of Education at the Institute of Education, University of London, UK.

Education plc

Understanding private sector participation in public sector education

Stephen J. Ball

Routledge
Taylor & Francis
LONDON AND NEW

First published 2007 by Routledge
2 Park Square, Milton Park, Abingdon, Oxon OX14 4RN

Simultaneously published in the USA and Canada
by Routledge
270 Madison Ave, New York, NY 10016

*Routledge is an imprint of the Taylor & Francis Group,
an informa business*

© 2007 Stephen J. Ball

Typeset in Times by
RefineCatch Limited, Bungay, Suffolk
Printed and bound in Great Britain by
Antony Rowe Ltd, Chippenham, Wiltshire

Every effort has been made to ensure that the advice and information
in this book is true and accurate at the time of going to press.
However, neither the publisher nor the authors can accept any legal
responsibility or liability for any errors or omissions that may be made.
In the case of drug administration, any medical procedure or the use
of technical equipment mentioned within this book, you are strongly
advised to consult the manufacturer's guidelines

British Library Cataloguing in Publication Data
A catalogue record for this book is available from the British Library

Library of Congress Cataloging in Publication Data
A catalog record for this book has been requested

ISBN10: 0–415–39940–8 (hbk)
ISBN10: 0–415–39941–6 (pbk)
ISBN10: 0–203–96420–9 (ebk)

ISBN13: 978–0–415–39940–1 (hbk)
ISBN13: 978–0–415–39941–8 (pbk)
ISBN13: 978–0–203–96420–0 (ebk)

The point is "to make the agony of decision-making so intense that you can only escape by thinking".

(Fred Friendly)

Contents

Illustrations

Figures

Tables

Boxes

Acknowledgements

I want to thank the ESRC for their support in funding the fellowship which allowed me to undertake this work. I also want to acknowledge the encouragement I received to start this project which came from talking with Tony Knight over coffee in Carlton, travelling on trains to conferences with Carol Vincent, hearing Dave Gillborn speak and having him listen to my preoccupations, and debating ethics in Balham with Alan Cribb in the Italian. Angie Oria needs special mention for her many hours of searching on the internet and other help, as does Lise Obi, who did all sorts of practical things in support of my fellowship work. Carol Vincent, Mark Olssen, Jane Lethbridge, Hugh Lauder, Alejandra Cardini, Stephen Crump, Bob Lingard, Janet Newman, Dave Gillborn, Brian Davies, Dennis Sargent, John Simpson, Ruth Lupton, Eva Gamarnikov, Michael Peters, Phil Woods and Meg Maguire, especially Meg Maguire, read and made very useful comments on various drafts of chapters.

David Hall of Public Services International Research Unit, Julie Hallam (Unison), David Budge (*TES*), Chris Abbott, Michael Apple, Heather Meakin and Norbert Pachler, David McGahey, Derek Foreman and Leisha Fullick all helped out with information and explanation for which I am grateful, and I thank Peter Gear for help with financial data. The participants in the ZES conference Bremen, EPRU privatisation seminar and ESRC seminar series on privatisation deserve a mention. I am very grateful to all my respondents for their time, frankness and friendliness.

Most of all I thank Trinidad Ball for putting up with me, and for her inspiration and belief, and I dedicate the book to Betty Ball.

Abbreviations

AC	Audit Commission
ACCA	Association of Chartered Certified Accountants
AIM	Alternative Investment Market
ARK	Absolute Return for Kids
ASB	Accounting Standards Board
ASI	Adam Smith Institute
ASST	Academies and Specialist Schools Trust
AST	Academies Sponsors Trust
BECTA	British Educational Communications and Technology Agency
BSF	Building Schools for the Future
CABE	Commission on Architecture and the Built Environment
CBI	Confederation of British Industry
CCT	Compulsory Competitive Tendering
CEA	Cambridge Education Associates
CEL	Centre for Excellence in Leadership
CEO	Chief Education Officer
CfBT	Centre for British Teachers
CIPFA	Chartered Institute of Public Finance and Accountancy
CLCs	City Learning Centres
CPA	Comprehensive Performance Assessment
CPD	Continuing Professional Development
CRB	Criminal Records Bureau
CSR	corporate social responsibility
CTC	City Technology College
DBFO	design, build, finance and operate
DETR	Department for Employment, Transport and the Regions
DfES	Department for Education and Skills
EAZ	Education Action Zone
EiC	Excellence in Cities
ESI	education services industry
FDA	First Division Association
FE	further education
FEFC	Further Education Funding Council

FM	facilities management
GATS	General Agreement on Trade and Tariffs
GEMS	Global Education Management Systems
HBS	Hyder Business Services
HCESSE	House of Commons Education and Skills Select Committee
HE	higher education
HEFCE	Higher Education Funding Council for England
IDeA	Improvement and Development Agency
ILAs	Individual Learning Accounts
ILEA	Inner London Education Authority
IOE	Institute of Education
IPPR	Institute for Public Policy Research
IWB	interactive whiteboard
KNWS	Keynsian National Welfare State
LA	local authority
LEA	local education authority
LEP	Local Education Partnership
LMS	Local Management of Schools
LSDA	Learning and Skills Development Agency
LSN	Learning Skills Network
LSP	Local Strategic Partnership
MCG	Major Contractors Group
MOD	Ministry of Defence
NACETT	National Advisory Council for Education and Training Targets
NAGM	National Association of Governors and Managers
NAHT	National Association of Headteachers
NAO	National Audit Office
NCSL	National College for School Leadership
NDPBs	non-departmental public bodies
NFTE	National Foundation for Teaching Enterprise
NGOs	non-governmental organisations
NLGN	New Local Government Network
NUT	National Union of Teachers
ODPM	Office of the Deputy Prime Minister
OECD	Organization for Economic and Cultural Development
Ofsted	Office for Standards in Education
PAC	Public Accounts Committee
PFI	Private Finance Initiative
PfS	Partnerships for Schools
Plasc	Pupil level annual school census
PPP	Public Private Partnerships
PPPF	Public Private Partnership Forum
PUK	Partnerships UK
PWC	PricewaterhouseCoopers
QAA	Quality Assurance Associates

QCA	Qualifications and Curriculum Authority
QIA	Quality Improvement Agency
RGfL	Regional Grids for Learning
RSA	Royal Society for the encouragement of Arts, Manufactures and Commerce
SEN	Special Educational Needs
SEU	Social Exclusion Unit
SHA	Secondary Headteachers' Association
SIFE	Students in Free Enterprise
SMF	Social Market Foundation
SPV	Special Purpose Vehicle
SRB	Strategic Regeneration Budget
SSP	Strategic Service Partnership
SWS	Schumpeterian Workfare State
TDA	Training and Development Agency for Schools
TES	*Times Educational Supplement*
TPS	Teachers' Pension Scheme
TTA	Teacher Training Authority
TUPE	Transfer of Undertakings (Protection of Employment)
UCLES	University of Cambridge Local Examinations Syndicate
Ufi	University for Industry
ULT	United Learning Trust
VTES	Vosper Thorneycroft Education and Skills

1 A 'policy sociology' introduction to privatisation(s)

Tools, meanings and positions

This book builds upon and extends my long-standing interest in the contemporary history of education policy. It uses the method of 'policy sociology' (Ozga 1987; Ball 1994) to describe and critically analyse changes in policy, policy technologies and policy regimes in the UK,[1] and some of the ethical and democratic impacts of these changes, although the purpose here is to understand rather than rush to judgement. As in my previous work theoretically and conceptually the book is pragmatic and eclectic. As such my examination of privatisation(s) involves the use of a variety of analytic tools to understand, interpret and begin to explain the phenomenon.[2] These tools are of three sorts and are employed self-consciously and tentatively to provide a methodological framework which is both ontologically flexible and epistemologically pluralist (Sibeon 2004) and a set of analytic concepts which are potent and malleable. They are respectively discursive,[3] structural and interpretive and they enable me to explore the complex interactions of social relations, economics and discourses without assuming the necessary dominance of any of these.

Discourse

Discourses are fallible but influential particularly in providing possibilities of political thought and thus policy 'but the extent to which they produce what they name is a matter for empirical research' (Sayer 2005: 76). They are also rooted within material contexts and networks of social interaction. Through narratives of plausibility, including the shared personal narratives 'of significant classes, strata, social categories or groups that have been affected by the development of the post-war economic and political order' (Jessop 2002: 93), policies accumulate credibility and legitimacy. These narratives offer language and practices in terms of which the public sector is being reformed. They are fundamental to the production of an obviousness, a common sense, a 'banality' (Rosamond 2002) and often an inevitability of reform, of a particular sort. "There is no alternative to reform. No one should be allowed to veto progress . . ." (Rod Aldridge of Capita[4] and Chairman of the CBI Public Services Strategy Board). They constitute what Angela Eagle calls a 'default model for any reform' (2003: 13) and a kind of reform readiness, or a 'systematicity' (Mills 1997: 17)[5] and a 'solidity and normality which is difficult to think outside of . . .' (p. 54). Voices on the 'outside' of normal find it difficult to be heard. The discourses of reform have distinctive generative effects but these effects are not determinate nor simply predictable and neither do they work independently from other extra-discursive mechanisms. They provide authoritative readings of prevailing economic and political conditions and problems (see below on globalisation) and mediate and render as 'sensible' the 'appropriate' solutions.

The prevailing discourse of education and public sector reform generates, as discourses do, subject positions, social relations and opportunities within policy. New kinds of actors, social interactions and institutions are produced (see Chapters 4 and 5). Specifically, the meaning, force and effect of this discourse are framed by an over-bearing, economic and political context of international competitiveness. "The purpose of our social model should be to enhance our ability to compete, to help our people cope with globalisation" (Prime Minister Tony Blair's speech to EU Parliament, 26 June 2005). The key ideas of these reform narratives are 'scaffolded' by and 'sedimented into institutions and operative networks' (Robertson 2006: 12) – they circulate and gain credibility and impetus through such networks. 'Those discourses which are commented upon by others are the discourses we consider to have validity and worth' (Mills 1997: 67). These are new ways of talking about ("personalised learning", "intelligent accountability", "leadership capacity building", "operational imperative", "activity streams") and realising education processes and relationships. They are spoken and authorised by a variety of types of (new) actors speaking from a variety of (new and newly) relevant sites and positions which map out possible uses of statements within the discourse. These statements are made up out of fragments – slogans, recipes, incantations and self-evidences (see Chapters 2 and 6). The recitations and rhetorics involved here are part of the process of building support for state projects and establishing hegemonic visions. As Fairclough (2000: 157) puts it, 'much of the action of government is language'. These statements are painstakingly reiterated but also constantly elaborated and inflected (retro-fitted) and this does not necessarily help to produce a clear and coherent vision of the future to which they point. What can count as part of the discourse is limited but is also diverse; the statements and fragments do not make a coherent joined-up whole. They do not have their effects by virtue of their inherent logic. Discourses often maintain their credibility through their repetition, substantive simplicity (see the discussion of Jessop later in this chapter) and rhetorical sophistication, for example in this case what Fairclough (2000: 10) calls 'the denial of expectations' which is central to the language of New Labour.

As indicated already, the naturalness of these discourses of reform arises in good part from what has been excluded from them and by them and rendered unsayable. Exclusion is indeed one of the most important aspects of discursive production. Nonetheless, discourses exist over and against these exclusions, they are always 'in dialogue and in conflict with other positions' (Mills 1997: 14) and accordingly the discourse of reform strategically appropriates from other sources in relation to its contrary objectives – trust, creativity and social capital are perhaps examples.[6] This is achieved in part by bringing together 'impossible alternatives' (Fairclough 2000) (see Chapter 7). This can very effectively undermine the possibilities of speaking 'otherwise' or in opposition to reform discourses. Despite their bricolage form, the discourses of contemporary reform have an agonistic dependency, even if this often rests upon a set of 'false dilemmas', that is they rest heavily for their legitimation on a particular 'discourse of derision' (Kenway 1990), one which pathologises the welfare tradition of public sector provision, which generates in turn what Torrance (2004: 3) calls a 'discourse of distrust'. As we shall see later there is a confusing interplay of trust/distrust inside the discourse and mechanics of public sector reform. A great deal of rhetorical effort and discursive work are expended on ensuring that the public sector is portrayed as ineffective, unresponsive, sloppy, risk-averse and innovation-resistant (except when it is not). Such portrayals also work to exclude or devalue particular voices, which thence have difficulty in inserting themselves into a discourse by virtue of the way in which they are spoken of by it (see Box 1.1).[7] But there is a contrary but concomitant celebration of public sector 'heroes' of reform and of new kinds of public sector 'excellence'. These are part of a new public sector, set over and against the old.

The discourse of 'the private', and 'the market', is examined in the next chapter.

The competition state

The second set of tools on which I draw are from Jessop's (1997, 1998a, 1998b, 2001, 2002, 2004) particular combination of economic geography and political sociology and his analyses of the capitalist state and state intervention, specifically the co-evolution of the economic and political aspects of what he calls the Keynsian National Welfare State (KNWS) and its 'potential replacement' by what he calls the Schumpeterian Workfare State (SWS) or 'competition state' (a term also used by Cerny 1990: 220–31).[8] The competition state 'aims to secure economic growth within its borders and/or to secure competitive advantages for capitals based in its borders' (Jessop 2002: 96) by promoting the economic and extra-economic conditions necessary for competitive success. In this account the conditions addressed are those produced within the education system. This is not an argument based on any kind of simple economic determinism but rather an account of 'structural coupling', a mutual conditioning and accommodation between accumulation and regulation: 'emerging modes of regulation themselves play a key role in constituting the eventual objects of regulation' (Jessop 2002: 134). In effect, Jessop's argument is that the changes that have taken place over the last 25 years in the

---

Box 1.1 Privileging the private

Allyson Pollack describes a meeting with Gordon Brown at which she questioned important aspects of PFI policy and notes that 'his response was simply to declare repeatedly that the public sector is bad at management, and that only the private sector is efficient and can manage services well' (Pollack 2004: 3).

> The era of state-only funding is over . . . we must remember that no public service model has ever delivered high quality services for every child.
> (DfES source quoted by J. Sutcliffe, *TES*, 13 April 2001, p. 20)

> Today David Crossley, headhunted by 3Es from a private international school in Brunei to be the new principal of King's College, ranges through his newly refurbished buildings, talking enthusiastically about a new ethos and innovative ways of teaching. Why does he think bringing in a private company was necessary at King's College? Education has suffered from a conservatism and command and control structure which has stifled innovation, he argues, but "it doesn't have to be private, that's a red herring. It's the quality of ideas and some money to implement them."
> (Felicity Lawrence, EducationGuardian.co.uk, 24 July 2001)

> Mr Neil McIntosh of CfBT Education Services told us that it was not possible to define specific qualities which private companies can bring to education, but that the "variety and competition" which private companies did bring helped to counter the tendency of monopoly providers to "atrophy over time".
> (House of Commons Select Committee on Education and Employment, Seventh Report, 2000, para. 14)

---

regime of capital accumulation have made the KNWS increasingly redundant and indeed obstructive, undermining of the conditions of accumulation. The relationships between the emerging accumulation regime (post-Fordism) and the institutional ensemble of the mode of regulation became increasingly incoherent. The KNWS became subject to mounting crises, *in* and *of* itself, that is both structurally and subjectively, which could no longer be managed or deferred. This was not as a result of some kind of disembedded economic logic, but rather a conjunction of crises, financial, economic, social and political – inflation, taxation costs, ungovernability, unemployment, demographic change, inequality, rigidity, changing national identities, family instability, movements of capital, ecological problems, etc., etc. – occurring at various 'moments' across the system. The form of the state/economy relationship, the settlement as it is sometimes termed or the 'spatio-temporal fix' as Jessop calls it, became untenable and a hindrance to international competitiveness. It produced a condition Cerny (1990: 221) calls the 'overloaded state' trying ineffectively to manage a 'lumbering' command economy creating 'rigidities which prevented private capital from playing its proper role in its own sphere' (p. 221). The KNWS has as a result become steadily de-legitimated and subject to systematic but not total dismantling and is in the process of being replaced or in part over-laid by the SWS, the logic and workings of which constitute a new 'social fix'. The new SWS, the new settlement, did not come into existence once and for all at some particular point in time, nor is it a stable or comprehensive settlement. Initial optimistic reformism was replaced by radical transformation which is itself always limited by the political reach of regulation.[9] The extent to which crises are solved or solutions attempted within the framework of an existing regime varies between nations. Therefore much of the generality of what is said here has a degree of specific relevance to England but a general relevance to many other national settings. England holds a particular position as a political laboratory of political transformation, first under Thatcher and then under Blair, which exports policy solutions across the globe (see Chapter 3).

The form of the SWS has not developed in a mechanical fashion but rather has crystallised out of the responses to and management of crisis tendencies and the promotion of 'economic and extra-economic conditions deemed appropriate to the emerging post-Fordist accumulation regime' (Jessop 2002: 95) and its new 'techno-economic paradigms' the informational, or digital or knowledge, economy (see Chapter 7). One of the aspects of the SWS, which is very relevant to the more specific analysis to come, is a shift from the state as a *decommodifying agent* to the 're-emergence of the state as a *commodifying agent*' (Cerny 1990: 230), that is a re-positioning of the state as commissioner and monitor of public services, and broker of social and economic innovations, rather than deliverer or even owner and funder. The new institutional architecture of the SWS is still emerging from 'fumblings' and 'muddling through' and is changing by trial and error, mediated by 'discursive struggles over the nature and significance of the crisis' (Jessop 2002: 92) and the inadequacies of neo-liberalism as an initial response (see Chapter 2). It is within parts of this new 'competition state' and its re-scaling and re-articulation that this research is set and the 'fumblings' and qualities of trial and error involved in 'reform' of state education will become apparent 'up close'. Indeed, education is itself now in almost permanent 'crisis' as it has taken centre stage in the complex relations between the state and the 'imagined economy' – a knowledge economy, an economy much simpler than the real one.

I aim to take education policy as an analytical case of state re-articulation and re-scaling which might purposefully be explored using Jessop's account of the characteristics of the SWS. Indeed he also offers a brief account of education policy (Jessop 2002: 162–8) and the discursive resolution of 'the crisis in education . . . through a growing hegemony of accounts that cast educational reform in terms of economic imperatives' (p. 163) within which 'learning is the key to prosperity' (DfEE 1998). However, I intend to deploy, elaborate and adjust his framework, where necessary, specifically in relation to the privatisation of education as one particular response to crisis. This will not, hopefully, be a simplistic process of just fitting the case into the framework but rather its use as a source of enriching insights: an interplay of exploration and modification between data and concepts.

In Jessop's analysis the building of the 'competition state' is a 'political response to the challenges *and opportunities*' which arise from the decomposition of Fordism and the 'economic and extra economic' (2002: 124) tendencies of 'globalisations'.[10] He sees globalisation(s) not as 'being a unitary causal mechanism' but rather 'as the complex emergent product of many different forces operating on many scales' (2002: 114). Globalisation is a heterogeneous process. It has economic, cultural and political dimensions and is made up of erratic but increasingly speedy flows of capital, goods, services, labour and ideas (including policy ideas – Ball 1998) which all contribute to an increasing synchronicity of demands, the weakening of traditional structures of meaning, and increasing but varying degrees of difficulty for nation states in the management of their economies. The term is used and the processes it refers to take place both in a transitive sense, something which is made to happen, and in an intransitive sense as something that happens (Lewin 1997). It is not just 'an "out there" phenomenon. It refers not only to the emergence of large scale world systems, but to transformations in the very texture of everyday life' (Giddens 1996: 367–8). However, 'to a large extent, globalization represents the triumph of the economy over politics and culture' (Kellner 2000: 307). For Western developed economies, globalisation is a threat to traditional forms of production and accumulation and the opportunity for new forms. While in some ways less nuanced, Leys (2001: 2) presents a case very similar to Jessop, that profound change in the structure and role of the state 'flows from a new political dynamic resulting from economic globalisation. It is not that the state has become impotent, but that it is constrained to use its power to advance the process of commodification' and 'from now on society would be increasingly shaped in ways that served the needs of capital accumulation' (p. 80). To quote Tony Blair again: "Of course we need a social Europe. But it must be a social Europe that works" (speech to the EU Parliament, 25 June 2005).

The political responses to all of this involve new forms of state relations, new institutions and levels of activity, new actors and agents of policy intervention, new policy narratives and the development of new forms of governance. To reiterate, this is not a single, conscious, explicit project, but is a set of trends which involve searches, discoveries, borrowing, and 'struggles to mobilise support behind alternative accumulation strategies' (Jessop 2002: 124), which are critically mediated through new discourses and which are also specific and path-dependent within particular political, cultural and accumulation histories. Within New Labour this involves a move away from Fabian planning modes of policy to the deployment of projects, initiatives and resources targeting and policy experiments from a variety of sources. These constitute a 'tendential emergence' (Jessop 2002: 124) on different scales – local, city, regional, national – of new forms of entrepreneurialism which are intended to promote structural or systemic competitiveness (see Chapters 6 and 7). Competition states typically have a 'self-image as being proactive in promoting the competitiveness of their economic spaces' (Jessop 2002: 124), always though in relation to an economy, the subject of policy, that they can control or influence rather than that they cannot. Indeed, 'National competitiveness has increasingly become a central preoccupation of governance strategies throughout the world' (Watson and Hay 2003: 299). 'So what is the agenda that we are carrying through?. . . It is to build on the platform of economic stability, the modern knowledge economy with the skills, dynamism, technological and scientific progress a country like Britain needs' (text of a speech by Tony Blair to the Labour Party's centenary conference in Blackpool, 10 February 2006).

Jessop (2002: 132) represents the replacement of the KNWS by the SWS as taking place through the articulation of a series of discursive-strategic shifts 'into new accumulation strategies, state projects and hegemonic projects' which reorientate and restructure the state and produce 'new regulatory regimes'. These shifts are mediated by discursive struggles over the meaning and causes of the crisis of the KNWS and its solutions, in particular the re-narration of the public sector in terms of economism, competition, performance and individuation. Following Gramsci, Jessop sees a 'key role' for intellectuals in this re-narration 'to consolidate an unstable equilibrium of compromise among different social forces around a given economic, political and social order' (2002: 6).

The centrepiece of Jessop's account then is the emergence of the Schumpeterian competition state, the central concern of which is 'with innovation, competitiveness and entrepreneurship tied to long waves of growth and more recent pressures on perpetual innovation' (2002: 132) and the development of innovation systems locally, nationally and regionally (see Chapter 6). One crucial aspect of this generalised orientation is the commodifying or collectivising of knowledge with its attendant contradictions – an assertion of intellectual property rights on the one hand and the fostering of productivity, communication and connectivity on the other. Another is the development of 'meta-capacities' which are intended to support the international economic competitiveness of the national economy (see Chapter 7) and a resulting expansion of the state's 'field of intervention' combined with a focused allocation of resources to innovation nodes and 'leading edges'. In Giddens's (1998: 99) terms, 'Government has an essential role to play in investing in the human resources and infrastructure needed to develop an entrepreneurial culture.' The emphasis of the state on structural and systemic competitiveness leads, among other things, to a redefinition of boundaries between the economic and the 'extra-economic'. The processes of the redefinition of boundaries are a major concern in the analysis which follows. Within all this, important distinctions between state and market, public and private, government and business, left and right are attenuated.

The following account by Amey plc of their involvement in sponsorship of an Academy school is a paradigm example of boundary crossing and the tying together of innovation, inclusion and regeneration in relation to the requirements of the workplace – the discourse of the SWS in action:

City Academy sponsorship
In Middlesbrough, Amey sponsors Unity City Academy. This is a major opportunity for the company to contribute directly to the improvement and opportunities of the children in an area with a history of under-achievement. The new state-of-the-art facility will be opened shortly and represents a radical departure from the conventional school model. With a specialism of ICT, the Academy will use new teaching methods and approaches to equip the children with the skills they need for the work-place of the 21st century.

I will return to look at the Academies policy in Chapters 6 and 7.

In relation to welfare, restructuring involves the use of social policy to 'enhance the flexibility of labour markets and to create flexible, enterprising workers suited to a globalising, knowledge-based economy' (Jessop 2002: 168) together with a reduction in the social wage. The achievement and enactment of the SWS also requires a shift from government to governance, a move from hierarchy to the greater significance of networks and 'self-organisation' or autonomy and responsibility as alternatives to the failures of both social planning and free markets. Increasingly individual learners and workers are required to become 'self-organising' (Colley *et al.* 2003). This involves the state in what Jessop (2002: 240) calls 'meta-governance', that is 'the organization and conditions for governance in its broadest sense' (p. 240) or the 'rearticulation and collibrating [of] different modes of governance' (2002: 242) founded on 'the judicious mixing of market, hierarchy and net-works to achieve the best possible outcomes' (p. 242) (see Chapter 5). Metagovernance also involves: 'the reflexive redesign of markets' – meta-exchange (see Chapter 4); 'the reflexive redesign of organizations . . . and the management of organizational ecologies' (p. 241) – metaorganisation (see Chapter 6); and 'providing opportunities for spontaneous sociability' and 'fostering trust' (p. 241), the conditions of self-organisation – metaheterarchy (see Chapter 6). The purpose of the state in these respects is to re-shape 'cognitive expectations' and 'try to modify the self-understanding of iden-tities, strategic capacities and interests of individual and collective actors' (p. 242) (see Ball 2000 and Ball 2003 for examples). Also involved here is the creation of 'linkage devices, sponsoring new organizations [and] identify-ing appropriate lead organizations' (p. 242). However, the emphasis on self-organisation is accompanied by a systematic prioritising of some out-comes over others – entrepreneurism and enterprise are key examples here.

Embedded in all this is the process of 'destatalisation' – 'the redrawing of the public–private divide, re-allocating tasks, and rearticulating the relation-ship between organizations and tasks across this divide' (Jessop 2002: 199). Clearly this re-drawing, re-allocation and re-articulation are very evident in recent education policy generally and the processes of privatisation of educa-tion particularly. They involve various forms of 'partnership' (see Chapters 4 and 5) in the management of economic and social relations. All of this 'could also be part of a more complex power struggle to protect key decisions from popular-democratic control' (Jessop 2002: 199–200), that is the replacement of democratic processes with technical or market solutions, like Trusts and Partnership Boards, Academy schools, Foundation Hospitals, that is 'at the heart of new localism lies a much more retrogressive agenda of privatization' (Centre for Public Services 2003: 10) – the privatisation of decision-making. At the same time an increased emphasis on regionalism and localism and new forms of local partnership is part of the 're-scaling' of the state and its 'denationalisation' (both a regional extension and a local devolution) and the regeneration of local economies through the creation of 'entrepreneurial localities' (see Chapter 6 where I will consider three such localities: Sandwell, Blackburn and Darwen, and Middlesbrough). Technicisation and subsidiar-ity work together. A set of diverse and multi-faceted shifts are involved here, not simply a move away from bureaucracy but also from democracy and a 'common equity' (Leys 2001: 71).

While it remains somewhat implicit, Jessop's account of state change also suggests a periodisation within the process of transition from the KNWS to the SWS. That is what I will call, for simplicity, a neo-liberal stage and a Third Way stage, the former approximating to Thatcherism and the latter to Blairism. However, these need to be understood in terms of both their con-tinuities and their differences. In the former the emphasis was on freeing the market and shrinking the state and a narrow definition of the social. Briefly at least during the 1980s and early 1990s, there was a flourishing of 'wild neoliberal triumphalist fantasies' (Jessop 2002: 169) with their almost exclusive 'emphasis on cost-containment' and the use of privatisation and 'market proxies' to reform the public sector and the reduction of civil society to the competing interests of consumer-citizens. In contrast, the post-neo-liberal, Third Way state retains key aspects of the capacity to man-age and remediate the social fragmentation and loss of trust produced by neo-liberal workfare policies based on 'a greater concern to recalibrate exist-ing institutions to deal with problems rather than to believe that the market can solve them' (2002: 171) together with the use of 'activation policies' (p. 155) and the deployment of performance measures and new forms of man-agement to encourage constant innovation. (I shall return to the continuities and differences between Thatcherism and Blairism in Chapter 2). However, despite this mix-and-match approach to governance, the combination of the 'invisible hand' with the 'invisible handshake' (Jessop 2002: 243), 'there is no Archimedean point from which governance or collibration can be guaranteed to succeed', as Jessop puts it (2002: 242). The complex tangle of initiatives and strategies and subsidiarities of post-neo-liberal policy-making is particularly significant in education policy within the general orientation to competitiveness on the one hand and development of networks and partnerships on the other and the role of 'experimentation' in both. Consequently an account that relies solely on an analysis of privatisation in terms of neo-liberalism is bound to be flawed. I shall argue that Third Way policies unstably and sometimes incoherently tie together the subordination of education to the demands of structural competitiveness and the re-articulation of state education through the production of 'plausible' new policy narratives (e.g. choice, diversity, personalisation – a middle-class ontology of welfare (see Ball 2003) – and enterprise, technology and innovation), with, nonetheless, a residual set of concerns with social inequalities or rather the underachievement and under-participation of some of the working class and some ethnic minorities in education – a social problem rendered economic. This is articulated in terms of individual responsibilities, and individual self-organisation (through schemes like Connexions, the ill-fated Individual Learning Accounts (ILAs), and notions like 'life-long learning'). All of this involves a significant re-working of the form of the welfare state and changes to the role it plays in social reproduction, and is a move away from collective consumption. As I shall go on to outline (in Chapter 3) the development of the education services industry (ESI) itself, as with other new public sector markets, is also marked by phases or stages of development.

What I will try to do in the remainder of this book is to examine the ways in which the general discourses (knowledge and practices) and material changes of the competition state drive, articulate or are resonant with concomitant changes, approaches, assumptions, logics and methods of appropriateness in the reform of education, in direct and indirect ways. That is the dissemination through the education system of a culture of competitiveness and its attendant social identities, not simply or even primarily competitiveness in the relations between institutions but in the orientation of institutions toward the logic of economic imperatives, of 'interdependence' and 'mutual learning' (Jessop 2002: 197) linked with the notion of 'collaborative advantage'. This generality and duality of competitiveness explains to some extent the different imperatives within education policy for educational institutions to compete *and* collaborate, to exploit financially their intellectual property *and* develop collective intelligence, to seek market advantage *and* attempt to ensure greater social inclusivity. These things do not necessarily sit together comfortably or coherently but they are all part of the public sector reform policy ensemble. While the former, schools as businesses, are perhaps evidence of the direct imposition of the neo-liberal market fantasy on to schools, FE and HE, the latter, collaboration, the dissemination of good practice and innovation, together with an agenda of social inclusion, are indications of the structural requirements of national competitiveness and the activities of the competition state within the global knowledge economy – Education plc. All of these issues will be returned to and explored more fully and in a more grounded fashion in later chapters. Thus, the analysis which follows focuses as much on the new forms of 'state education' as it does on the inroads of the private sector into state education. Indeed I will suggest that they are parts of the same project of competitiveness. The title *Education plc* refers to both the privatisation of education and the tying of education to the requirements of international competitiveness and the competition state.

Private actors

The third positioning in this account and its conceptual resources are inter-actional. I deploy the words and utilise the perspectives of a range of actors within the ESI whom I interviewed (21 in all; see the Appendix and Box 1.2). I take their accounts very seriously but situate these within the discursive and structural frameworks adumbrated above. These accounts provide important insights into the new subject positions which are made available within 'entrepreneurial governance' (Hall 2003). These actors represent subjecti-vities which fit within the complexity of new forms of governance and these are blurred and elude simple categorisations. There are strong common ele-ments across the interviews in terms of motives, purposes and values which are meaningful and powerful within the context of destatalisation and the re-articulating of 'the relationship between organizations and tasks' (Jessop 2002: 199) across the public–private divide. These actors embody a new kind of self-understanding and a new set of strategic capacities and interests. They

---

Box 1.2 The interviews

The interviews were tape-recorded and the transcripts were sent back for comment, editing or elaboration. Only three people took up this opportunity. I explained what I was trying to do at the beginning of the interviews and assured the interviewees that I would not attribute anything that seemed to me to be 'sensitive'; consequently you will see that a few extracts quoted are simply attributed to 'a respondent'. I sent draft chapters to five of the interviewees and received some helpful comments and corrections back.

I also drew on a large number of secondary sources and with help conducted thousands of internet searches and explored hundreds of websites. I have tried throughout not to rely too heavily on any particu-lar of these sources.

The publishers asked me to remove three pieces of 'data' from the text for legal reasons. None were of great substantive importance.

move within and in relation to government and governance and blend private interests and public service in a variety of ways. They are constantly engaged in networking and negotiation. They are the flesh and bones of new discourses and structures, its subjects and disseminators and relays. Their insights were also of great strategic importance to my understanding of privatisation(s) and its complexities and conundrums. Their accounts of the work of the ESI and of their companies also play an important role in my mapping of privatisation(s) and the relationships between ESI companies and the state. Partly by virtue of the nature of my questioning the interviews with these actors 'inside' privatisation were also in part narratives of personal histories, of journeys and boundary crossings, accounts of themselves as well as of the ESI (see Ball 1994). The private sector is here constituted by relationships and encounters and personalities. They were keen, as we all are, to give a morally adequate account of themselves and affirm 'preferred identities' (Convery 1999). I was asked to do this for myself in a couple of interviews and did not find it easy. The interviews were astonishingly open and frank but still of course partial. At times we hedged around things which could not be said or described. Most of my respondents knew each other – the ESI is a close-knit community – and were aware of me and my research.[11] This enabled me to cross-reference between interviews. It also meant that the interviewing was cumulative. Information and insights from one interview could be rehearsed, probed or checked out in the next. The interview process was also a complex learning process, the accumulation of background knowledge across a wide range of technical areas, but I was also trying to grasp something of the culture of this small part of the private sector. The status of this data raises interesting questions. As noted already, there were commercial sensitivities involved which meant some things were not said or said in confidence. There was also a range of sensitive political or ethical issues which were discussed in the interviews. The respondents were to some extent representing their company and the private sector in the interview as well as themselves. These considerations have to be taken seriously but all interviewing involves some aspects of these 'sensitivities' and 'presentations'.

Collectively these actors within the private sector are part of what Whitfield (2001: 10–13) calls the emerging 'corporate welfare complex' but many other companies not represented in the interviews make up the totality of this complex. Whitfield identifies three main elements to this complex. The first part is based on relationships between public (client) agencies and a relatively small number of private contractors. Both clients and contractors share a similar ideological position and a set of vested interests which dictate that the state will outsource an increasing range of services and functions. This goes beyond direct service delivery per se to include the huge army of consultants that advise on the best model of service delivery, ways of outsourcing, and arm's length performance management systems. The second part is based on an owner-operator infrastructure largely supported by the rapid and continued extension of PFI contracts in which the financial institutions, contractors and facilities management companies take control and ownership of what are ostensibly public buildings and facilities, paid for with public money. It is important to note that the impact of this goes far beyond the narrow technical and financial scope of the contract to have implications for employment, local economic development and public space. The third part is based around regulatory and financial concessions to business. Public money is used to give tax breaks, subsidies and local and regional grants and to remove obstacles to entice businesses to locate in particular areas (Whitfield 2001; Centre for Public Services 2003: 5).

Privatisation(s)

Let me try to delineate now my use of the term 'privatisation' because it is at the centre of my concerns and will be used as a shorthand throughout the book. I say a shorthand because a variety of processes is actually involved here. It is more appropriate perhaps to think about 'privatisations'. There is a wide variety of types and forms of privatisation involving different financial arrangements and different relationships between funders, service providers and clients (see Chapter 3). Clearly, privatisation in general terms also has a long history. It has been the normal way of going about things in terms of things like textbook production and sales (see Apple 1986), testing programmes, equipment and building for many years. Privatisation is old but also very new. 'The state has always bought and sold property, purchased services and encouraged enterprise but the scale of privatization in the past two decades has been unparalleled', a 'relentless rolling process' (Whitfield 2001: 75). Contemporary privatisation is part of a much broader and more fundamental re-design of the public sector, as outlined above. This involves private and not-for-profit companies and voluntary and community organisations and NGOs and parastatal organisations in income-generating activities inside the public sector. There is also a relatively new kind of 'philanthropic privatisation', to which I shall return in Chapter 5. The newer forms of privatisation mean that the distinction between 'hard' and 'soft' services, books and educational media, etc., on the one hand, and 'those services which require human interaction' (Boyles 2000: 118), on the other, is now thoroughly breached – the private sector operates across this divide. There are no service areas which are exempt from private sector participation, although there are some where it appears, as yet, only infrequently. The state is increasingly re-positioned as the guarantor, not necessarily the provider (White 1998: 3) nor the financer, of opportunity goods like education. This is not a 'free market' in any simple sense; neither is it simply imposed by the state. However, as I shall demonstrate later the state is very much a market-maker or broker in relation to the ESI.

As for a categorisation of types, I want to suggest a set of categories that are practical and flexible rather than absolutely precise and fully comprehensive (presented in Chapter 3) but which takes account of both first-order privatisation – in terms of ownership, organisation forms, financial relations, etc. – and second-order privatisation – in terms of the implications for social relations, social space, family responsibilities, citizenship and democracy, and which also incorporates the privatisation of governance or what Mahony *et al.* (2004) refer to as 'privatising policy'. In education there is a further, specific dimension to privatisation or more precisely commercialisation (Molnar 2005) or what is called in the US 'cola-risation' – 'where income is derived from vending machines, displays of sponsors logos and advent of TV advertisements streamed at students via Channel One television' (Fitz and Beers 2002: 140) (see Education Policy Studies Laboratory, Arizona State University). This is what Boyles (2000) describes as 'schools as sites for consumer materialism'. In this country the Food Commission, and others, have raised concerns over the Cadbury's chocolate and Walker's crisps promotions which target school children through schemes to collect tokens towards school equipment. The major supermarkets also regularly run such schemes. The NUT estimates that brands are now spending £300 million a year targeting classroom consumers. In addition commercial companies are also increasingly involved in the production of formal or informal curriculum materials and educational resources, sometimes unacknowledged,[12] and Buckingham and Scanlon (2005: 42) note that 'Parents are being placed under increasing pressure to "invest" in their children's education by providing additional resources at home'. Together with the growth in the use of private tutors (Ireson 2004) and other enrichment activities for children (Vincent and Ball 2006) and the increasing importance being given to home-based e-learning, this points to yet another form of privatisation, the privatisation of learning itself; 'the overall value of the educational resources market (including print and digital media) in the UK is around £350 million per year' (Buckingham and Scanlon 2005: 42). It seems clear that the child and childhood are now thoroughly saturated by market relations and, within this saturation, the meaning of childhood and what it means to be well educated are subject to significant change. As Kenway and Bullen (2001: 3) argue, 'we are entering another stage in the construction of the young as the demarcations between education, entertainment and advertising collapse'. The typology also draws attention to the global context of educational privatisation, which is undoubtedly of increasing importance. But while I will address some aspects of the international dimensions of educational privatisation I will not deal specifically with the impact of GATS (see Rikowski 2001, 2003, and on the role of the private sector in European Community policy-making see Hatcher and Hirtt 1999 and Robertson 2006). I also make use of the distinction between what Hatcher (2000) calls exogenous and endogenous privatisation. Where the former involves private companies entering education to take over directly responsibilities, services or programmes, the latter refers to changes in the behaviour of public sector organisations themselves, where they act as though they were businesses, both in relation to clients and workers, and in dealings with other public sector organisations.

The existing literature on social and educational privatisation in England is extensive but is also narrowly focused, fragmentary and primarily discursive and tends to under-estimate and homogenise the impact and spread of privatisation in English education. Green's (2005) account is the most comprehensive, and Farnsworth (2004: 1) investigates 'business views and influence on social policy outcomes' including education. Much of the other work rests on rather lazy binaries which contrast a particular version of 'the private' with a particular, often rosy, version of 'the public', which Green avoids. I want to move beyond a simple juxtaposition of public/private to explore the blurrings and elisions between them and to analytically audit in a critically constructive fashion the different privatisations currently under way, as well as to re-insert and re-assess the role of the state in relation to privatisation. I shall consider the possibility that privatisation can have paradoxical effects, good and bad together, and that the small particulars of privatisation might contribute to larger-scale social and political changes.

Research and ethics

Political argument and policy-making have out-run research in this field. Key components of the dynamics of public sector privatisation are still relatively poorly understood, some market sectors are dramatically under-researched and many of the concrete first- and second-order effects of the market remain almost totally unexamined. In part these lacunae exist because of the divisions within the field of academic practice. Sociologists, policy analysts, economists and philosophers ask their questions separately and differently and researchers tend to pursue their specialisms within particular sectors of the education system (HE, FE, school, pre-school and life-long learning). (I do not escape from this; because of the limitations of space this account is heavily focused on schools.) Most discussion of education markets still remains at the level of 'abstraction'; little is written about the actual buyers and sellers, forms of labour, constraints and regulations in lived, 'concrete' markets. Markets, of any kind, are complex phenomena but 'all market processes are amenable to sociological analysis' and 'such analysis reveals central, not peripheral, features of these processes' (Granovetter 1985: 505). They are multi-faceted, untidy, often unpredictable and both creative and destructive. Any comprehensive attempt to review and analyse the privatisation of education needs to address: competition, supply and demand, producer and consumer behaviour, commercialisation and commodification, values and ethics and distributional outcomes. The account which follows ranges across these concepts with greater or lesser detail and precision although the last is only addressed in passing.

The challenge of finding an ethical position from which to speak about privatisation is difficult in a practical sense, especially when my own institution has a number of collaborations and other relationships with the private sector (the HSBC Chair of Educational Leadership, work with CEA, Teachers' TV,

Goldman Sachs, Teach First)[13] and generates 'profit' from overseas activities and full-fee students from which I indirectly benefit. This illustrates again the need to move beyond a simple public/private binary. Thus, within the analysis that follows I attempt to avoid rhetorical condemnation and avoid the taking up of simple positions, a false neutrality and a rush to closure.

As well as drawing on a number of theoretical resources the book is also written and presented using different genres and techniques. It includes descriptive mapping, commentary, critique and analysis. There is some ethnographic-style use of and interrogation of interview data. There are some case studies of companies, policies and events. There is theoretical interpretation and the development of some concepts which will hopefully have some lasting value in the analysis of privatisation phenomena. While the book is about the here and now of privatisation (or the there and then by the time this is read) it is intended to provide a set of possibilities for understanding and analysis of education policy which, as was the case with *Politics and Policymaking in Education* (1990), have a transposable relevance across topics and settings. Most importantly the book is intended to suggest ways of thinking about and tools for analysing the privatisation phenomenon; it opens up lines of enquiry, maps out issues that need further work and points to omissions in and problems with the current understanding of and debate about public sector reform.

Through the analysis presented there is a series of recurring substantive themes and concepts. Blurring or boundary redefinition is one, the multi-dimensional breakdown or increased porosity of the public–private divide; flexibilisation is another, the breakdown of welfare state categories, particularly forms and categories of labour, as a project of 'modernisation'; what Ken Jones (2003) calls 're-agenting' is a third, the insertion of new players into the field of education policy and education service delivery; new forms of governance are another, the role of the private sector as a means of transformation and discipline; and the state and its changing form and methods are constantly returned to. The analysis and the substantive account of privatisation(s) build recursively chapter by chapter as these themes are tackled in different ways. As will become apparent there is a problem of language in this account, that is a problem of knowing how to describe or refer to new forms, structures, roles and relationships in the general field of privatisation. I will be precise when and as far as I am able but some slippage in the use of terms is inevitable.

2 Privatisation(s) in contexts

In this chapter I outline an analytic history of privatisation and introduce the primary policy technologies of public sector reform. I intend to situate education policy within a broader framework of public sector reform. Following from the previous chapter, the changing role of the state, from the KNWS to an SWS, is a central feature of the account, alongside and in relation to new political narratives. More specifically, I shall seek to demonstrate that recent education policy moves have established a framework of possibility and legitimacy for privatisation and I will look at some of the elements of a 'discourse of privatisation' which re-articulates public services as commodities that can be bought and sold but which also facilitates the modernisation of the education system and its re-articulation in terms of the requirements of international competitiveness.

A brief and crude history of privatisation(s)

The privatisation of education in England is relatively new but it has a history – a history which unfolds through a process of public sector reform and reformation of the state beginning in the 1970s. It has become embedded in policy and the possibilities created by policy over a period of 30 years and I will trace its beginnings back, at least symbolically, to the intellectual and political influence of Keith Joseph. Like Jessop (2002), Kavanagh (1987) sees 'political activists who have "political leverage" and are willing to push their ideas' (p. 114) as having a role in 'changing the climate' or 'in developing alternative economic strategies, state projects and hegemonic visions', as Jessop (2002: 6) puts it. Joseph was the 'first Conservative front-bench figure to offer a sustained and broad-ranging challenge to the direction of post-war British economic management' (Kavanagh 1987: 115). Young (1990: 83) describes him as 'a pathfinder'. In a series of speeches in 1974–5, and through the work of the Centre for Policy Studies (directed by Joseph's friend Alfred Sherman), Joseph argued the case for a social market economy and for monetarism and claimed that, in 1984, for the first time he had become a convert to Conservativism. He outlined an economic and social policy position that became known as New Right or more broadly neo-liberalism (Joseph 1975).

This rested on a rejection of extensive state regulation, high taxation, high levels of public spending, borrowing and subsidies, and the role of unions as monopoly suppliers of labour, and argued generally that the public sector was a drain on the wealth-creating private sector. What was needed was 'more market, less state' – deregulation, liberalisation and privatisation. He wanted the Conservative Party to abandon what he called 'the middle ground' and find 'the common ground' 'where the real lives and aspirations of most people were in practice acted out' (Young 1990: 103). His case was that the Keynesian National Welfare State (KNWS) with its reliance on 'imperative coordination' (Jessop 2002: 234) had failed and 'that economic "realities" must be faced' (Green 1987: 218). In a speech in June 1974 he said: "We are now more socialist in many ways than any other developed country outside the Communist bloc" (quoted in Young 1990: 84). During this period Joseph also began to influence the political ideas of Margaret Thatcher and this 'supplied the base for the decisive leap' (Young 1990: 88) in her career – leadership of the Conservative Party. Joseph's 'conversion' and his impact on Thatcher were to bring about what was in effect a reversal in post-war economic policy with its concerns with low unemployment, welfare state funding and economic intervention. Margaret Thatcher encapsulated this reversal in her first Party Conference speech as leader: "Let me give you my vision: a man's right to work as he will, to spend what he earns, to own property, to have the state as servant and not as master: these are the British inheritance." This signals a key facet of what Giddens (1998) calls 'the neo-liberal outlook', that is its 'antagonism to the welfare state' which is 'seen as the source of all evils' (p. 13). And what is the alternative? 'The answer is market-led economic growth' (p. 13). As Green (1987: 218) put it, 'after a long absence from the political agenda, markets are back'. During Thatcher's terms as prime minister the landscape of economic and political understandings of welfare changed irrevocably; a new discourse was established which expressed the relationships between the state, the economy and the public sector in new (or very old) ways. The boundaries between them were discursively reconstituted. In particular this reconstitution destroyed the specificity of understandings which had articulated the role, purpose and conduct of the public sector. This meant that some public services could simply be sold off (water, gas, electricity, telephones, etc.). Their special status as public services no longer applied. Other services remained in the public sector but were 're-thought' in terms of their conditions of operation, inter-relationships and modes of planning and financing, and made subject to competition and choice, for example. In other words, the New Right or neo-liberal discourse travelled across the public sector (see Ball 1990), enabling the insertion of 'market proxies into what remains of public provision financed by the state' (Jessop 2002: 162). The market form and the logic, modes and visions of the private company, as a model, were to be the primary vehicle for the internal reform of the public services. 'Within two decades the omnipresence of business and business culture had become as commonplace and apparently inevitable as the rain' (Leys 2001: 55). By changing the relationships between providers and between users and providers and tying budgets much more closely to patterns of choice within these new relationships, public sector providers were required to act like businesses and in a business-like way – endogenous privatisation.

Let me offer one pertinent example of the movement of discourse. In 1981 Joseph became Secretary of State for Education and in an interview I conducted with him in 1989 I asked him what his major contribution had been in this post. After a great deal of agonising he claimed that what he had achieved was to change the way in which schools are thought about and think about themselves: "I think the national agencies tend to be producer lobbies, like nationalised industries. One of the main virtues of privatisation is to introduce the idea of bankruptcy, the potential of bankruptcy" (quoted in Ball 1990: 63). During the 1980s and 1990s a framework of reform based upon the model of the private sector was set in place which led to 'a gradual dismantling of the welfare state through cuts and privatization, deregulation and a new emphasis on individual choice and consumption' (Kirkpatrick and Martinez Lucio 1995: 23) or, as Taylor-Gooby and Lawson (1993: 2) put it, 'Spending constraint and privatization have been the central themes in policy debate throughout the past 15 years.' Having said that, in education the changes introduced under the Conservatives between 1979 and 1997 were primarily endogenous. The inroads of business into state education were limited but still important – Compulsory Competitive Tendering, City Technology Colleges and the National Nursery Voucher Scheme, for example (see Box 2.1). The first two were taken up and developed further by New Labour. The Conservative moves produced an infrastructure of possibilities within which business could establish a presence within state education services, and other policies like the Local Management of Schools (LMS) both positioned schools as 'buyers' of services and began to displace the infrastructure of LEA services.

In both discursive and some very practical ways the public sector monopoly of services provision was broken and some key functions were 'privatised'. The private sector was made a legitimate participant in new areas of public service delivery.

Changes in education and social policy since 1988 can be understood as a 'ratchet effect' of changing practical and discursive possibilities (see Ball 1990). This has continued to be the case under New Labour, a step-by-step process of breaking up established modes of operation and taken-for-granted practices, introducing new 'freedoms', new players and new kinds of relationships. Sometimes these are modest, sometimes bold. "If anything we have not pushed fast enough and hard enough" (Tony Blair, Labour Conference 2005). Each move makes the next thinkable, feasible and acceptable. The process of 'modernisation' or transformation involved here is both creative and destructive, a process of attrition and re-invention. Whitfield argues that, 'although the transformation process may sometimes appear to be disjointed or uncoordinated' (2001: 69), it has an internal logic, a set of discernible, if not

Box 2.1 Conservative privatisations

CCT Compulsory Competitive Tendering	Broke the LA monopoly of service provision by requiring councils to contract services to the lowest bidder and transferred workers to private providers (Hoggett 1994). Replaced under Labour by 'Best Value', which shifted from an adversarial to a partnerships relationship between councils and the private sector and from cost reduction to quality (Kirkpatrick 1999).
CTCs City Technology Colleges	Encouraged businesses and business people to 'sponsor' and run state schools with a vocational orientation. Provided part of the model for Academies.
LMS Local Management of Schools	Gave schools control of their budgets with a freedom to make spending decisions.
Parental choice	Encouraged schools to compete for recruitment and employ promotional techniques (see Gewirtz *et al.* 1995).
Ofsted Office for Standards in Education	Inspections of schools and colleges contracted to private companies.
NNVS National Nursery Voucher Scheme	A short-lived scheme intended to allow parents to 'spend' their voucher in state or private nurseries – abolished by New Labour.
School Vouchers	A small pilot scheme initiated by Keith Joseph but deemed a failure by the civil service.

necessarily planned, facets. The destructive facets of transformation involve *destabilisation, disinvestment* and *commodification*. I will say something about each in turn.

Destabilisation is driven by an 'unrelenting criticism of public services, often by generalising individual failures' (Whitfield 2001: 69) and this produces the 'discourse of derision' which deploys exaggeration and 'ludicrous images, ridicule, and stereotypification . . . a caricature has been developed and presented to the public as an accurate depiction of the real' (Kenway 1990: 201). The deployment of derision is a way of creating rhetorical spaces within which to articulate reform, e.g. Alastair Campbell's criticisms of 'bog standard' comprehensive schools (http://archive.thisiswiltshire.co.uk/2001/2/14/225660.html).

Over and against this is the construction and dissemination of the new hegemonic discourse, a romantic discourse of perfection which represents the private and markets forms as magical solutions to the 'problems' of the public sector (Stronach 1993). This new hegemonic discourse is romantic in the sense that it excludes markets failures and negative externalities. However, in some important ways the initial New Right version of this in the UK, with its clarity, its antagonisms and its simple binarisation of economic and social policies, also ensured the inevitability of its failure. It was dogmatic and conservative (Brown and Lauder 2001: 135), relying exclusively on the market fantasy to solve all social and economic problems. It was out of this dogmatism that the possibility of 'something different', of New Labour, of Blairism, of a post-neo-liberalism, was established. Newman puts it that the Third Way signalled 'something different from the hierarchical governance of social democracy and market-based governance of the 1980s and 1990s' (2005: 719) but goes on to say that 'the something different is hard to pin down' (p. 719).

The conventional academic wisdom on the educational policy of the Labour Party since they won the UK general election in 1997 is neatly summed up in a comment by Michael Novak in a pamphlet for the Institute of Economic Affairs, a New Right pressure group: 'the triumph of Tony Blair may in one sense be regarded as the triumph of Margaret Thatcher' (Power and Whitty 1999: 545). Giddens (1998: 25) also notes that critics of the Third Way, or at least Blair's version of it, see it 'as warmed-over neoliberalism'. Nonetheless, there are both significant continuities and decisive ruptures between Thatcherism and Blairism, between 'open' and 'structural' competition, between neo-liberalism and the Third Way. While neo-liberalism rests on a fairly unreflexive belief in markets and the private sector as the engine of national economic competitiveness, a 'free-market fundamentalism' (Eagle 2003) which regards state invention as almost always counter-productive, the Third Way rests on a more reflexive adoption of a 'flexible repertoire' of state roles and responses. My point is that neo-liberalism and the Third Way are the same and different. They are different kinds of policy mixes. The Third Way draws 'selectively on fragments and components of the old' (Newman 2001: 46) but it is novel and distinctive (Hall 2003: 11). It would not be possible without neo-liberalism but it differs in important ways in terms of the role of the state and its relationships with the public and private sectors, among other things. Paterson (2003) suggests three key elements to the Third Way repertoire: a version of progressive liberalism, with an inclination toward individualism, and a concomitant suspicion of the state; developmentalism, the explicit promotion of competitiveness by the state and a concomitant interventionism; and New Social Democracy, with elements of moral authoritarianism (made up of reciprocity, responsibility, strong values and community – Driver and Martell 2003), new localism and a 'continuing insistence on the inadequacies of unregulated capitalism' (Paterson 2003: 166), but this element, Paterson suggests, is more evident in Wales and Scotland. The outlines of a new form of regulation, a controlled decontrol, is discernible here and from this ideological mix comes a combination of policies and levers of change which no previous government has attempted (with the exception perhaps of that of Ramsay MacDonald). In particular it develops a 'range of networks, partnerships and other models of economic and political governance' (Jessop 2002: 243) within which the state is 'a prime source and mediator of collective intelligence' (p. 243). The Third Way does not look back to a pre-welfare market heyday; it is about moving on; it is centred on the project of modernisation, the appeal of which 'as a political formula for a new settlement . . . is obvious' (Brown and Lauder 2001: 179). It 'cannot simply be portrayed as Thatcherism Mark II; it is a much more complex political phenomenon' (Atkinson and Savage 2001: 15). 'Modern government has a strategic role not to replace the market but to ensure that the market works properly' (*Labour Party Manifesto* 1992: 11). As noted in Chapter 1, this does not mean that the state is less active or less intrusive – but it acts differently. 'In this context, paradoxically, the total amount of state intervention will tend to increase, for the state will be enmeshed in the promotion, support and maintenance of an ever-widening range of social and economic activities' (Cerny 1990: 230). Jessop (2002: 244) argues that the destructive impact of the Conservatives' 'neo-liberal hostilities' 'deprived the central state in the short term of an adequate range of modes of coordination'. Saltman and Von Otter (1992: 8) offer exactly this analysis of the Conservatives' National Health Service reforms: 'The liabilities that accompany neo-classical economic logic strongly suggest that it is unable to provide an appropriate replacement paradigm upon which to order health policy decision-making within publicly operated systems.' The limits of the market mechanism had to be 're-learned', and other forms of coordination to supplement, complement or compensate for the inadequacies of the market had to be re-invented albeit 'disguised behind changed names, innovative discourses, policy churning and institutional turnover' (Jessop 2002: 244–5). The Third Way, I suggest, in the form of the competition state, embodies that re-invention, although the Third Way also contains its own instabilities and failures.

The second strategy identified in Whitfield's account of the destructive effects of public sector reform is *disinvestment*, but this needs some clarification (and could perhaps be thought of as *re-investment*). Under the Conservative governments of the 1980s and 1990s there clearly was a series of withering public spending cuts. However, under New Labour such cuts have not been a priority; it is new forms of financial control and financial allocation that are of importance, in two senses. First is a form of redistribution of funding within the public sector related to indicators of performance or competitive success and an increasing use of targeted funding and systems of programme bidding to achieve institutional re-focusing and re-design.

> You can't run on your ordinary budget, everyone knows that, so you have to get involved in various initiatives and cater for that, the initiative's

priorities, and bend your curriculum and your priorities in order to get hold of that bit of money.

(Deputy Headteacher, Merchants' School)

Second is a redistribution of funds away from direct funding of public sector organisations and local authorities to contract funding of private, voluntary and quasi-public organisations for the delivery of public services and a concomitant process of making state agencies into free-standing, self-financing organisations.

Education Action Zones (EAZs), an initiative launched in 1998 (see Gewirtz 1999), offer an example of a short-lived policy experiment which brought together a number of the new forms of funding and of local social relations which typify the Third Way aspects of the competition state. First, there is the use of contracting as a means of resource allocation, by which local partnerships, including business partners, had to tender for Zone status. Applicants had to demonstrate their willingness to incorporate the goals and structures laid down by government into their Zone plans. The documentation for bidders was very explicit about what was expected. Once approved, Zones were expected to bid for funding for other government initiatives – specialist schools, work-related learning, family literacy schemes and early-years excellence centres – and to 'build on national initiatives such as literacy and numeracy hours' (DfEE 1997: 8), and part of the assessment of bids was to be based on their 'value for money'. The guidance notes for Zone applicants also made clear the need for bidders to 'Identify relevant performance indicators, where possible directly attached to targets for improvement' (DfEE 1998: 3).

In addition, Zones were encouraged to put forward proposals for innovative staff contracts and the flexible use of staff. Zones which chose to dis-apply the Teachers' Pay and Conditions Order could, for example, make weekend and school holiday working a contractual obligation. EAZs are one example of what I term a *policy condensate* (see also Chapter 7), an ensemble of focused policy ideas which work to tie education to 'the knowledge-based accumulation strategy' (Jessop 2002: 167) of the New Labour competition state. Several elements recur in later policy examples (see Chapter 5) – partnerships, including cross-sector working and institutional collaborations, a local rather than institutional focus, private or voluntary sector participation, deregulation, target setting and innovation. In particular relation to education, although the precept was applied elsewhere, EAZs are also an example of 'standards not structures'. The EAZs contracts were fixed-term and did not bring into being new permanent structures and relationships. Rather the EAZs provided a test-bed for strategies and ideas which would be developed further in later policies. They also served to push back the limits of reform, to make ideas for more reform plausible and therefore possible. Again key boundaries within the public sector and between the public and private sectors were breached and re-worked. I will return to these in later chapters.

Commodification is the third key facet of the destructiveness/creativity of reform – in making transformation possible by re-working forms of service, social relations and public processes into forms that are measurable and thus contractable or marketable, and in creating spaces for privatisation within the public sector (of both hard and soft services). I shall return to this point a number of times. Commodification is both then cause and effect in relation to privatisation. The replacement of social relations with exchange relations is an effect of 'privatisation' but is also a pre-condition and has involved packaging services in ways that 'prioritise the interests of contractors' (Whitfield 2001: 73); they are 'reconfigured'. 'What makes something, or some service, a commodity is that it is produced for sale, which means producing it in such a way as to make it saleable' (Leys 2001: 87). This is done in part to encourage the development of new markets and attract private providers; where none existed. Whole new forms of commercial activity have emerged – like teacher supply agencies, 'improvement' products, etc. (see Chapter 6). Cerny (1990: 230) argues that:

> what we are seeing in the world today . . . is . . . the re-emergence of the state as a commodifying agent . . . A new state capitalism will come to the fore. The dividing line between public and private, in this context, is being eroded.

As I shall argue, part of the work of performativity is the technical and discursive re-imagining of education as a commodity.

At a practical level of organisational re-design there are three distinct but related facets to the destructive 'creativity' of the transformation or reform process. Three different policy technologies were brought to bear upon and within the public sector – markets, (new) managerialism (or New Public Management) and performativity. Working together they have brought about the 'modernisation' of the 'organisation ecology' (Jessop 2002) of schools – and each has also contributed in particular ways to the processes of privatisation. Each technology is a form of discipline and regulation, and together they constitute a new regime of public sector regulation. I have written about these elsewhere and will rehearse them only briefly here (see for example Ball 1998, 2001, 2002).

Markets

The market, through the medium of various forms of choice and competition, as with the other technologies, is polymorphic; it is organised and applied in different ways in different parts of the public sector, beginning with CCT, which opened a whole range of hard services up for profit and offered public sector agencies the possibility of choice of supplier, through to parental choice of school and per capita funding and thus competition between schools for 'valued' students and families (Ball 1994), to systems of competitive bidding for targeted funds. Once the model of bidding is established it becomes both technically and culturally feasible to extend the range of those who might be able to bid beyond established public sector providers.

The intimate imbrication of managerialism, markets and the increasing presence of the private sector in public service provision is well illustrated by the example of social care. The creation of social care markets came a little later on the Conservatives' agenda of public sector reforms. They were initiated by the 1990 NHS and Community Care Act and implemented between 1991 and 1993 based on the principles of needs-led and user-centred services and they were intended to deliver 'choice, cost-effectiveness and innovation' but what was different here was that the reforms also involved the promotion of the interests of private care service providers. Local authority social service departments were to assume the responsibility for making and managing local social care markets as purchasers of services from independent providers and withdraw from or massively reduce their service provision role. This is a precursor of current developments in educational service. Indeed some of the private providers of social care services would later develop an interest in the education services market.

(New) managerialism

New managerialism is the logical concomitant of the market and logical antidote to the 'failings' of public sector bureaucracy and culture. 'The *new* managerialism emphasized innovation, creativity and empowerment' (Clarke 2004: 117). The new managers are policy entrepreneurs, 'motivated, resourceful, and able to shift the frame of reference beyond the established norms and procedures' (Exworthy and Halford 1999: 6). The new manager is the competition state writ small, although in both rhetoric and practice new managerialism is a ragbag of models, values and purposes – as is the competition state. At heart managerialism 'is a normative system concerning what counts as valuable knowledge, who knows it, and who is empowered to act in what ways as a consequence' (Clarke *et al.* 2000: 9). In application to the public sector this involves a decisive reconstitution of power relations. In line with the periodisation of reform suggested above several writers have made the point that in terms of the form of managerialism in play 'there is an important difference between the New Right model and New Labour's modernization strategy' (Thrupp and Willmott 2003: 31). While the New Right model was outcomes-based, 'New Labour's version is much more interventionist, and considerably more managerialist. Outcomes remain the focus but they are now constituted as targets and benchmarks rather than comparisons with other institutions' (Fergusson 2000: 208). Fergusson goes on to characterise this change as a shift from norm referencing to criterion referencing.

The spread of (new) managerialism through the public sector began in the civil service, in the early 1980s, with the Financial Management Initiative (1982). This was quickly followed by the creation of trading accounts and new executive responsibilities in local government and the changes brought out in the NHS by the implementation of the Griffiths Report (1983). In education the incursions of management began somewhat later via the introduction of Local Management of Schools (Education Reform Act 1988). A report commissioned by the then DES from accountants and management consultants Coopers & Lybrand (1988) described the implementation of LMS in schools as requiring 'a new culture and philosophy of school organization' (p. 2). The private sector was crucial in setting or informing the reform agenda from the outset, bringing its commercial wisdom to bear, and the model of using consultants to advise on, draft, implement or evaluate key aspects of the reform agenda was established early. Increasingly policy was articulated in the language and methods of business. LMS was also the first move in a series of shifts away from local democratic control of education budgets towards a combination of central and indirect 'devolved' financial controls. In an interview at the time a senior civil servant explained to me that "the Bill, it seems to me, is about reducing the power of local authorities, that's what the Bill is about" (quoted in Ball 1990: 69).

Again though, management is not simply a means to effect change in the public sector; it is an opportunity for business for the private sector (see Box 2.2). Management has moved over the past 20 years from being an imperative in the public sector to being a commodity, for which the public sector is an increasingly important customer (see Chapter 6 on 'selling improvement').

Generally, while the 1980s began with a policy emphasis on financial restraint, by the end of the decade the emphasis had shifted to a much broader concern with the re-design of the organisation and management of public sector institutions or, as Schick (1990: 26) explains, the objective of such interventions, and there were similar developments in other English-speaking

---

Box 2.2 Transformation as a business opportunity

Kable business transformation services in the UK public sector 2005 (Price: £1,950 + VAT)

The market for business transformation services is set to grow substantially over the next four years as the government embarks on a series of initiatives described by analysts as "the most significant restructuring of public services for a generation". Efficiency drive creates new opportunities. Greater public sector efficiency is creating business transformation opportunities associated with process improvement modernisation of procurement. Market in public sector business transformation services is set to grow to £2.3bn by 2007 as government initiatives drive demand.

(http://www.kable.com/Default.asp)

and north European countries, was to foster 'a managerial environment which is attentive to performance when funds are parcelled out' or in other words to tie resources to results and to turn spenders into managers. The manager is a subject and means of public sector change, a cultural re-engineer who through vision and leadership re-works the organisational ecology of their institution. This involves an ongoing attrition, made up of incremental larger and smaller changes which are many and disparate. As the OECD put it in terms which are echoed in the Third Way: 'A "selective radical" strategy for implementing reform may be the preferred solution . . . reform is a journey rather than a destination' (1995: 9).

Performativity

The final key component in the triumvirate of reform is performativity, which ties the effort of management to the information systems of the market and customer choice-making and/or to the target and benchmark requirements of the state. Indeed the contraction 'performance management' denotes a particular form and dynamic of managerialism. According to Husbands (2001: 10) performance management works on and through schools in two ways: in a limited way 'to the extent to which [it] focuses school leadership on the core tasks of enhancing pupil progress against measurable criteria; but expansive in the extent to which the language and assumptions of perform-ance management describe a cultural refocusing of schooling', that is 'schools become increasingly subject to "bottom line" judgements of their standards or outputs' (Fitz and Beers 2002: 144). Performance management does not simply change the ways in which schools work; it changes the way we think about schools and learning and it changes how teachers think about their work and their relationships with pupils.

Performativity is a culture and a mode of regulation. The performances of individual subjects or organisations serve as measures of productivity or out-put, or displays of 'quality', or 'moments' of promotion or inspection. They stand for, encapsulate or represent the worth, quality or value of an indi-vidual or organisation within a field of judgement. Performativity is about driving out poor performance, inefficiencies and redundancies – it is about focus. It is insatiable. It is achieved through the construction and publication of information and the drive to name, differentiate and classify. Performativity is intimately intertwined with the seductive possibilities of a particular kind of economic (rather than moral) 'autonomy', what Edwards (2000: 154) calls 'coercive autonomy', for both institutions and in some cases individuals – like headteachers. Performativity works to 'tie things together' and re-make them. It facilitates the monitoring role of the state: 'steering-at-a-distance', 'govern-ing without government', 'the politics of clarity' (Giroux 1992). It allows the state to insert itself deeply into the culture, practices and subjectivities of public sector organisations and their workers, without appearing to do so. It changes that which it 'indicates'; it changes meaning; it delivers re-design and ensures 'alignment'. It objectifies and commodifies public sector work; the knowledge work of educational institutions is rendered into 'outputs', 'levels of performance' and 'forms of quality', that is this process of objectification contributes more generally to the possibility of thinking about social services like education as *forms of production*, as 'just like' services of other kinds and other kinds of production. The 'soft' services like teaching which require 'human interaction' are re-made to be just like the 'hard' services (book supply, transport, catering, instructional media). They are standardised, calculated, qualified and compared. More generally performativity works to edge public sector organisations into a convergence with the private sector.

Through the combination of these policy technologies a new relationship of the state to the public sector is produced and at the same time service provision is made 'contestable and competitive' and 'corporatization and privatization are important policy options in this context' (OECD 1995: 9). The reform process and the changing role of the social democratic state is then part of a broader transformation in political architecture. The shift from responsibility for delivery to responsibility for commissioning, contracting and measurement and audit opens up the possibility of two further policy moves. First, it becomes possible for the state to consider a variety of potential service deliverers – public, voluntary and private. This introduces contestability, competition between potential deliverers on the basis of 'best service' and/or value for money and involves the use of commercial models of tendering and contracting. Second, it becomes possible to consider alternative models of funding and the participation of private funders in the development of the public sector infrastructure. One version of this, in the UK, is what is called the Private Finance Initiative (or Public Private Partnerships). These arrangements involve private sector providers in the building and management of schools, hospitals, university plant, etc. on a lease-back and management contract basis. In most of these cases public sector direct labour is replaced by the contractor, and some commentators fear that at some point such contract labour may extend beyond catering, cleaning, maintenance, security, etc. (hard services) to the core tasks of teaching, research, etc. (soft services). In fact this move is already under way – not only through contracts to run schools, but in the design and management of Academies, through advice, consultancy and CPD and the provision of teaching and learning software by whiteboard companies.

Within social policy research there is a series of hotly contested debates around these issues and the appropriate ways of theorising changes in the welfare state. However, there is also a lot of common ground (Cochrane *et al.* 2001). Several key points within these debates are helpful in making sense of education policy. First, as Esping-Andersen (1996) points out and as noted already, in the UK as elsewhere in Europe these are 'welfare states in transition', that is moving and changing from where they were to somewhere else; the changes are not ended. Second, the ongoing changes are not absolute, the replacement of one welfare regime by another; rather there is a new 'welfare mix' or 'welfare pluralism' (Rao 1996) or 'mixed economies of welfare' (Johnson 1 999). Furthermore, not only are these changes partial, involving 'residual attachments' (Clarke 2004: 154), but they are neither in one direction nor one-dimensional – 'complete design of governance structures is impossible' (OECD 1995: 9). Clarke does go on to say that the status of these residuals and the degree of attachment to them are questionable. All this means that, as Clarke *et al.* (2001: 104–5) put it, 'it is hard to produce a satisfactory synoptic overview of these changes because they are uneven, contradictory and contested. There is no single trend of direction of change'. The composite and sometimes incoherent nature of change is a characteristic of the SWS.

However, there are problems with these social policy accounts; they are almost exclusively focused on the state at a national level and on citizenship and tend to neglect the relationships of welfare to the economy, either as functionally related to competitiveness or as a focus for profit, that is the subordination of 'social policy to the demands of labour market flexibility and/or employability and the perceived imperatives of structural or systemic competitiveness' (Jessop 2001: 298). Privatisation or what is called 'corporate welfare' is generally given little attention in these accounts and, when it is, the focus is on the 'famialisation' of welfare, or the rewriting of 'the relationship between state and citizen, while reforming the state' (Clarke 2004: 67).

We do need to think about and theorise welfare changes in relation to changes in the state and citizenship and that is central to my analysis, but also, and perhaps especially in the case of education and training, we need to explore their relations to the economy – in at least three senses:

- the economics of education – funding and cost (e.g. PFIs);
- education and the economy – labour and knowledge, competitiveness;
- the economy and education – commodification and profit.

The technologies of public sector reform work in complex ways to bring about practical, cultural and discursive changes. They combine to re-work organisational ecologies and the ecology of the state. They change the ways in which we think about the public sector and its relationships and practices. In particular they have the effect of making the public sector amenable to privatisation(s) – endogenous and exogenous. They constitute a political imaginary more subtle and elusive than that of the New Right. I want to move on now to look at some of the ways in which this imaginary is disseminated within education policy, that is the ways in which Third Way education policy celebrates the virtues of diversity, entrepreneurship and privatisation and links education in direct and indirect ways to globalisation and international competitiveness. One of Tony Blair's declared aims is to "make this country at ease with globalisation" (27 September 2005).

Discourse of privatisation

The discourse of privatisation and of 'the private' is ubiquitous in education policy statements. It is pervasive, polymorphic and insidious. Within this discourse, education is re-articulated as a resource for the economy, that is as productive, as income-generating and as a commodity (see Box 2.3 for examples).

Box 2.3 Discourse of privatisation

Inflation pressures threaten university viability
Official figures from the Higher Education Statistics Agency, released yesterday, showed income to all British universities rose by £1.2bn in 2002–3 to £16.6bn, with an operating surplus that had grown to £241m.

(*Financial Times*, 27 April 2005)

Public pleasure over private regret
In an interview with the *Financial Times*, schools minister Stephen Timms put forward the idea that individual school departments might be handed over to private management.

(*TES*, 21 September 2001)

From Delhi to Dudley
It is one of Britain's unsung success stories: the phenomenal growth in the number of fee-paying overseas students ... Derby has 400 overseas students of whom 50 are on full-time fee-paying courses. It is also targeting China, Taiwan, Hong Kong and Japan for recruitment ... *Positioning for Success*, a British Council consultative paper, wants £5m pumped into a drive to ensure Britain stays a world leader in educating foreign students.

(*TES*, FE Focus, 13 August, 2004)

Entrepreneurial spirit
The new education Bill gives schools powers to create companies and run post offices.

(*TES* Weekly Newsletter, 24 November 2001)

Higher education spin-offs push Britain up entrepreneurial league
Spin-off companies created from higher-education institutions have risen sharply in number, challenging the view that British universities are less entrepreneurial than North American ones.

(*Financial Times*, 7 December 2001)

Pioneer of school–business links: Kings Hurst established a blueprint for the education innovations the government hopes to encourage

The school has online video links with its partner schools in the Kings Hurst Federation – all run by 3Es. Students build websites and are in regular touch with partner schools in the US. One room in the school is 'The Academy', a software design studio financed by 3Es surplus. It is a growing business with 100 schools buying Kings Hurst's GNVQ science course online at £3000 a time ... "We've got business and industry in our bloodstreams" says Mrs Bragg [Headteacher].

(*Financial Times*, 16 July 2001)

Lester Davies looks back on his year-long secondment to the Bass brewery as one of the best professional development experiences he has ever had. So when he heard of a programme that turns the secondment process on its head and sends people from business into schools, he decided to give it a try ... Heads, Teachers and Industry (HTI) matched the school with Izzy Ali-McLachlan from the Technology Innovation Centre at the University of Central England. Mr Ali-McLachlan has a background in product design.

(School Leader, *TES*, 20 May 2005, p. 27)

These examples of media coverage of educational issues serve as illustrations of the dissemination of the discourse of privatisation (or perhaps more accurately in some cases competition). Key terms within the discourse recur – 'entrepreneurism', 'partnerships', 'companies', 'innovation', 'business', 'private' – and the 'knowledge economy' is very much in evidence. These words represent new ways of thinking about education, new ways of acting and relating for education workers. Schools and universities 'exploit' their knowledge, selling to generate 'surpluses'. Success is measured in terms of income, 'spin-offs' and turnover – as well as creativity, dissemination and technology transfer. This constitutes a powerful meta-narrative, 'a web of interlocution' (Somers 1994: 614) which 'joins up' a diversity of activities, interactions and organisations. Nonetheless, the contradictions noted previously between 'commodified and collectivised' knowledge are apparent also, although in these examples it is the commodified form which is most in evidence. There is a 'judicious' mix of networks and markets, competition and collaboration. What is being outlined here is key elements of what Osborne and Gaebler (1992) describe and advocate as 'entrepreneurial governance' with its enterprise, responsiveness and devolved responsibility to agencies separately accountable from government for their budgets and their performance in relation to targets or contract requirements. This is 'the reimagination of previously distinct domains of existence as forms of the economic' (du Gay 2000).

The boundaries between what is state and what is private are blurred. Schools and universities and business are literally 'joined up' in joint enterprises, and schools are 'joined up' in networks and federations, via video links and ITC. Social relations, organisational forms (companies), modes of operation, and culture and language in the public sector have all changed, and it is change that makes these items newsworthy. This is part of the re-design of schools, colleges and universities, organisational and discursive, which shifts both structure and purpose. We see glimpses of the global economy (UK and US entrepreneurism compared), the market in educational services (overseas student recruitment) and the production of new kinds of learners and workers; all of this uses 'collective consumption to promote transition to a globalizing, knowledge-based economy' (Jessop 2002: 162). Education is no longer 'extra-economic':

> We can already see how important education and skills are for individual and collective prosperity . . . On a global scale, half the increase in the annual growth of productivity comes from new ideas and ways of doing things. The fastest-growing cities in America and Europe are those with the highest proportion of knowledge workers.
>
> (Tony Blair, 'Knowledge 2000', Conference on the Knowledge Driven Economy)

In its directness and single-mindedness this discourse is increasingly familiar and inescapable. Public sector institutions are being 're-thought' as profit opportunities. Underpinning this is an effective policy trope which celebrates the 'superiority' of private sector management, in 'partnership' with the state, over and against the conservative, bureaucratic and unresponsive modality of public sector management, although the public sector is not without its own pockets of 'excellence' and not all experiments in privatisation succeed.

> The weakness of our public services has not been their inability to achieve excellence, but the fact that it is too thinly spread, with opportunities and high quality provision too often restricted to a minority . . . Sure, there are risks. It won't always work. But taking risks is part of change leading to improvement.
>
> (Prime Minister's speech on public service reform, 16 October 2001, available online: http://www.number10.gov.uk/output/ Page1632.asp from www.direct.gov.uk)

Finally, here I want to examine New Labour policy talk a little more and point up some of the components of the political discourse of privatisation and the variety of ways in which they are intimately tied to competitiveness on the one hand and the role of the private sector in the re-design or transformation of the public sector on the other. This will highlight a number of themes and terms which recur through the book, and the use of some of these terms and the 'work' they do will be addressed more fully in later chapters. This is an initial foray into a programmatic discourse that 'highlights the contrast between terms that represent a stereotyped and demonized past and those offering a visionary and idealized future' (Clarke and Newman 1997: 49). I have chosen to give special attention to the words of Tony Blair but there are innumerable other sites for and sources of the discourse in White Papers, government websites, other political utterances, etc.

Within the complex and expansive rhetoric of New Labour the terms I want to drawn attention to are: 'transformation', 'modernisation', 'innovation', 'risk', 'dynamism', 'creativity' and 'competitiveness' (for the relationship of these to technology see Chapter 6); other terms like 'partnerships', 'flexibility' and 'collaboration' are given attention in other chapters. These are terms, except 'competition' perhaps, which have no necessary exclusivity to the private sector but are often deployed as though they did, for example 'the celebration of "creativity" as an essential element of business' (Jones 2003: 164). They are taken to be qualities of and to exemplify entrepreneurism and enterprise, key signifiers that also recur. They often appear in texts as collocations – co-occurrences; that is they are linked together as an ensemble and are chronotopically related to a sense of the pace, movement and constant change that are taken to define globalisation, the globalised economy and world cities. They set the inadequacies, particularly the slowness and unresponsiveness and risk aversion of the public sector prior to reform, over and against the 'idealised' alternative.[1] The shift from the former to the latter is taken to be necessary and inevitable and related to economic rather than social pressures and needs, the urgent demands of globalisation. 'Complaining about globalization is as pointless as trying to turn back the tide. Asian competition can't be shut out; it can only be beaten. And now, by every relative measure of a modern economy, Europe is lagging' (Tony Blair, *Newsweek*, http://www.msnbc.msn.com/id/11020913/site/newsweek/). This is the 'necessarian logic of New Labour's political economy' (Watson and Hay 2003). The public sector must be re-made to respond to the exigence (Edwards and Nicoll 2001), that is to globalisation, and to play its part in the economics of competition. Individual and institutional actors and their dispositions and responses are tied to the fate of the nation within the global economy.

> The purpose of the reforms is to create a modern education system and a modern NHS where, within levels of investment at last coming up to the average of our competitors, real power is put in the hands of those who use the service, the patient and the parent, where the changes becoming self-sustaining, the system open, diverse, flexible, able to adjust and adapt to the changing world.
>
> (Prime Minister Tony Blair reflects on 'pivotal moment'
> for education, 10 Downing Street, 24 October 2005)

There is an easily graspable narrative here, an 'insistent singularity' (du Gay

2000: 78) which links the intimacies of educational practices to the global economy. As Fairclough (2000: 158) explains, 'the work of politics or government is partly done in the material of texts – it gets into the texture of texts'. Urgency, inevitability and radical change are part of this texture, creating a policy ontology within which public sector actors are made new kinds of subjects. The lack of clarity and coherence in these statements, how the elements are joined up, is unimportant and is overcome by reiteration, and within the texts there is a constant play of key binaries, some of which are collapsed while at the same time others are ramified and reified often in fantastical ways as what Fairclough (p. 10) calls 'impossible alternatives'. "Enterprise and fairness. That is our goal" (Tony Blair, 'Knowledge 2000', Conference on the Knowledge Driven Economy, http://mbbnet.umn.edu/doric/economy.html). The rhetoric here writes a history of the public sector that is epideictic, an allocation of praise and blame. There is a dialogue that places the 'old' public sector in contrast to a 'modern' public sector and the 'new' economy and as a threat to competitiveness; it is cast as an anachronism, an irrelevance.

> Do we take modest though important steps of improvement? Or do we make the great push forward for transformation? Let me spell it out. In education . . . we open up the system to new and different ways of education . . . There's nothing wrong with the old principles but, if the old ways worked, they'd have worked by now.
>
> (Tony Blair, Labour Party Conference, Autumn 2002)

The rhetoric conjures up the need for new kinds of policy and a new kind of government, which is New Labour; and the policy itself is timely and dynamic.

> [W]e must let the systems change and develop. The old monolithic structures won't do. We can't engineer change and improvement through bureaucratic edict. Hence the reform programme . . . It is not our tax and fiscal positions which are holding us back as a nation. It is productivity and the state of our public services.
>
> (Prime Minister's speech on public service reform, 16 October 2001, available online: http://www.number10.gov.uk/output/Page1632.asp from www.direct.gov.uk)

Bureaucracy stultifies creativity and inhibits innovation, which are sometimes natural qualities (of the nation) that are being suppressed and must be 'released' but sometimes need to be imported (from the private sector). 'Today the British people are characterized by creativity, ingenuity, and imagination. There is a new dynamism in our country . . . education is our No. 1 domestic priority. That is the key to economic success and social justice' (Tony Blair, 'The New Britain', DLC, *New Democrat*, 1 March 1998). The rhetoric of reform also tightly couples social justice, equity and maximising social and economic participation to enterprise and economic success. Modernisation and change are all-embracing; they are meritocratic, an escape from old social divisions, again in this way a form of liberation which will allow creativity and passion to flourish unhampered. Here individual and collective well-being are totally elided. Equity and enterprise, technological change and economic progress are tied together within the efforts, talents and qualities of individual people (see Chapter 6 on this and on 'peoplism') and the national collective – the 'us' and the 'we'.

> It is to modernise our country, so that, in the face of future challenges, intense and profound for us and like nations, we are able to provide opportunity and security for all, not for an elite, not for the privileged few, but for all our people, whatever their class, colour or creed. It is to build, on the platform of economic stability, the modern knowledge economy with the skills, dynamism, technological and scientific progress a country like Britain needs. And above all, they are about realising the enormous creative energy and passion that people feel in all walks of life for education, for its liberating power, for its unique ability to correct the inequalities of class or background.
>
> (Text of a speech by Tony Blair to the Labour Party's Centenary Conference in Blackpool, 10 February 2006)

Reform will not only deliver greater equality; it is also intimately tied through the development of skills and 'new' knowledge' to the requirements of the imaginary Knowledge Economy: and the forging of "a nation where the creative talents of all people are used to build a true enterprise economy for the 21st century – where we compete on brains, not brawn" (Tony Blair, Colorado Alliance for Arts Education, http://www.artsedcolorado.org/advocacy.cfm).

> Successful countries need a stable economic framework so firms, and families, can plan with confidence. They need open markets, strong encouragement of enterprise with labor-market flexibility to foster dynamism and adaptability. And, more important today than ever, they need sustained investment in science, education and lifelong learning to make the most of the skills and talents of all their people – to create, in fact, true knowledge economies.
>
> (Tony Blair, *Newsweek*, http://www.policy-network.net /php/article.php?sid=4&aid=528)

Central to the process of education reform and to the insertion of dynamism and the achievement or release of innovation is the participation of new players in the field of public service delivery – the private and voluntary sector. Blair himself plays a key role in providing recurring rhetorical legitimation for a 'diversity of providers' and the 'failures' of uniformity. The private sector is not a simple ideological preference as it was under Thatcherism; it is a means to an end, a mechanism rather than a belief system. There is a convergence of interests. 'The public sector is looking to the private sector for expertise, innovation and management of appropriate risks. The private sector is looking for business opportunities, a steady funding stream and a good return on its investment' (DfES Public–Private Partnership website, May 2004). Indeed, the task of modernisation is presented as beyond ideology and politics, which are distractions from what must be done. "It is not just investment that has held back reform. We have also been held back by ideological clashes, going back decades, which have distracted from the real challenge of improving our public services" (Prime Minister's speech on public service reform, 16 October 2001, available online: http://www.number10. gov.uk/output/Page1632.asp from www.direct.gov.uk). Service delivery itself is 'depoliticised' – policy, management and practice are discursively integrated. The private sector also acts as a form of discipline, an alternative to the public sector if modernisation is resisted or fudged. "If you are unwilling or unable to work to the modern agenda, then government will have to look to other partners to take on your role" (Tony Blair's address to public agencies, 1998, cited in Newman 2001: 51). The private sector is a comparator and a model to be emulated: 'we need to make sure that government services are brought forward using the best and most modern techniques, to match the best of the private sector' (Cabinet Office 1999: 5). As Jones puts it: 'Blair combines a market-based recognition of "porosity" and the limits of government action with an assertion that governments should act decisively within those fields where directive action is possible' (Jones 2003: 149). 'Prime Minister Tony Blair used his monthly press conference to make clear his determination to use private-sector practice to push through public-sector reform. It would be a mistake of "fundamental historic importance" to change course now, he said' (Jon Slater, *Guardian*, 2 May 2003).

> In developing greater choice of provider, the private and voluntary sectors can play a role. Contrary to myth, no-one has ever suggested they are *the* answer. Or that they should replace public services. But where use of them can improve public services, nothing should stand in the way of their use. In any event, round the world, the barriers between public, private and voluntary are coming down . . . if schools want a new relationship with business in their community, as many do, let them . . . What I'm saying is let the system breathe; develop; expand; let the innovation and creative ideas of public servants be given a chance to flourish.
> (Prime Minister's speech on public service reform, 16 October 2001,
> available online: http://www.number10.gov.uk/output/
> Page1632.asp from www.direct.gov.uk)

The discursive ensemble adumbrated above is constantly reiterated and re-worked and expanded into new fields; it builds, sediments and elaborates, supplanting other possibilities, appropriating other uses and meanings. The key terms are insinuated into the everyday language of the public sector, changing the landscape of meanings and imagination. The dynamic of transformation and the need to seize opportunities, constantly innovate and constantly improve performance are everywhere.

> Schools at the cutting edge of innovation and collaboration will be selected from amongst the country's best schools as a lever to transform secondary education, to engineer the growth of collaborative learning communities and federations, and to promote innovation, research and development to push the boundaries of current teaching practice.
> (Leading Edge Partnerships, DfES website, 2004)

> Constantly, I meet public servants whom I find truly inspiring; people who are change makers and social entrepreneurs every bit as capable and creative as the best private sector entrepreneurs. We need to encourage them, to let diversity break down the old monoliths.
> (Prime Minister's speech on public service reform, 16 October 2001, available online: http://www.number10.gov.uk/output/ Page1632.asp from www.direct.gov.uk)

Such a discourse works in a variety of ways to re-draw boundaries, label heroes and villains, create space for action, exclude other possibilities, legitimate new voices, construct events into sequences (narratives) and re-write history, attribute cause and effect, and make some things seem natural and others inevitable. It privileges certain sorts of knowledge and human qualities. The public sector is re-imagined (see Chapters 6 and 7 on icons).

Within this discourse is a single, iterative and embedded ontology of reform based on an idealisation of the firm as a generic model of social and economic behaviour – creativity, innovation, risk-taking, flexibility and adaptation (joined and animated by charismatic, resolute, committed and visionary leadership, for which Blair himself is the model) in a changing and dynamic and competitive economic context are the model for the nation, public sector, local state (see Chapter 5), institutions and rational, self-interested but responsible individual actors. The expectations, assumptions and standards within policy discourse require the public sector to imitate the outlook and practices of the private sector and a transfer (or release) of the characteristics of the firm into the public sector. What this amounts to is what Hodgson (1999: 240–1) calls an 'evotopian scheme of thought', made up of uncertainty, experiment, variety and the impossibility of omniscience and stressing the link between pluralism and innovation, that is the idea that innovation comes about 'from a repertoire of opportunities' (p. 252).

As part of this re-imagining of the public sector there are opportunities and possibilities for and legitimacy lent to various forms of privatisation and a re-working of the relationships between the state and the private sector.

There are both opportunities for new sources of profit, the 'restless develop-ment of capital' (Rikowski 2001), and a concomitant exploration of new forms of public sector management and delivery. Both are intended to enhance the state's 'capacity to project its influence and secure its objectives' (Jessop 2002: 199) – economic stability and international competitiveness. While privatisation is a 'necessary' and decisive component of the transform-ation of education it is as much about changing the public sector as it is about replacing it. Indeed, the state is highly active in the organisation and man-agement of new public sector markets.

This is not a single, simple or finished move, nor simply a move 'to privat-ise' as such. It is the pragmatism of New Labour and its commitment to 'what works'. This is nicely captured in the policy aphorism 'standards not structures'. In displacing and dismantling the institutional and professional foundations of a monolithic public sector and moving to a system which is more diverse, responsive (signal-alert) and malleable by the use of fixed-term delivery systems (contracts and initiatives), the state builds flexibility and reflexivity into its competitiveness and coordination strategies at the oper-ational level. Failures can be more quickly dispensed with – both in financial and in electoral terms – and learned from; 'relative success in coordina-tion over time depends on the capacity to switch modes of coordination as the limits of any one mode become evident' (Jessop 2002: 244). The 'de-privatisation' of rail maintenance is a case in point. In this respect the examples I shall give in later chapters of the state as a *market-maker* indicate the managed development of educational privatisation, the limits set to some forms of privatisation and their experimental use and as part of all this the 'publicisation' (Sellers 2003) of private provision.

The opportunities for business within public sector reform rest on the variety of meanings and practices of the Third Way discourse as realised within an ensemble of policies and statements – Best Value, CPA, School Acts and White Papers, EAZs, contestability, failure, measurement, inspec-tions, outsourcing, connectivity, infrastructural investment, partnerships and Academies. Such ideas and initiatives and their scaffolding within prime min-isterial speeches and other policy utterances make meaningful and practical the doing of privatisation. On the one hand, the state underwrites private failure by ensuring, in some cases, a favourable point of entry into the new markets, making them attractive. However, on the other, these new markets can contain surprises for business and profits can be elusive, especially in educational 'retailing' where the margins are small (see Chapters 4 and 6). As a result, as will be demonstrated, the ESI is potentially unstable and unpredictable. It is to a detailed examination of the ESI that I now turn.

3 Scale and scope

Education is big business

In this chapter and the next I look in some detail at the scale and scope and complexity of the education services industry (ESI) and some of its internal workings in the form of a descriptive analysis. Such an exercise will provide, I hope, some clarity and precision regarding what is meant by privatisation(s) and specify some of the diversity of arrangements to which this term refers. The chapter will also introduce substantive issues which are taken up in more detail in the following chapters.

Some bits of the ESI are high-profile and have received considerable press and public attention – LEA intervention contracts, for example, or the Academies programme or PFIs – but many other facets of this extensive market remain rather obscure or neglected – like prison education, consultancy work within the DfES, induction schemes for overseas-trained teachers, work with children out of school, project management, etc., etc. I will argue that the extent and 'value' (to business) of private participation in public education is generally misunderstood and under-estimated and 'blurred under a thousand half-truths' as Pollack (2004: vii) puts it in her examination of the privatisation of health care. Furthermore, not only are the privatisations which the ESI represents very diverse, but so too are the companies and groups which participate. The chapter will profile some of the 'players' and detail some of their differences in terms of size, ambition, values and history. The chapter concludes with some preliminary generalisations about the ESI and privatisation and their relationships to the changing role of the state.

Profiting from reform

The 'reform' of the public service sector is a massive new profit opportunity for business – a key point that I shall revisit several times in this study. "Fast growth in the local government and education outsourcing market is certain now that the government has made education its key priority" (Mike Henebury of Gresham Trust, private equity investors in Tribal Group). The school rebuilding and refurbishment programme Building Schools for the Future (BSF) is worth between £5 billion and £8.5 billion. In 2003 the PFI debt market stood at £8.2 billion, up from £4.9 billion the previous year.

New investment in PFIs in 2003 was £6.7 billion. The outsourcing of education services is worth at least £1.5 billion a year, and outsourcing across the public sector as a whole at least £10 billion a year. The Tenders Electronic Daily Service (http://www.scottishenterprise.com/sedotcom_home/about_se/ procurement/tenders/teds.htm) estimates the total value of the public procurement market (contracts for public sector work of all kinds) at £500 billion annually. However, within all this, private sector participation ranges from multimillion-pound building projects and national contracts for systems management to involvement in the small-scale, everyday activities of schools and with teachers.

Private companies run national programmes, like the National Literacy Strategy (CfBT and now Capita), provide school inspections, advice for school leavers, and school meals,[1] and supply teachers and IT and office support systems for LEAs and individual schools. Additionally, and often confusingly, many schools and LEAs are involved in 'partnerships' and joint ventures with private companies, and many state agencies and quangos also seek and obtain contracts for commercial work, often in direct competition with private companies. Furthermore, schools were enabled by the 2002 Education Act to form themselves as companies and market goods and services to other schools. The school examination boards, including Edexcel (annual turnover £112 million), AQA (£128 million) and OCR (Oxford, Cambridge and RSA) (£77 million), are now fully fledged international businesses. University student loans and university bursaries are handled by SLC, the Student Loans Company, etc., etc. In other words, privatisations are everywhere and are very diverse.

Most of the major UK management services companies and accountancy and consulting firms are now or have attempted to become involved in the ESI; several of the largest building firms in the UK and overseas-based now devote all or significant proportions of their investment to Private Finance Initiative (PFI) work; private equity banks and City institutions see the public sector as an 'opportunity' and are now investing in educational 'enterprises' or buying up existing contracts. On the other hand, there are still large, but declining, numbers of sole traders and small and medium-size enterprises who do consultancy work, CPD and back-office work for schools.

Box 3.1 Retail services

Succeed and have Fun with Differentiation, Modelling and Plenaries. Key Stage 2 Teachers of English Literacy – Fee £135

Pupils' Spiritual, Moral, Social and Cultural Development – Ofsted Licensed course – Fee £240

(HBS CPD Course Portfolio 2004–5)

The private sector is now embedded in the heart and sinews of state education services at all levels, inter-twined in the day-to-day business of decision-making, infrastructural development, capacity building and services delivery. The ESI has also generated significant but largely unacknowledged secondary markets (e.g. in PFI facilities management (FM) contracts and lease contracts), and a subsidiary 'transition' business which provides a constant stream of work for 'the Big Four companies of auditors and management accountants, and the corporate law firms responsible for drawing up hundreds of thousands of contracts and subcontracts with all those private providers' (Pollack 2004: 214). Furthermore, the policy work of the state is routinely informed, monitored or taken over by private providers in the form of consultancies, evaluations or reviews; this is what Mahony *et al.* (2004: 207) call 'privatizing policy' – 'we contend that such has been the central involvement of some of these companies that they should be seen as part of the policy creation community' (see Chapter 4).

> Figures from the Office of Government Commerce show that spending on consultants rose by 42 per cent last year from £1.76 billion in 2003–04.
>   Some private consultancies are now focusing entirely on public sector contracts, which can attract fees of up to £2,000 per day. Firms are being hired to advise on outsourcing, to 'manage change', to set up IT systems, to advise on advertising and communications and to conduct polls and surveys ... Douglas Johnson-Poensgen, director of Serco Consulting, said that his firm had seen a 250 per cent increase in public sector contracts in the past two years, particularly from the NHS ... Andy Ford, head of local government consultancy at PricewaterhouseCoopers, said his firm's public sector contracts had doubled over the past three years, particularly in local government. This was partly due to council league tables, Sir Peter Gershon's drive to save £20 billion in the public sector and local efforts to improve frontline services.
>
> (*Times*, 24 September 2005)

Through these involvements, networks of social relations are established between politicians, civil servants and business (and charities and voluntary organisations) which inform and influence policy thinking about education, and in addition there is considerable movement of personnel between state and public services and the private sector and some in the other direction.

Within these networks, the distinctions between advice, support and lobbying for work are sometimes hard to see. Private consultants are routinely contracted to give advice on the future organisation of government or local government services or are members of taskforces which almost without exception produce recommendations for further privatisations and outsourcing. Within these networks, privatisation in one form or another is 'the obvious' of policy. Prevailing policy discourses which circulate in and are legitimated by these networks privilege privatisation(s) as the solution to almost every problem of government.

There are two further aspects to the ESI which need to be noted. First, this is not just a national phenomenon, and I do not mean this simply in the sense that more and more countries are engaged in privatisation, to greater or lesser extents, although this is the case (Kenway and Bullen 2001; Hall and Lubina 2004; Crump and Slee 2005; Molnar 2005; Saltman 2005). Rather the ESI is international. British firms sell their services abroad and foreign firms are engaged in the delivery of education services or infrastructure here. In 2003–4 the Swedish construction firm Skanska did the most PFI business in the UK at £3 billion, followed by Balfour Beatty, and Japanese company Kajima is another major PFI investor. Two state schools in Surrey, King's College and Frenchay, which are contracted out, are run by a company owned by General Education Management Systems (GEMS), a Dubai-based international education business. Vinci, a French construction giant, has bought out most of the PFI work of construction and services company Jarvis ('Beleaguered', http://news.scotsman.com/topics.cfm?tid=571&id=1194522004). Second, there is a massive and growing adjunct market in educational services, that is the selling of 'educational' products and services directly to parents and learners. This includes private schools – and GEMS is also a provider here – and nursery schooling and childcare, private tuition, enrichment activities (e.g. Stagecoach,[2] Tumbletots and Crescendo), learning materials (books and software) and educational toys and materials or what Kenway and Bullen (2001: 83) call 'edutainment' – 'fun with a purpose', which encourages parents to 'seek consumerist solutions to parenting problems' (p. 85). In a broader sense, what Kenway and Bullen (2001: 90) call 'promiscuous corporations' also see children themselves as a lucrative market via 'sponsorship, philanthropy and commercial opportunism'. Schools are now targeted as a means of reaching the child consumer – "So, it is a question of coming up with a method whereby one can actually get into schools" (Marketing Manager, quoted in Kenway and Bullen 2001: 91). I will explore each of these different aspects of the ESI in more detail below.

Representing the ESI

I intend to explain and represent the development and structure of the ESI using heuristic devices which highlight different aspects of it and different ways of thinking about it. Later I will offer a typology of private sector companies and in the next chapter look at the work of a number of ESI companies, drawing on interviews and documentary research. As intimated above, the role of public sector organisations and quangos in the ESI also needs some consideration – as, for example, Warwick University establishes a Far East campus, Dulwich College sets up schools in Malaysia and China, and the Qualifications and Curriculum Authority competes to win government contracts.

The education market within which private companies participate is in fact a series of often discrete sectors and specialisms which some companies work across and others specialise within. Many of the companies introduced below reappear at points in later chapters – indicating their multi-faceted engagement with the ESI. One way of representing the sectors is offered in Figure 3.1. As Kay (2004: 11) says, 'a good model is like a biblical parable and like parables, is neither true nor false, only illuminating or unilluminating'.

Figure 3.1 indicates four major kinds of involvement with and relationships with and within state education by the private sector (the cross-axes within the circle), although they are in practice not always mutually exclusive. The forms of involvement range from hard services like buildings, IT hardware and connectivity (*infrastructure*), through management systems at LEA and institutional levels, and office, payroll and HR services, benchmarking and performance monitoring (*contracts*), to softer services related to CPD, curriculum materials and 'performance enhancement' (*services*), and pedagogy in the case of the National Strategies for Numeracy and Literacy, and careers advice in the case of Connexions (*programmes*). Several other market

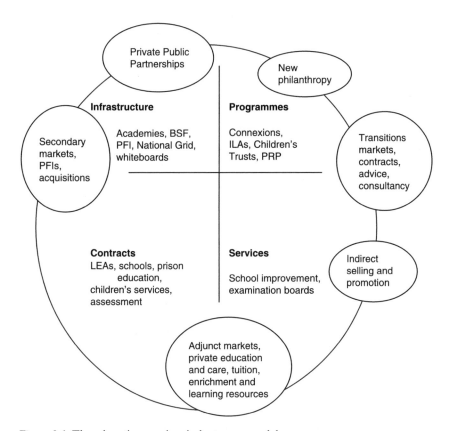

Figure 3.1 The education services industry – a model.

sectors are indicated in the figure (on the rim of the circle) inter-woven in different ways with the main ESI sectors. I will work through each of these sectors and markets (with the exception of new philanthropy, which is discussed in Chapter 5). I will also look at the processes of vertical and horizontal integration in the ESI. The scope and complexity of these sectors and markets mean that I can only offer a glimpse of what goes on in each, enough I hope to convey a sense of the scale and range of activities.

Infrastructure

Infrastructure mainly concerns capital works, the building or major refurbishment of school or university buildings and the installation of ITC systems and connectivity (e.g. Regional Grids of Learning). The Private Finance Initiative is in some respects the most radical form of the privatisation of public services, involving the use of private sector funding and ownership to provide new buildings and major refurbishments. I do not intend to rehearse too much of the details of these schemes and initiatives here (some further explanation appears in Chapter 6). Rather I want to register the size and significance of PFI commitments and the interest of the construction industry in them and to note some of the disputes about PFI financing and some issues about ownership. It is important to note that PFI schemes operate right across the public sector. I also want to draw attention later to the attempts of some of the infrastructure companies to diversify into the softer end of education services, that is to move across the boundaries between ESI sectors.

The UK Private Finance Initiative was launched in late 1992 by the Conservative government. It encourages public authorities to 'consider' contracting for major capital assets and the facilities services associated with their operation as a combined package – DBFO (design, build, finance and operate). Bidders for these contracts are normally a consortium (or special purpose vehicle) made up of builders, banks or private equity companies and sometimes a management services company. See Box 3.2 for examples.

Box 3.2 PFIs: examples

Renfrewshire Schools
Operis acted as financial advisors to the Bank of Scotland on the Renfrewshire Schools PPP Project which reached financial close in March 2005. The Bank of Scotland was the senior debt provider. The £135 million contract is between Renfrewshire Council and the Renfrewshire Schools Partnership Limited ('RSP'), a joint venture company owned by Amey Ventures Investment Limited, Carillion Private Finance and the Bank of Scotland Corporate.

Under the 32 year contract, RSP will assume responsibility for the construction of ten new schools, which will comprise six primary and four secondary schools, two community nurseries and a community learning centre. The schools, which carry a build value of just under £100 million, were designed by Carillion and will be managed by Amey on behalf of the consortium. It is expected that the first facility will be completed by the middle of 2006 with the remainder due for completion by the end of 2007.

(http://www.operis.com/refrewshire.htm)

Balfour Beatty reaches financial close on £140 million North Lanarkshire schools PPP project
8 June 2005
Balfour Beatty plc, the international engineering, construction and services group, announces today that it has reached financial close on North Lanarkshire Council's Education 2010 PPP schools project. The project involves capital works to the value of approximately £140 million and over £100 million of long-term service revenue.

The 31-year concession involves the construction of 21 new schools, including three large secondary schools in Airdrie and Coatbridge, six primary schools and a further 12 primary schools provided over six joint campus facilities. Also, there is a potential for a further three schools to be constructed.

Commenting on today's announcement, Balfour Beatty Chief Executive, Ian Tyler, said: "We are delighted to be working in partnership with North Lanarkshire Council in realising its objective to provide the very best education opportunities for the area. Balfour Beatty will provide the Council with a greatly enhanced education environment through the design, construction and servicing of new, modern, state-of-the-art buildings and facilities. We intend to bring the same level of professionalism and service as we are providing through our public–private partnerships in Stoke and Rotherham schools."

North Lanarkshire Council Leader, Councillor Jim McCabe, said: "I am pleased to report that after a lot of hard work behind the scenes by the Council and Transform Schools, we are a step closer to providing brand new schools and community facilities for the people of North Lanarkshire."

Balfour Beatty will invest £8 million of equity in the project. Balfour Beatty Capital Projects and its joint venture partner, Innisfree Limited, have established Transform Schools (North Lanarkshire) Ltd as the concession company. This is the highest value concession contract awarded to Transform Schools, which now has responsibility for providing services to over 150 schools in England and Scotland.

> Construction work by a joint venture of Balfour Beatty subsidiary companies, Balfour Beatty Construction and Balfour Kilpatrick, began under an advance works contract in October 2004. Completed schools will be handed over between January 2006 and October 2008. Facilities management for a range of hard and soft services will be provided by Haden Building Management, Balfour Beatty's building management and building maintenance arm.
>
> Balfour Beatty is preferred bidder on two further schools PPP projects, in Nottinghamshire and Birmingham, which are expected to reach financial close during 2005.
>
> (http://www.balfourbeatty.com/bbeatty/media/pr/ 2005/2005 –06–08/)

By late 2004 there were 86 PFI schools projects in England worth £2.4 billion involving over 500 schools, 15 in Scotland worth £553 million, and two in Wales. The overall value of PFI deals in 2004 was estimated by the Treasury to be £7.7 billion, including £900 million for educational and skills projects.

Under PFI contracts the private sector company is responsible for meeting output specifications set by the public sector authority. These may be expressed in a wide variety of ways reflecting the nature of the desired services facility or system. The private sector company carries the responsibility and risk for design, financing, project management and ongoing service quality and delivery. However, many critics of PFI, like the Association of Chartered Certified Accountants and the National Audit Office, argue that the 'risk-costing' of these schemes, which is part of the value-for-money calculations (in relation to a public sector comparator, an estimate of the cost of the project if it were publicly funded), is typically exaggerated. Risk-costing tends to ensure a built-in advantage to private sector tenders over the public sector comparator, and this is in turn a source of short-term profit when borrowing costs are renegotiated when construction is finished. These windfalls are now shared with the public sector. PFI contracts and buildings and facilities management normally last for between 25 and 35 years, over which time the public agency (LEA, health trust) pays a monthly lease and FM fee. These fees are an ongoing cost to the public authority annual budget.

PFIs are enormously attractive to construction companies and have provided a new stability and considerable growth in the industry. The Major Contractors Group (MCG), which lobbies government on behalf of the construction industry, accepts that companies involved in PFI work 'expect to make between three and ten times as much money as they do on traditional contracts'. Bill Tallis, the Director of MCG, said 'construction firms traditionally received rates of return of 1.5% to 2% on contracts but were now expecting margins of 7.5% to 15% on PFI building schemes' (*Corporate Watch*, 19 March 2004).

Once building is complete, the contractors are responsible for FM and operational services, although these contracts are also sold on in some cases (see page 63) and they normally take on or replace the existing workforce through TUPE arrangements[3] (http://www.businesslink.gov.uk/ bdotg/action/layer?&topicId=1074450319&tc=000KW021904512). For this and other reasons PFIs and PPPs are staunchly opposed by public sector trade unions like the NUT and Unison:

> Public services are labour intensive and labour costs can be a major source of potential savings and profit to the private sector. Until employees are fully protected against contractors creating a 'two-tier workforce' by giving new staff inferior pay and conditions, this will remain a central issue for trade unions.
> (Unison, 'What is PFI?', p. 18, http://www.unison.org.uk
> /acrobat/B1062.pdf)

In 2003 the *Best Value Code of Practice on Workforce Matters* was introduced, which stated that contractors who intended to cut costs in this way 'will not be selected to provide services' (para. 3). Nonetheless, the transfer of workers from the public to the private sector and changes to their conditions of work is one of a number of examples of the flexibilisation of labour which privatisation(s) bring about and part of a gradual break-up of national union and professional arrangements for the employment of education services workers which 'disaggregates public services' (Rutherford 2003: 44) and disentangles 'service provision from its social ties' (p. 44). Public services are made objects of commercial calculability. Perversely several local authority pension funds (London, Newham and South Yorkshire) are now investors in a £400 million fund put together by the Mill Group to invest in small-scale PFI projects.

PFI projects are forms of Public Private Partnerships (PPPs), but PPPs now embrace a much wider range of possible contractual and collaborative relationships between public authorities and private sector companies. The term has become widely used to describe initiatives to form partnerships between the public and private sectors 'to enhance the value of public sector assets or to deliver more efficient services' (Serco website). Such schemes are attractive to government in that they appear to reduce public borrowing requirements, although there are heated and technical debates about the 'real' costs of PFI to the taxpayer. They are also attractive to local authorities in so far as they provide funding for capital building which might well not otherwise be forthcoming. At a conference in 2000 the Finance Directors of Birmingham and Glasgow local authorities, both major users of PFI, both cast doubt on the value-for-money claims being made for the scheme. George Black, the Finance Director of Glasgow, said "I'm not sure it is value for money. But it's the only game in town. It is the way you get money back into your services." The multi-faceted nature of PFIs re-works the landscape of public sector provision and is part of the re-positioning of local government as service commissioners.

The BSF programme is a parallel state-funded infrastructure development programme which is intended to 'rebuild or renew facilities for all secondary pupils in England within 10–15 years from 2005–6' (PfS website). The Labour government have committed £5 billion to the programme. Not surprisingly this has also elicited eager interest from construction and IT companies (most of the major companies refer to BSF schemes on their websites). In this case local authorities must select a private sector partner for their renewal works and establish a Local Education Partnership (LEP) (see Green 2005, Chapter 5).

The 'delivery vehicle' for BSF is Partnerships for Schools (PfS), which is

---

Box 3.3 Building schools for the future

Amey-led consortium selected as Preferred Bidder for £400 million Bradford Schools project

The Amey-led consortium, Integrated Bradford, has been announced as preferred bidder for the Building Schools for the Future (BSF) programme in Bradford.

The £400 million, 30-year project with Bradford Council is designed to transform education in the city, delivering 21st century learning environments that will raise attainment, create a high-tech workforce and extend learning opportunities to the whole community.

BSF is the government's biggest investment in education for half a century, intended to promote a new approach to the design, construction and operation of secondary schools. During the next 10–15 years, the programme will renew and rebuild all the secondary schools in England, creating learning facilities that exploit information and communications technology, supported by operational services that allow teachers to focus on teaching.

In Bradford, the first phase of BSF will deliver three fully operational new schools by 2008, with a second phase creating further new schools that integrate special needs facilities with mainstream secondary education.

Following the construction phases of the contract, Integrated Bradford will take responsibility for the facilities management of the schools. This will incorporate services from caretaking through to cleaning, ground maintenance and security.

Each school will also be equipped with integrated IT systems providing every pupil with access to wireless laptops. This will allow teachers to offer personalised learning tailored to meet the individual needs, interests and aptitudes of pupils.

According to the council's director of education and life skills, Phil Green, Integrated Bradford's success was the result of strong alignment between its proposals and the council's educational aspirations. He said: "The BSF programme gives us a one-off opportunity to transform our secondary school provision. It is both an exciting opportunity and a major challenge, and we have involved the first three schools extensively in the development of their new schools. We believe that Integrated Bradford's holistic and education-led proposals offer a solution designed to deliver our vision of education as a vital part of Bradford's regeneration over the coming decades."

(http://www.amey.co.uk/html/news_752.htm)

jointly managed by the DfES and Partnerships UK (PUK), which are interesting in their own right and examples of new kinds of 'linkage devices' between the public and private sectors and part of a re-culturation of the public sector (see Box 3.13).

The Academies programme also involves the building or refurbishment of schools, again paid for mainly from state funds; sponsors contribute up to £2 million, against an average cost to build of £25 million to £30 million (*Hansard*, parliamentary answer at http://www.publications.parliament.uk/pa/cm200506/cmhansrd/cm060612/text/60612w0861.htm#06061315000629). Again there are opportunities here for construction companies and project management contractors like Mouchel Parkman, Tribal, Alligan Consulting, and 3Es which are involved in the feasibility studies for Academy projects (£250,000) and the project management (£650,000) of these new schools.[4]

ITC is another infrastructure (as well as retail) opportunity. Research Machines (RM) is the market leader here and by 2002–3 had a 35 per cent share of the IT education market; Learning Technology, Granada Learning and to some extent the BBC are major competitors. (The BBC's coverage of the National Curriculum is limited to allow commercial providers 'space' to operate.) The RgsL (consortia of LEAs) are led by commercial partners (connectivity companies).

Interactive whiteboards (IWBs) are another example of a multi-faceted policy opportunity for business from infrastructural developments which as a new pedagogical technology has received considerable encouragement from government. There is the sale of boards, technical support contracts, training (pedagogical and operational), installation, software sales (EasyTeach, BoardWorks), and work for freelance trainers. The whiteboard companies (Cleverboard, Clevertouch, GTCO, SMART, Hitachi, RM Classboard, Promethean[5]), market their goods to LEAs (the London Challenge has provided at least one whiteboard to every secondary school in London). The IWB software bites deep into the pedagogical core of classroom work.

'When we provide interactive classroom solutions we also provide the training, support and advice that you need to bring out the magic of classroom technology' (Promethean newspaper advert).

Programmes

Programmes is a rather loose category used here to refer to national schemes of various kinds which are contracted out to private providers. These can range from IT and management systems to pedagogical or curricular initiatives (see Box 3.4).

Box 3.4 Privatised programmes

Teachers' TV – the channel will be run by Education Digital, an independent consortium made up of Brook Lapping Productions, ITV and the Institute of Education with an annual budget of £20 million.

Connexions – a national scheme of careers and training advice for young people. VT Education and Skills is the market leader here and nationally the largest provider, but Prospects is also a major provider: "careers guidance, Connexions, that bit of the business, still accounts for about 50 per cent of our turnover" (RA).

Gridclub is a PPP developed by Channel 4, Oracle Inc. and Intuitive Media, with an investment of £6 million by the DfES to create a virtual learning environment for children aged 7–11. It was launched in 2001 with 'content' covering the whole of the National Curriculum.

Cocentra supports the DfES School Improvement Adviser Initiative, working with 650 secondary schools in challenging circumstances. £1.9 million.

A £1.8 million contract to cut paperwork for teachers has been awarded to consultancy firm Serco and Manchester Metropolitan University. The scheme is aimed at school administrators and will be overseen by the National College for School Leadership.

The Threshold Assessment of Teachers' Pay and Performance involved six private providers at the national level. Hay McBeer were contracted to develop standards; CfBT were contracted to train assessors; CEA were contracted to verify judgements; TLO and QAA were sub-contracted to write training materials; and Ernst & Young were brought in to design and monitor the implementation of the programme.

Among the former are various systems management contracts held by Capita including Plasc, TPS (Teachers' Pension Scheme, £62 million), ILAs (Individual Learning Accounts), school admissions, education smart-cards (£100 million over seven years) and Children's Trust accounts (£430 million over 20 years). Capita is the specialist provider of such services but a number of these programmes have run into difficulties or been delayed (http://management.silicon.com/government/0,39024677,10004285,00.htm (CRB), http://www.publications.parliament.uk/pa/cm200102/cmhansrd/vo-020627/debtext/20627-30.htm (ILAs), http://news.bbc.co.uk/1/low/education/4330245.stm (school admissions), http://society.guardian.co.uk/ppp/story/0,,515808,00.html (benefits)). In 2005 Capita also took over the contract for the National Learning Strategies (Literacy and Numeracy) from CfBT (worth £177.5 million over five years).

Here the private sector is both taking over existing in-house government or local services (careers advice) or taking up new opportunities (like Gridclub and Teachers' TV) but mainly the latter.

Contracts

This again is a broad category but refers to specific, time-limited contracts to run services or provide support for local authorities and institutions or to provide educational services outside the mainstream. This is a lower-margin field of private sector activity and indeed some of the early LEA service contracts are probably 'loss leaders', that is they serve as indications of interest and demonstrations of effectiveness intended to attract further business rather than generate short-term profit (see Chapter 4). The outsourcing of LEA services is probably the best-known example of these (see Box 3.5) and, by the end of 2005, 14 contracts had been awarded to private companies. The possibility of such outsourcing has now been extended to local authority children's services, although as of the end of 2005 only one such major contract had been awarded – North East Lincolnshire (NEL), a three-year £200,000 p.a. contract to Mouchel Parkman and Outcomes UK.

These contracts normally arise from serious concerns about LEAs' performance and capacity identified in Ofsted (see Campbell *et al.* 2004) and subsequent 'recommendations' made by consultants (PWC in many cases) to the DfES and negotiations between the authorities and the DfES about appropriate remedial action. However, not all authorities in difficulties have been outsourced, and outsourcing is one of a number of 'experiments' by the DfES to encourage 'new ways of working' by LEAs. The evaluation of these 'experiments' by Bannock Consulting (Bannock 2003) identified 44 (*sic*): 11 interventions leading to outsourcing; 11 interventions of other kinds; 10 New Models funded by the DfES; and 11 independent innovations. Then again some of the funded examples (e.g. Surrey/VT (see page 70), Black Country Partnership, Wirral) and independent examples (e.g. Bedfordshire, a 12-year contract with HBS – now terminated) did involve contracts with

---

Box 3.5 Islington privatised

An outsider in the bidding to take over Islington's school services, Cambridge Education Associates nipped in at the last to take the prize from bigger rivals Nord Anglia and the CfBT. The £86.6m (over seven years) deal – the biggest privatization of state school services so far – is expected to more than triple the private company's turnover. Having finalized the Islington deal this month [including a profit cap of £600,000 a year (interview DF) and large penalties if it fails to perform – http://www.gh.accaglobal.com/publications/public_eye/32/22724], the company says it will not be in the market for another privatization contract until it has digested its catch. If everything goes well in north London, it is likely to be a major player in privatized education for years to come. Other names to conjure with are the international accountancy firm Arthur Andersen, The Education Partnership, Capita, Windsor and Co, and the CEM consortium. All of these companies are on the approved government list to tender for local authority services. The list also has non-private-sector partners including the local education authorities of Birmingham (with Arthur Andersen), Essex (with Windsor and Co), and Hampshire.

(www.tes.co.uk/section/story/?story_id=330332& window type=print–21k-)

---

private companies and in several other cases external consultancy support and advice was commissioned (Capita worked with Oxfordshire, West Berkshire and Wokingham), most but not all from the private sector.

In some cases (Leicester, Liverpool, Rotherham and Sandwell – see Chapter 5), the outsourcing involved contracted or seconded interim management of various kinds, usually undertaken by serving or retired LEA officers (see Chapter 4). Two of the outsourced authorities, Swindon and Haringey, have subsequently returned to local authority control; Islington is negotiating with its provider (CEA) for a voluntary extension to the contract. Of two others, Hackney is outsourced to a not-for-profit trust, and Education Leeds is run on a not-for-profit basis by Capita. In these terms local authority outsourcing has not, thus far, proved to be the sort of major market opportunity (or privatisation nightmare) it was originally thought to be (see Chapter 4).

However, in some ways the LEA contracts are the tip of the iceberg as regards outsourcing at this level. Large numbers of local authorities have whole or partial outsourcing of their other services driven by the findings of Best Value reviews – Housing Benefits and other financial services in particular. Four companies dominate in the provision of these services – CSL (Sheffield, Southwark, Newham, North Somerset, Taunton, etc.), Capita

(Lambeth, Westminster, etc. – see Chapter 4), EDS (Brent, Kingston, Wandsworth, etc.) and ITNET (Islington, Hackney, etc.). In some cases these contracts take the form of Strategic Partnerships (Lincolnshire, Norfolk, Sheffield, etc.) within which private contracts take over a wide range of often very different local authority services. In June 2001, HBS (see page 72) was awarded a 12-year £267 million Strategic Service Partnership (SSP) by Bedfordshire County Council covering financial, information technology, human resources and schools support services and contracts/facilities management. Some 550 staff were transferred to HBS (see Centre for Public Services 2005). In 2005 the County terminated the contract; 'The Council considers and is so advised that HBS was in breach of a number of its obligations under the Services Agreement' (http://www.publictechnology.net/modules.php?op=modload&name=News&file=article&sid=3646). The cost of the termination to the Council was £6.75 million.

The point here again is the scale, complexity, diversity and in some respects invisibility of private sector involvements. Furthermore, the majority of the private sector involvements with local authorities and LEAs did not stem from interventions, although they may have been encouraged in various ways or made necessary by Best Value and CPA reviews.[6]

And at the heart of Best Value, this time around, is going to be contestability. So, why is this, you know, this service might be delivering – why do you think it's the best service and why do you think it's the most efficient way of delivering it? How have you tested it? What alternatives have you looked at? And can we see your evidence, please? So there's going to be an increasing focus around that.

(BH, Mouchel Parkman)

However, in many examples the initiation of private sector involvement came from the authorities themselves. These examples at least suggest that there is no coordinated policy push towards wholesale LEA outsourcing although there is 'policy talk' by Prime Minister Blair and others (see Chapter 2) about moving local authorities to become commissioners rather than service deliverers and an emphasis on a greater role for the private and voluntary sectors as providers. However, the Bannock (2003: 34) evaluation of 'new ways of working' notes a lack of incentives for headteachers and LEA officers to procure services from the private sector and a lack of skills and capacity to do so and recommend 'additional investment in brokerage or other agencies to support purchasers and procurers'. The Bannock evaluation also notes 'policy developments that might have blurred the message that private sector providers have a bigger part to play' (p. 33). Nonetheless, the private sector is making inroads and their 'market share' of services is growing and some local authorities are moving towards the model of what is called 'virtual authorities'. Perhaps the message here is that the 'contract market' should be neither over-estimated nor under-estimated. There is a more detailed and close-up account of some of this work in the following chapter.

The second level of this 'contracts market', the outsourcing of schools, is much less developed. Only three secondary schools, all in Surrey, are fully outsourced, two run by 3Es (Frenchay and King's College) and one (Abbeylands) by Nord Anglia. Another primary school in Tower Hamlets, Rams Episcopal, was managed for a short time by CfBT. This level of outsourcing is much more developed in the US but still small-scale, with Edison as market leader. In 2003 Edison ran one-quarter of the 417 contracted-out schools in the US, teaching 132,000 students in 20 states – a tiny proportion of US schools. The major inhibitors in terms of further developments in the UK are a lack of interest on the part of LEAs and on the part of providers, most of whom see little opportunity for efficiency savings and profit in running single schools. Neil McIntosh of CfBT explained:

> essentially being the managers of a group of schools is what we aspire to. And I've been saying, since, well, since the beginning of the Labour government that the model for us exists in the independent sector, which is the Girls' Public Day School Trust, which has 25, 30 schools. I'm not saying that everything in that model we would mirror and we are certainly not interested in it being intellectually or socially exclusive, come to that, but in terms of a managerial model it's interesting.

> In principle that's something we would be quite interested in if the government now, or at any point in the future, was to do a Sweden and allow the private sector to operate schools within the state system, then we would certainly be interested in that . . . in Scandinavia at the moment there are some, I think, some very interesting examples of school systems that are owned in different ways: private sector, voluntary sector, faith, state . . . this is the sort of thing that could be in either or both political manifestos the election after next.

> (DM, VTES)

There are some developments in policy that do gesture to such a possibility (see the 2005 White Paper). One is the Academies programme: a number of sponsors have undertaken or indicated an interest in running clusters of such schools – ULT, Oasis Trust, Peter Vardy and ARK. Another is through the development of federations of schools. Federations offer the possibility of a new kind of private sector involvement through partnerships. Graham Walker of Edunova explained:

> And we're now working with a collaborative in Weston-super-Mare, which are four secondaries and two specialist schools. We've been working with them for over a year now – we've helped them forge a vision as to where they would like to take that group of schools. And they're working

as a pretty coherent team now. They've got new governance structures and they've got processes by which they're supporting each other. So it's a new school model, the concept of federations, of collaborations, of schools working in a hard-edged way together . . . a) you have 26 federations out there already who've got these federation grants, and b) you have piles of network learning communities who are already in an early stage of collaboration, albeit soft. You've also got a whole lot of old EAZs that are coming to the end of their life who perhaps have got the potential. There's actually an awful lot of potential collaboratives out there if they were just given, you know, a bit of the wherewithal to speed up the process.

It may also be that private school ownership is, or is seen by some companies as, a 'route' into the management of groups of state schools. In 2003 (*TES* Archive, 21 March) the *TES* reported that CEA, Nord Anglia and CfBT were 'talking to ministers about taking over and setting up schools' and 'want control of teaching and learning in schools contracted out to them for up to 30 years in deals that would enable them to employ staff'. The article went on to say that 'leading education entrepreneurs believe the Academy initiative does not give them enough control and want to extend PFI contracts to cover teaching and learning'. CEA Operations Director Vincent McDonnell was quoted as saying "This could take private sector involvement in education to another level."

There are also various 'efforts' ongoing within the context of policy influence to keep the possibility of large-scale school outsourcing on the policy agenda. A meeting organised by the Social Market Foundation (27 April 2004) is an interesting example of such policy 'work'. Representatives of Kunskapsskolan (Sweden's largest education company, which operates 22 taxpayer-funded schools) and Sovereign Capital and GEMS (see page 77) were invited to speak about 'the value and the innovation that independent and private sector companies and organisations can bring to education' (http://www.reform.co.uk/site/display.aspx?mn=41580&s= f928e6e0–2ffb–436c-b124-c208995439ac&).

A third level of contracts is a massive variety of local provision for children out of school with special needs and specific learning needs which are delivered outside the mainstream, like pupil referral units, as well as post-compulsory programmes of work-based learning, return-to-employment skills, Learndirect, Jobcentre Plus, etc. and prison education (see Box 3.6).

Private companies also provide specialist residential care and related childcare services. Again the diversity and size of this market are difficult to convey. A couple of examples will have to suffice:

We do a lot of European Social Fund projects, some quite exciting ones. In Southwark we're running what we call Elephant Angels, which is a community support project, where our staff act as advisers, supporting,

---

Box 3.6 Education of offenders

The successful rehabilitation of offenders is a vitally important strand of the government's aims to create a more inclusive society. Reed Learning offer education and resettlement services to the Prison Service which focus on overcoming barriers to learning and improving prisoner employability.

(Reed website)

---

stimulating people to get back into employment or to take control of their lives and develop themselves, go back into learning in what is effectively a very deprived area.

(RA, Prospects)

So we now find ourselves in our fourth year of trading, having become the largest private provider of work-based learning in West London, and probably the most significant provider of foundation programmes for 16- to 19-year-olds. We probably work with 90 to 100 companies at any one time and we see in the region of 900 to 1,000 people over a 12-month period across everything we do. So it is life-long learning that is going on here, because we could have a 65-year-old doing a Learndirect course in one of our offices, or you could have a 16-year-old doing an entrance-to-employment programme.

(VF, Capital)

Services

This is the retail end of the education services business. That is the sale of single services or packages of services to individual schools or LEAs ranging from 'hard' office, financial and facilities services to 'soft' school improvement and CPD work and what Tribal call 'turnaround services' aimed at supporting weak or 'failing' institutions. Services companies will also help schools prepare themselves for Ofsted inspections and mentor and train senior staff in the management roles (see Chapter 6). Various 'human resources' services also fit here, like interim management and teacher supply agencies (see Box 3.7) (by 2002 the teacher supply business was worth £600 million per annum (see Hutchings 2006).

A significant part of this 'soft' work responds to government policy changes and initiatives in relation to curriculum requirements and related developments. The private sector fills the gap left by the reduction in funding of local education authorities to interpret and mediate policy for schools. Peter Dunne described HBS's education business as "95 per cent curricular and national agenda activities, standards funds, 5 per cent back office . . . we're

---

Box 3.7 Teacher supply

Reed Education Professionals
Providing Best value for schools and Best pay for teachers, Reed Education Professionals is an autonomous, dedicated division, entirely staffed by experienced teaching personnel. Reed Education Professionals meets the needs of schools, colleges and Local Education Authorities by providing a quality, total staffing solution. Reed Education Professionals meets the needs of teachers, lecturers and nursery nurses by finding the work that suits them best.

(Reed website)

---

directed primarily at school improvement and enabling change in schools". Back office work also includes such things as the supply and training of laboratory technicians and school ground maintenance. Performance management systems, like benchmarking, are a part of this market. The ESI companies engage with the services market in different ways. HBS does a considerable amount of business in this area, whereas Bob Hogg of Mouchel Parkman described this as "bits of work we don't go near . . . nothing in it for us 23k customers". Some of the softer work, 'the management of change', is also a niche market for smaller companies – like Edunova, Edison and Cocentra.

New technology adoption provides opportunities in which the private sector has expertise and experience which has never existed to any great extent in the public sector, although some of the software development companies which now sell to schools (like Intuitive Media and SEMERC and Inclusive Technology) and areas of activity like SEN software did originate from public sector services or innovations – "a lot of these companies have been specifically targeting teachers for their employees" (CA).

Let's move on now to some other facets of the ESI which are related in different ways to the main areas of the edu-business.

Secondary markets

Acquisitions and mergers

One absolutely key point about the ESI is that it is dynamic and fast-changing. It is a relatively young industry and the market is not yet stable or mature. A great deal of growth in the size and capacity of companies is driven by acquisitions and mergers. This means that the number of participating players is declining but they are growing in size (see Box 3.8). In part this is one of the 'natural' tendencies of markets, a result of the need to diversify, which is in turn in part a response to the uncertainties of a business that

Box 3.8 Tribal Group

Tribal Group can serve as an illustration here of how ESI businesses grow and particularly the role of acquisitions in this growth.

Tribal Group was set up in September 1999 (founder Henry Pitman of Pitman Publishing) and quickly listed on the AIM. It was rated by Ernst & Young as the second-fastest-growing company floated on the Stock Exchange between 1998 and 2002. Turnover for 2000–1 was £17.5 million, for 2001–2 £45.7 million, for 2002–3 £105.7 million, and for 2003–4 £185.7 million with an operating profit of £23.2 million but in late 2004 the company issued a profits warning based on six-month losses of £4.4 million. Tribal lost nearly a quarter of its value after the NHS awarded a contract for a national network of walk-in centres to Swedish firm Capio (http://www.unison.org.uk/acrobat/B2916.pdf).

As well as education and health care, Tribal works with local authorities, police and housing – 97 per cent of its income is from the public sector and approximately 65 per cent of its staff were recruited from the public sector. Head of Education Services John Simpson is ex-CEO of Brent.

Acquisitions include:

2000   Instant Library Ltd
2000   SfE, a teacher training company
2002   Yale Consulting
2002   Kingsway Advertising
2002   Riley Consulting (public sector recruitment)
2003   HACAS (consultancy business in the social housing sector)
2003   Geronimo (PR and CSR)
2004   Recruitment firm GWT
2004   SITS (software and technology)

Tribal trains teachers and lecturers, inspects schools, provides library services, holds Academy project management contracts, sells school improvement through its Pupils Champions scheme (part of which is funded by the DfES through the London Challenge), held the intervention contract to run Swindon LEA, runs benchmarking schemes for FE colleges, works with 80 per cent of all secondary schools and 70 per cent of all LEAs in England (materials from company website and interview).

Tribal is one of the five national inspection companies recognised by the DfES with a current contract worth £50 million over five years.

"So we have a property division, which is now I think the third-largest architecture practice in Britain, and that's specialising in schools,

FE colleges and hospitals. We've got a communications division, a technology division, a consultancy division" (JS).

is driven and constrained by the 'opportunities' of state policies. Policies change; political priorities shift; contracts come to an end. This consolidation is a product of procurement practices and the 'market-making' activities of the state. The ESI cannot be understood except in relation to changes in and the requirements of the state. Inspection is an example. When inspection was contracted out in 1992 the number of contractors grew rapidly to around 120 of varying sizes. In 2005 Ofsted issued seven regional and sectoral contracts to just five providers, five of the 'big players' in the ESI – Nord Anglia (North-West and FE), Prospects (South/South-East), CEA (Midlands and independent schools), CfBT (North-East) and Tribal (South-West and West Midlands). Many of the small inspection companies had in the meantime been swallowed up by the bigger providers.

Here there are forms of horizontal and vertical integration but primarily the former. That is, company expansion takes the form of the acquisition of similar or related areas of business. Inspection services are added to school improvement work; 'turnaround' and interim management and inspection preparation and human resources services are added to leadership mentoring and CPD work; youth work is added to after-school activities; community programmes complement careers advice and return-to-work courses, etc.

> Educare is one of those scenarios, handled properly, would be wonderful, in terms of a full managed service which provided the eight-to-six wrap-around but left the pedagogues doing what they do best . . . So therefore we're looking at partnerships, joint vehicles, special purpose vehicles, and acquisitions for the educare.
>
> (PD, HBS)

In a few cases, like Tribal, contracts for educational services have led on to work with the health service and housing associations via acquisitions.

This process of consolidation seems likely to continue.

> I still get phone calls on a very regular basis, usually from people acting on behalf of major companies, because I suppose we're probably one of the largest of the 'independents' still out there. But we're rather stoutly independent, and we see our future as being independent and developing that way. And that's strongly the view of my board.
>
> (RA, Prospects)

The two companies which have been most aggressive in terms of growth and integration strategies through acquisitions are Capita and Serco (see page 71), which have been grown into vast and extremely diverse management services multi-nationals.

In 2005 GEMS, a Dubai-based company headed by Sunny Varkey (part-owner of the Dubai Plaza Hotel), bought not-for-profit education services company 3Es which holds contracts to manage two Surrey secondary schools and works with three Academies. In 2004 GEMS paid £11.9 million to Nord Anglia for ten private schools and plans to acquire 25–30 more and build up to 20 on greenfield sites. GEMS also has schools in the UAE, Qatar and India, 42 in all worldwide, and owns the Emirates Diagnostic Clinic and other health care services. "Education is a business and we have acquired a lot of expertise over a number of years which can be beneficial to everyone. It does not matter if the individual is paying or the Government is paying" (*TES*, 25 March 2005).

Private equity funds are also increasingly interested in education services. In 2004 Cognita, a company chaired by ex-Chief Inspector of Schools Chris Woodhead, bought Asquith Court's chain of 17 private schools for £60 million and Quinton House school in Northamptonshire with funds from WestAb Private Equity Ltd which is backed by Englefield Capital, a German private bank, and the Bank of Scotland. In 2003 HCTC and ServiceTeam acquired Sedgemoor College in a £13 million deal (see Box 3.9).

Sovereign Capital has acquired Pelcombe Training, and Cliff and Silver-wood schools (see Box 3.10).

It is also possible to identify some forms of vertical integration in the ESI, that is acquisition of or expansion into up- and downstream activities that are part of the 'overall manufacturing process'. The relevance here is that some companies now operate at different points in the 'policy process'. Involvement in advice, consultancy and evaluation work with central government secures inputs into education policy formation or policy influence; the running of programmes involves the production of training and curriculum materials; CPD, school improvement and 'turnaround' services mediate and

---

Box 3.9 Private acquisitions and consolidation

Sedgemoor are leaders in child care education and residential care for children and young people. As a child care provider we provide emergency assessments for children and young persons. We are also a fostering services provider. Sedgemoor has a single sex specialist care provision providing residential facilities and education for young people and children, including those with hearing impairment and learning difficulties. Sedgemoor operates EBD Schools & Education.

(http://www.sedgemoor.net/content/ed_overview.htm)

Box 3.10 Sovereign Capital

Sovereign Capital is the UK's largest owner of independent main-stream and special education needs schools – a market with high barriers to entry and stringent regulations. Sovereign's investments include Alpha Plus Group and SENAD Group. The recent investment in Pelcombe Training in December 2004 has broadened our scope into the large and fragmented adult training sector.

Sovereign Capital Partners LLP announces that it has led the £25 million institutional buy-out of one of the UK's leading private education businesses Davies Laing & Dick Limited which operates 11 schools and colleges across the UK. The education sector is large and fragmented. The supply for quality independent schools is a growing market, particularly in the Central London area. This is primarily due to the increase in first time fee payers generally dissatisfied with the state provision (a position amplified in London), and the competition for places in leading schools.

Paul Brett, Strategic Director of Serco plc's educational business, will become the new Chief Executive Officer of DLD. While at Serco, Paul built a £50 million business providing educational services across the UK.

(Sovereign website)

---

disseminate policy and programmes; and inspection work involves setting and monitoring standards of performance.

The other side of these kinds of secondary acquisitions comes in the case of companies that run into difficulties and must sell their assets. Jarvis is the case in point here, although Amey has also had liquidity problems. Both companies over-stretched themselves financially in the PFI market and both made abortive attempts to expand into the education services market (see later in this chapter and Chapter 6).

Selling contracts

A secondary market of a different kind has grown up around the PFI, that is the selling on of contracts by builders or FM companies once projects are completed. Construction contractors use this route once their active role is complete to generate funds for further PFI work. Sometimes a whole portfolio of PFI investments come up for sale. Buyers include banks and investment funds that specialise in the long dates and predictable nature of PFI income (see Box 3.11).

What these examples point up is both the attractions of PFI as a source of investment and profit and again the internationalising of UK public service

Box 3.11 Contract sales

In November 2003 Carillion sold its stake in the Derwent Valley Hospital for £5.2m to the Barclays UK Infrastructure Fund.
(http://www.carillionplc.com/privatefinance/assets/
documents/darent.pdf)

In July 2003 John Laing with the Commonwealth Bank of Australia bought Carillions PFI road scheme shares.
(http://www.laing.com/460_535.htm)

Innisfree is the leading infrastructure investment group in the UK sponsoring and making long term investments in PFI and PPP infrastructure projects. Innisfree currently has a platform of 47 PFI infrastructure projects with a capital value of some £8 billion covering health, education, transport and government accommodation.

Innisfree provides the principal channel for institutional investors to invest in PPP/PFI assets and has to date raised £1.12 billion for investment in PFI and PPP project companies. Innisfree's investors include leading UK institutional investors such as the Prudential and Hermes and local authority pension funds. Overseas institutional investors from Sweden, Germany, Switzerland, USA, Canada and Japan currently provide 42% of Innisfree's funds.

Innisfree is the largest investor in NHS hospitals and healthcare after the NHS. It has committed some £280 million to 17 hospital projects costing £4.3 billion. These comprise 26 hospitals representing some 13,000 beds in the UK.

Innisfree is also the largest private sector investor in PFI education projects in the UK. It has current commitments of some £90 million to 16 education projects costing £1.4 billion. These comprise over 270 schools educating over 100,000 children.

(Innisfree homepage)

Innisfree is backed by Hermes, Prudential and John Hancock.

Star Capital Partners a 581mEu private equity fund acquired Secondary Market Infrastructure Fund (joint venture between Abbey National and Babcock and Brown) in 2003. SMIF acquires interests in infrastructure assets from investors and developers in PFIs. (E.g. Varndean school, Brighton from Jarvis and HSBC's equity interest in the Falkirk Schools project for £18m). In 2003 SMIF had assets of £120m in 23 interests in education, local authority and health (with an underlying asset value of £2bn).

STAR is backed by a network of core partner European banks, including The Royal Bank of Scotland Group, Santander Central Hispano, Espirito Santo and One Equity Partners.

(STAR website)

Having personally been involved in the PFI since its beginnings, I have always believed in the attractions of the PFI market and its euro equivalents as an investment class that is resilient to economic down turn and produces good risk adjusted returns.

Tony Mallin, STAR Chief Executive (STAR website)

Engineering firm Jarvis is to back out of its controversial £105 million schools contract. A new company, the Secondary Market Infrastructure Fund (SMIF), will take over the refurbishment and maintenance of Dorothy Stringer, Varndean and Patcham high schools in Brighton this week. Jarvis has been forced to sell its private finance initiative (PFI) contracts across the country follow-ing interim losses of more than £283 million. SMIF today pledged to transform the way the schools were run. Since the agreement to turn over the management of the three schools was signed in 2002 it has been beset by problems. The governors of Varndean blamed Jarvis in their annual report of 2003 for delayed term open-ings, rooms without equipment and a lack of cleaning and other day-to-day maintenance.

(http://archive.theargus.co.uk/2005/1/27/105931.html, from the archive, first published in the *Argus*, 27 January 2005)

assets. More and more of the UK public service infrastructure is built, owned or run by overseas companies.

The transitions market

The operation of the education services industry and processes of privatisation involve transition costs of various kinds particularly in the writing of contracts and other legal work, the use of consultant reports and 'scoping' reviews and evaluation and research reports. By 2002/3 PWC had involvements in con-sultation and reviews for 132 PFI schemes. PWC holds the contract for the five-year evaluation of the Academies programme, and wrote 'recommenda-tions' on several 'failing' LEAs including Rotherham, Sheffield, Leeds, Waltham Forest and Hackney, before also writing several of the outsourcing contracts for these LEA services (http://www.teachers.org.uk/resources/word/failing_leas_2003.doc). PWC also drafted the outsourcing contracts for Islington (interview LF), Walsall, Swindon and North East Lincolnshire. Of the latter, one respondent commented: "This is Swindon, because that's what they used. And then they just added ... they put a children's services umbrella on the Swindon contract, basically. Same lawyers involved."

Another respondent described the contract writing process:

> And I think the problem was you had the blind leading the blind. You had Pricewaterhouse, or whoever was doing that side of it, negotiating and advising, and they didn't understand education budgets and budget streams. You had, very often, councils who were having financial difficulties anyway, so they weren't very clear on it. And then you had people on the private sector side who didn't understand the education budget.

This kind of work not only produces significant income streams but also furthers the work of rendering education into a commodity form and re-articulates educational processes within the discourse of commodities.

The Gershon Review of the Civil Service (http://www.hm-treasury.gov.uk/) has led to further use of private consultants within government, to replace permanent civil servants, as a way of reducing costs and 'increasing flexibility':

> the FDA, which represents senior civil servants, said it had repeatedly raised concerns about the use of management consultants who were often former civil servants being paid more to do the same work. "There is no accountability for the money spent," a spokesman said. "Nobody knows how much money is spent, it often doesn't appear in department running costs, and it is just spiraling out of control".
> (http://www.timesonline.co.uk/article/0,,2–1798183,00.html)

Green (2005: 70) quotes a school governor involved in a PFI scheme saying "All the fees spent on the process would have built a primary school."

Adjunct markets

Alongside the direct privatisation(s) of public sector services there is a whole variety of more subtle, indirect and intimate privatisations involving education and educational services as part of what Clarke (2004: 122) calls 'double privatizations', that is shifts from the public to private sector and from the public to private realm. In a whole variety of different ways children and childhood are now 'saturated by the market' (Ball 2004). As Baudrillard (1998) puts it, 'consumption is laying hold of the whole of life'. Research by advertising agency WAA found that the average family spends £1,500 per child between the ages of 6 months and 8 years on additional classes and activities (outside school hours). Most activities are given up within five weeks (*Loving and Family Life – London's Child Magazine*, Autumn 2004, p. 9).

> "Parents are driven by a fundamental anxiety", says Stacy DeBroff author of 'Sign me up! The Parents' Complete Guide to Sports, Activities, Music

Lessons, Dance Classes and Other Extracurriculars', "we perceive the world as increasingly competitive and specialised, so we think the choices we make for our four-year-olds are relevant to success in life. We think if we don't give our children an edge, we're being a bad parent".

(Dianne Devlin, in *Loving and Family Life – London's Child Magazine*, Autumn 2004, p. 16)

Parenting itself is a marketing opportunity. There are an expanding number of parenting magazines which offer advice on childrearing, and children's fashion and entertainment in equal measure. Companies also sell advice, support and training to anxious parents. The Parent Company offer evening seminars for £45 per person on topics such as 'Raising boys' and 'Raising girls'. They also offer parenting classes over the phone. The Parenting Practice offer 'Skills for transforming family life'; upcoming workshops (all £38 per person, £60 per couple) include 'Reducing sibling squabbles' and 'Improving adult–child relationships' (flyer).

Parental anxieties also fuel the market in personal tutoring (Ireson 2004) and home learning. The 2001 OECD PISA study reported 20 per cent of UK students as using tutors (Ireson 2004: 113). There are now several national tutoring businesses, including Personal Tutors (with 10,000 tutors nation-wide), TopTutors (established in 1985 and directed by 30-year ex-teacher Bill Fleming) and Stepping Stones Tuition. BrightApple Tutoring (www.Brightappletutoring.com) in the USA, where 'tutorbrokers' operate to match student needs with tutors, notes a 10–12 per cent increase between 2000 and 2006 in students using tutors. Software and hard texts which supplement school work are also now big international business.

> The UK's 4 leading educational software companies are all owned by global multinationals: TLC (formerly the Learning Company) – US toy company Mattel, and Europress – US toy company Hasbro. Havas is owned by the French-based media corporation Vivendi, and the 4th is Disney.
>
> (Buckingham and Scanlon 2005)

These are privatisations in several different and complex senses: a privatisation of parts of the work of learning through the use of tutors, crammers, software and learning toys, etc.; a privatisation within the family of responsibility for managing children's learning and their educational careers; and a privatisation or commercialisation of aspects of the intimate life of families as things like enrichment activities, developmental experiences, birthday party events and parenting itself are commodified and marketed.

The market in private schools is also changing. Alongside trusts and charities and small traders, business 'chains' like Cognita, Sovereign and GEMS (which plans to create 120–200 low-cost schools in the UK over five years) are becoming a more significant part of the private school market. The Girls'

Day School Trust remains the largest provider of private education in the UK, running 25 schools and employing 3,500 staff. 'GEMS recently sent a promotional DVD to 2,000 private schools to persuade them to contract out their management. It featured interviews with Mike Tomlinson, Sir Michael Bichard and Dulwich college head Graham Able' (*TES*, 2 July 2004).

For older students whose families can afford them, there is a range of private sixth form colleges and crammers. University students are also now a business opportunity: Inforl.uk.com 'specialises in assisting students in the compilation of all manners of assignments and projects' (company flyer). More and more of the work of learning or learning-related problems is subject to commodification and the possibilities of profit; in effect parts of individual learning can be 'outsourced' to commercial providers. In the USA the latest development in the privatisation of learning is the creation of 'virtual' charter schools, which use 'the Web to link home-based students with educational programs, and in turn collect state funds ordinarily directed to public schools' (Molnar 2005: 110).

Indirect selling and promotion

In part what I am referring to here is what is called in the US the 'cola-isation' of schools, selling to school children through vending machines,[7] and the development of brand identity and loyalty through displays of logos, sponsorships and equipment promotions (see Molnar 2005). As Molnar notes, 'schools by their nature carry enormous goodwill and thus can confer legitimacy on anything associated with them' (p. 7).

As a result of campaigns by the Food Commission and others, Cadbury's scrapped its campaign for free sports equipment after it was revealed that pupils would have to eat 5,440 chocolate bars – containing 33 kilograms of fat and nearly 1.25 million calories – to qualify for a set of volleyball posts. In some kind of contrast, the Weetabix 'Energy for Everyone' pack, which includes advice on planning sports days and free (branded) equipment, was requested by 48 per cent of all English primary schools (*TES*, 25 June 2004). Tesco run 'Tesco Sport for Schools and Clubs' and Sainsbury's 'Kids Active'. Bennett and Gabriel (1999) found that 58 per cent of 171 state-funded secondary schools in Greater London had participated in voucher collection schemes. Companies like McDonald's and Cadbury's also use 'educational' websites to promote their products (Buckingham and Scanlon 2005).[8]

Markets of any kind are complex phenomena. They are multi-faceted, untidy, often unpredictable and both creative and destructive. It seems clear that the child and childhood are now thoroughly saturated by market relations and within this saturation the meaning of childhood and what it means to be well educated are subject to significant change. As Kenway and Bullen (2001: 3) argue, 'we are entering another stage in the construction of the young as the demarcations between education, entertainment and advertising collapse'.

The international education business

I have already indicated the penetration of the UK PFI market by overseas companies like Skanska and Kajima. We can add to this the purchase of Amey and parts of Jarvis by overseas companies (see Chapter 7) and the buying into other aspects of UK edu-business, directly or indirectly, by overseas companies or capital, as well as the presence, albeit small-scale, of US companies Edison and Brighter Horizons Family Solutions (now the fourth-largest provider of private nursery places in the UK). Edexcel the (University of London) examination board was recently bought by US testing and publishing giant Pearson Media. Some Edexcel GCSE exam answers are now marked in Iowa and Sydney; time differences allow for 24-hour marking, which speeds up the turnaround of marks (*Education Guardian*, 17 August 2004, p. 2).

However, the internationalising of the edu-business is two-way. In 2003 UK education and training 'exports' were worth £8 billion (http://www.overseas-trade.co.uk/). UK education businesses are expanding into overseas markets – Capita and Serco are established multi-national businesses. Other ESI companies work overseas:

> At the moment we're doing some work in Hong Kong. Through our Ofsted inspection company, we're doing some advisory work in Macedonia, looking at the establishment of an inspection regime there. So they're picking up on the idea of Ofsted-type inspections of their schools. We've got a number of smaller collaborative projects where we collaborate with youth services in Finland. We're particularly interested in the medium term and our people who are doing the work in Hong Kong are also, I believe, starting to do some work in mainland China now. So that's clearly a big potential market for education, as is the whole of Eastern Europe. So I think that probably the next decade will see us looking a lot more externally as well as developing in the UK.
>
> (RA, Prospects)

> China, people are building flagship schools, but if they can now have English lessons going out to the rural community . . . And I have been approached by somebody who's in that business in Hong Kong who knows that we do that kind of technology.
>
> (PD, HBS)

> . . . the discussions we've been having to look at moving into Wales, where it seems that hardly any of the private companies are working. We had a colleague who has a background in schools and LEAs, who's come to talk to us this morning about Wales, so it's not only developing these products but actually saying, okay, where are we going to take them now? Which regions?
>
> (RG, Tribal)

Nord Anglia runs schools in Moscow, Pudong (Korea), Warsaw, Shanghai, Bratislava and Berlin and in 2005 entered into a joint venture with UAE company ETA Ascon Group to launch Star British schools in the UAE. The Nord Anglia CEO commented that "We hope Star British School will be the first of many such schools in the region and beyond" (www.asdaa.com). Also in 2005 it sold its stake in two schools in the Ukraine for £1.3 million. Global Education Management bought the British International School in Berlin from Nord Anglia (GEMS website, 10 December 2004). GEMS with the Alokozay Group, also based in Dubai, plan to create a network of fee-paying schools in Afghanistan: 'This project is in line with the company's corporate policy of continuously expanding ongoing services and forging new partnerships to pioneer new developments' (http://www.gemseducation.com/server.php?search_word=Alokozay&Go.x=13&Go.y=8&chan).

> The Alokozay Group describes itself as a 'leader in the cigarette industry' and is the sole distributor for cigarettes made by the Korea Tobacco and Ginseng Corp in Africa, Asia, Eastern Europe and the Middle East . . . Hugh MacPherson, chief operating officer of Gems, said the project was "a small step towards achieving a brighter future for the children of Afghanistan".
>
> (Michael Shaw, *TES*, 20 August 2004)

The UK provides a model and a laboratory for educational innovations, and policy is being exported. Increasingly the work of international policy transfer is done by the private sector (see Crump and See 2005 on Serco in Australia).

> CEA has been in the forefront of developing local management of schools and has assisted in transferring this to environments beyond Britain. The UK experience has served as the underlying model for much of the development internationally of SBM.
>
> (www.cea.co.uk)

These are all indications of the re-scaling of education policy and the relative decline in significance of the nation state as the dominant scale of policy-making (as was ever the case for developing countries). Overall structural coherence in education policy may no longer be automatically secured by Western states – the Bologna Declaration and its effects in terms of higher education is another kind of example, and GATS may bring further scalar changes (see Rikowski 2001).

At this point some readers may want to skip to the concluding section – the remainder of the chapter introduces in more detail the major companies and other organisations that participate in the ESI.

The players

The ESI can also be viewed via a typology of the companies and other main players involved. The constructors are not included here (see Chapter 7) and neither are the banks, private equity funds and ITC providers. Rather I concentrate on those companies and other organisations whose activities are focused on the direct (hard and soft) education services sector. I want to use the typology in a number of ways: to reiterate the diversity of what we might call private; to reiterate the blurring of the public/private boundary – indeed such a boundary is not so much blurred as obliterated; to indicate some values differences between companies; and to highlight differences in history, scope and scale among the companies and other players. The typology is purely heuristic and not particularly robust and the fact each category contains hybrids and mergers, acquisitions and joint ventures means that some companies have in effect moved between categories. It looks like this:

Engineering/management services companies

Specialist management services providers

Public service start-ups

Niche start-ups

Primitive capitalists

Accountancy and consultancy services providers

Public sector and NGOs

Partnerships

Engineering/management services companies

Here there are six companies of interest. They are engineering and construction companies which have diversified into management services and from there into educational services – with more or less success. VT Education and Skills, Mouchel Parkman and Mott MacDonald through its joint venture with CEA (see page 73) are the successes. Jarvis, Atkins and Amey failed for various reasons to sustain their forays into the education services market – Jarvis and Atkins are discussed in Chapter 7.

- *VT Education and Skills* is a division of Vosper Thorneycroft Engineering, originally a boat-building company. The Director of Education was until recently David McGahey, ex-CEO of Buckinghamshire, who previously worked for Amey's education division. The 2003–4 turnover of VT was £700 million; VTES accounted for £100 million (interview DM).

> Building ships migrated into providing services in support of ships once they're built, including, importantly, training. VT group do a lot of training in the defence world; we are the trainers for the Royal Engineers, for the Navy. So training would be a core competence of the company.
>
> (DM)

Services now account for 80 per cent of VT's business. VTES runs modern apprenticeship programmes, Connexions careers services (of which nationally it is the largest provider), school inspections, and DfES and LA contracts. "By 2008, the company has an ambition to double the size of its education business as part of an overall expansion plan for the group" (DM). In 2004 VTES launched a joint business venture/Strategic Partnership with Surrey CC – VT4S; 4S was set up in 2000 as an in-house operation, and Surrey CC will retain a 19.9 per cent holding. Also in 2004 VTES secured £25 million extensions to their vocational training contracts and had six of eight careers guidance contracts renewed (VTES website).

- *Amey* has a similar trajectory to Jarvis, and has faced similar travails. Amey evolved from aggregate production and road building and "realised that there was more value in the support, in managing contracts than delivering them, so got into the managed services, support services, procurement contracts and so on" (DM). Amey is interesting here as a sponsor of an early, and 'failing', Academy, the Unity Academy, Middlesbrough (http://www.ofsted.gov.uk/reports/manreports/2661.pdf). Edunova (see page 75) has worked with Unity, and I will return to Unity in Chapter 6. Amey is also a partner with Nord Anglia in EduAction, which holds the contract to deliver 28 of the 47 Waltham Forest LEA service functions and share 14 others. EduAction was awarded the £200 million Waltham Forest Council contract in September 2001 with a mandate to deliver major improvements in educational standards over a period of five years (http://eduaction.com/index.cfm?fuseAction= SM.nav&UUID=A490390D–1143–37A1–3602F34B9EE4B9C6).
- *Mouchel Parkman* is the product of the merger of an engineering firm and education consultants (Mouchel Consulting) in 2003 and now employs 4,250 people. Its core market sectors are property, rail, water and expanding involvements in gas, waste, education and housing. The leaders of the education section are John Turner, ex-Senior Education Adviser at the DfES (Director of Educational Consultancy), and Bob Hogg, ex-Executive Director of LifeLong Learning and Leisure of Southampton City Council (Director of Learning Services). Mouchel sells school improvement strategies, does SEN work, offers infrastructure support

to LAs, training and development, and support and advice for PPPs and PFIs and is the latest company to win a contract to run LEA services (NE Lincolnshire), and they are project managers for a number of Academies. The group turnover for 2003–4 was £217 million, up 22 per cent from the previous year; pre-tax profits were up 43 per cent from £13.5 million to £19.4 million (company website and annual reports, and interview with BH).

Specialist management services providers

There are three major players in this category: Serco, Capita and HBS. Serco has the longest history – it was founded in 1929 – and has extensive worldwide public sector contracts ranging from London's traffic light system and the Docklands Light Railway to air traffic control systems, IT training and waste management for the MOD, to running theme parks and science laboratories. Capita is more recent and was spun off from the IT division of CIPFA in 1984. HBS has its origins in the privatisation of public utilities and an LEA-based school services business. All three moved into educational services work through horizontal integration and the acquisition of existing education services companies.

- '*Serco*'s product is the management of change' (website). The company dates back to 1929 as subsidiary of RCA. In the 1950s it installed and commissioned Fylingdales early-warning system, the beginning of a long-standing relationship with the Ministry of Defence. It was the subject of a management buy-out in 1987 and Stock Exchange listed in 1988, and has 35,000 employees worldwide. Serco acquired QAA Consultants (Ofsted inspections and school leadership), now Serco Learning, in 2000 (Serco website). Serco profits in 2001–2 were £46.4 million; the education business turnover in that year was £35 million, including contracts to run Walsall and Bradford LEAs. The Head of Children's Services division is Elaine Simpson, ex-CEO of Sefton.
- *Capita* has been FTSE listed since 1989 and by 2000–1 had a turnover of £453 million and profit of £53 million. By 2004 Capita's turnover had grown to £3.5 billion with average annual profit growth of 42 per cent (Capita website). Growth has been achieved in part by an aggressive acquisitions policy, over 40 small and medium-size businesses or government agencies since 1989, including four inspection companies (TWA, Lynrose, Evenlode and QICS) and three teacher supply agencies – Capstan Northern, LHR and ESS (for £12 million). But it did not win any of the national inspection contracts. The company was founded by Rod Aldridge (who in 2004 was listed 337th in the *Sunday Times* Rich List with personal wealth of £80 million) in 1984 with CIPFA. He led a management buy-out in 1987 (acquiring the business for £350,000). Capita provides management software to schools as well as finance, ICT,

property consultancy and personnel services. The education 'trouble-shooting team' is headed by Ian Harrison, ex-CEO of Newham – 16 per cent of company income comes from education, and public sector contracts make up 60 per cent of turnover and 90 per cent of profits. Among other contracts, Capita administered ILAs (subject to a critical report by the NAO and closed down, http://www.audit-scotland.gov.uk/news/press_releases/2003/ILAs.pdf), Criminal Records Bureau (£400 million), Teachers' Pension Scheme, school admissions, Child Trust Fund Accounts (£430 million over 20 years), Connexions Card Scheme (£100 million) (judged to have failed to achieve its aims and outcomes according to a DfES report, http://www.dfes.gov.uk/research/programmeofresearch/projectinformation.cfm?projectid=13564&resultspage=1) and the Education Maintenance Allowance (£48.4 million over five years), and took over the National Strategies contract in 2004. It has an alliance with Microsoft to provide educational Internet services. It manages Education Leeds as a not-for-profit company and provided interim management for Haringey LEA. Capita is described as 'the Government's favoured external provider' (NUT website).

- *HBS (Hyder Business Services)* originated from a Strategic Partnership between Bedfordshire's Teaching and Media Resource Service (spun off in 1996) and Hyder (a spin-off from the privatisation of Welsh Water) headed by John Jasper (ex-DCE of Warwickshire and for six years a member of the Board of Capita). HBS is now part of the equity portfolio of Terra Firma (headed by Guy Hands – see Box 3.12). HBS Education turnover in 2003–4 was £28 million (interview PD). The Education Services division is headed by Peter Dunne, ex-Education Officer of Bedfordshire LEA. HBS Education also does considerable work directly with schools (420 in 2005) and LEAs, providing bespoke service and support packages.

    HBS also serves as illustration of the increasing complexity of ownership of some of these education services companies, and the way that education services are tied in some cases through such ownership to the ownership of other privatised public services and utilities.

Public service start-ups

There are four main players in this category: Tribal, Prospects, CEA and CfBT. The latter is a not-for-profit company. The other three are companies which were founded specifically to take advantage of the emerging education services market in the 1990s. Prospects and CEA were started from scratch by defectors from the public sector. Significantly, these companies between them hold four of the five national contracts for school and college inspection services; Nord Anglia (see page 77) holds the other. These companies distinguish themselves from those in the previous two categories in seeing education as their 'core business' (see Chapter 4).

Box 3.12 Guy Hands

Pennon spurns £1bn cash bid by Guy Hands
Pennon, owners of South West Water, will today reject outright a
£1bn cash approach from Guy Hands' Terra Firma investment
company to take over the water and sewerage group.

Terra Firma, which owns the UK's biggest landfill company,
Waste Recycling, has let it be known that it will walk away if the
Pennon board sticks to its takeover plans for Shanks. It prefers to
merge Waste Recycling with Viridor.

Guy Hands previously worked with Nomura, the Japanese banking group; his last deal with Nomura was the £1.9bn buyout of the
Le Meridien luxury hotels group.

(David Gow, *Guardian*, 17 May 2004; see also http://
www.thisismoney.co.uk/news/article.html?in_article_id=319402
&in_page_id=2&in_a_source=Evening%20Standard)

- *Prospects Services* was founded in 1995 and in 2003–4 had a turnover of
  £44.5 million. It has 1,200 staff and consultants (interview RA). A
  limited company, Prospects is a 'not-for-distributable profit' company
  and re-invests its profits in the communities it serves. It is a major
  Connexions provider and does youth service work and Ofsted inspections, community regeneration, consultancy and school improvement.
  Chief Executive Ray Auvray is an ex-senior LEA officer who headed a
  'spun-off' service prior to the creation of Prospects.
- *CEA* was established in 1987 by Derek Foreman, ex-Deputy Director of
  the ILEA, and Brian Smith, ex-Deputy Director of Cambridgeshire
  LEA. It deals in LEA consultancy and outsourcing and currently runs
  contracts in Islington, Southwark and the Scilly Isles. It conducts Ofsted
  inspections and does ICT training, offers interim management and
  PPP support and administers the Teacher Pay Reform programme,
  and project-manages several Academies. It has an annual turnover of
  around £50 million. In 2000 CEA entered into a joint venture with Mott
  MacDonald (turnover 2003–4 of £342 million and profit of £7.8 million),
  an international engineering project management consultancy working
  in transport, property, health care, communications, energy, leisure and
  utilities (company annual report).
- *CfBT* is a not-for profit company established in 1965, and employs
  around 1,000 staff. It 'uses commercial disciplines to encourage efficiency
  and generate surpluses' (CfBT website). It operates in the UK and
  abroad, with work in Africa and the Far and Middle East mainly funded
  by the British government, the EU and the World Bank. CfBT runs the
  Teaching Agency and careers services (e.g. Thames, West London and

Bedford). It was awarded the contract to manage the national roll-out of the Connexions Service Accredited Training Programme. It also has responsibility for managing key elements of the Fast Track Teaching programme and held the first contract for management of the National Strategies. It owns a private school and a small number of private nurseries, runs after-school clubs and offers school improvement services. It managed Rams Episcopal primary school in Hackney for a short time.

Niche start-ups

These are smaller companies with turnovers of £1 million to £5 million. Five companies are profiled here: Cocentra, Edunova, Capital, Edison UK and Alligan but there are others which could have been included. Many similar-sized companies have been 'swallowed up' by the larger companies.

- *Cocentra*, previously Jarvis Educational Services (the name was changed to distance itself from Jarvis's difficulties), was a joint venture between Jarvis and private finance subsequently 'bought out' and now operating independently. It is headed by Nick Blackwell, an ex-Director of HSBC Bank whose initial experience of public sector education came through involvement in Atkins work with Southwark LEA (see Chapter 7), who explained:

> I think bringing some of that [high-level business expertise] together with some senior educationists is what we've done now. The hope is that bringing those things together, that two and two really does add up to more than four. And the early signs of that are promising. I wouldn't say they're overwhelmingly, that people are running over themselves to do business. But the early signs are promising. The issue for us is how long will it really take for the market to wake up to some of these things that we've got.

Cocentra has a twin strategy for establishing itself in the ESI:

> We've got two lines to our strategy. One is what we call demand side, which is where there will be tenders that come out and we will continue to tender like everybody else does. And we won the national SIA contract . . . but there is the other side of our business that we've deliberately built, proactively, which is our supply side, which is broadly the products and services that we sell, most of that will be in to schools; some of it will be via the LEA market. But we see, in fact, the overarching philosophy comes through in our brand values . . . I believe that the only way of unlocking this market over the longer term is to have a reputation that is better than anybody else's by a huge margin [see Chapter 6].

At the time of interviewing the business had 12 staff, with an ambition to increase that to 100 and achieve a turnover of £5 million to £10 million.

- *EduNova* is a small independent provider headed by Graham Walker, whose background is in accountancy with Accenture and Cap Gemini, with 12 full-time staff. The business focuses on school transformation and learning: "this is what we call the Edunova wheel, which is, if you're trying to bring about effective learning for the individual student then we believe you have to manage at least these five key things" (GW). The approach of the company is to work collaboratively with schools or groups of schools:

> If you're moving into a world of collaborative working across schools and collaboration with other learning communities outside the school there's a whole business about how do you develop new partnerships and make them work and make them integrate with the way your school is operating.

The business plan is to grow to 50–60 staff and a £4 million turnover by expanding in the UK and elsewhere: "So I think we would hope that probably in five or six years' time we'd maybe have another country started."

- *Capital* is a London-based employment training company with three offices and 45–50 staff which opened for business in 2001. It is headed by Vic Fairlie, who has a long-term background in local government as both officer and councillor, in FE as a deputy chief executive, and working for a Training and Enterprise Council. He came to the education business with a thorough knowledge of all sides of the education and training market. In 2003–4 the company turnover was £2.5 million and growth was partly achieved by the acquisition of another small provider. Capital found its niche in the opportunity 'gaps' created by policy turbulence:

> The principal opportunity was a public policy one. The Training and Enterprise Councils were being abolished and being replaced by the Learning and Skills Councils, and various services just fell between the cracks. A number of organisations that were consumed by this change didn't really understand the kind of processes that were at play here. And I could see, looking at how things were organised on the ground, that a number of services were just disappearing, and that there was an opportunity for someone to create an organisation that could supply those services.
>
> (VF)

> I found a training provider in Kingston, the guy wanted to sell up, I went to the bank, the bank agreed to loan me the money, I bought

him out, and that took us from employing five people to 45 people. So we had a very classical development strategy where in business terms you grow organically, but you also grow through acquisition. And the synergy was that we had developed, in the first year, strong systems. What they got historically was strong delivery. That, then, enabled us to expand, so from when we secured the acquisition in May 2002, with that level of staffing, it also enabled us to secure about another three-quarters of a million pounds' worth of LSC contracts that that provider had.

(VF)

- *Edison Schools UK* is a wholly owned subsidiary of the Edison Corporation, which has been operating since 1992 and is the largest of the private partners to state schools in the USA. Edison Schools UK was set up by ex-CEO of Essex Paul Lincoln in 2003. A school teacher for 20 years, he is now Education Director UK, and Mark Logan (previously of Serco) is the Managing Director in the UK. The focus of the business is on school improvement design, and they began work with four Essex schools – against the objections of the County Council. By 2005 this had risen to 30 schools, and 18 staff had been appointed. The business turnover in 2005 was relatively small. Paul Lincoln explains that: "the core business is very much school focused and all about school improvement and we've set out to differentiate ourselves clearly from our competitors in a variety of ways."
- *Alligan* was founded in 1995 as a one-man consultancy to do support work for FE colleges struggling with the demands of incorporation by Graham McAvoy, whose background is in teaching, FE management, research and DfES policy work. He explained: "because I got offered more work than I could handle I started finding people that I wanted to work with." Alligan is now almost exclusively concerned with project management work for Academies, and hopes to expand into BSF work, but also does some work with schools in North Africa. It does feasibility studies and project management for Academies and has "developed an expertise in furniture and equipment consultancy" (GM) and the design of school uniforms. It has an annual turnover of £3 million to £4 million and employs consultants (GM).

I see our role as we're translators and we do take seriously this listening to the sponsor. Some are informed, in the sense of ULT have been running schools for – or their parent company – for many years, and others are not. But even where they're not they still know what they want to achieve. And it's our job to articulate it for them, back to them, in a way that people would understand within the education sector.

(GM, Alligan)

Primitive capitalists

Included here are Nord Anglia, Cognita, Sovereign Capital and GEMS, and they have featured several times already in the account above. These companies are distinguished here for three reasons. Firstly, they operate across the public/private divide, and in the private sector they 'sell' directly to the public (or to LAs) through ownership of private schools, care homes and nurseries. Second, they are buyers and sellers of these direct education businesses. Third, they compete with as well as sell services to the public sector.

- *Nord Anglia* is a stock market listed company founded in 1972 by Kevin McNeany to teach English as a foreign language. The company moved into for-profit schools in the UK in the 1980s, and latterly into private day-care nurseries. It runs British International Schools in several countries, but Kevin McNeany reported in an interview in 2003 that "the largest proportion of revenue comes from the outsourcing business". In 2004 it acquired Leapfrog and Jigsaw nursery groups to become UK market leader with 101 nurseries and 10,262 places. In 2004 it sold ten of its private schools to GEMS for £11.9 million. Turnover in 2003–4 was £45.5 million, up 10.4 per cent on the previous year, with a profit of £1 million, down from £2.1 million in 2003, substantially as a result of a loss of £536,000 by EduAction, a joint venture with Amey to run parts of Waltham Forest LEA (http://www.unison.org.uk/acrobat/B1512.pdf). Nord Anglia also manages Abbeylands Comprehensive in Surrey. In 2005 a downturn in the nursery business led to the issuing of a profits warning, and shares fell 3p to 197p. In 2004 Kevin McNeany stepped down as chief executive and sold 2 million of his company shares, netting £4.3 million.
- *GEMS* is headed by Sunny Varkey, a Dubai-based entrepreneur. It runs private schools in several countries and, as noted on page 60, bought a UK group of private schools from Nord Anglia in 2004 with the intention of building up a chain of 200 'economy class' schools by "cutting personnel costs" and increasing class sizes (Varkey – AMEinfo fn, 11 January 2005). GEMS also runs private health care facilities in the Middle East. In 2005 GEMS bought education services company 3Es and made an offer to sponsor two Academies in Milton Keynes, later withdrawn (http://news.bbc.co.uk/1/hi/education/4443512.stm). *The Business* (6/7 March 2005) reported that 'Blair is considering issuing a contract to GEMS to build and run schools' in the state sector.
- *Cognita* was founded in 2004 and is backed by £500 million equity fund Englefield Capital LLP. It bought 17 private schools from Asquith Court, which is the UK's second-largest private nursery provider (http://www.catalystcf.co.uk/pressreleases/Aquimonth.pdf). Other schools have since been added to the Cognita portfolio (making 22 by mid-2006). The company is chaired by ex-Chief Inspector of Schools Chris Woodhead.

In May 2005 Cognita announced a discount scheme to attract parents from the state sector, which could save parents up to £25,000 over the education career of one child (*TES*, 20 May 2005, p. 16).

- *Sovereign Capital* is a UK 'lower mid-market' equity firm which has made several acquisitions in private education and social care (e.g. Herts Care Group and Orchard End) since 2000 (see page 61) but has a diverse portfolio across support services, leisure, health care, a chain of funeral homes, and waste/environmental services. Sovereign's acquisitions illustrate again the way in which education services are viewed as profitable assets and the integration of these into sets of diverse services holdings.

Accountancy and consultancy services

This is a large and diverse category and I will not deal with the companies in any detail here. Much of what they do is 'behind the scenes' and difficult to access but they have been 'at the heart of government policy on privatisation acting as secondees to government departments' (Unison 2002: 1). There have already been several references to growth in the sales of consultancy services to the public sector, which now accounts for around half of the profits of the accountancy giants (PWC, KPMG, Deloitte Touche Tohmatsu, and Ernst & Young). PWC has already been mentioned several times; it employs 150,000 staff worldwide and in 2000 handled 222 privatisation deals worth $5.1 billion. Other important players to note here are Bannock, McKinsey, Hay Group and PFK, and previously the now defunct Arthur Andersen. These companies both work inside the state and appear on several of the DfES and Treasury Framework listings as approved service providers, and they are often the beneficiaries of policies they endorse and recommend (like PFI). The complex and sometimes startling involvements of these companies in policy work not infrequently see them acting for both sides in contracting and tendering processes. They earn consultancy fees from central and local government and audit fees from contractors. Unison (2002: 1) identified 45 cases where 'the adviser to the public sector [in PFI deals] was also the auditor to at least one of the consortium members of bidders on the contract'.

Public sector and NGOs: blurring the blur, or drowning in alphabet soup

The key point here is that some of the players in the ESI are public bodies – like the British Council (BC), the Learning and Skills Development Agency (LDSA) and the Qualifications and Curriculum Authority (QCA) – or institutions (like schools and universities) or privatised or semi-privatised non-departmental public bodies (NDPBs) that part of the time are acting as businesses and competing for contracts or deriving income from other sources either working alone or in partnerships or joint ventures with private providers on which in many cases they rely heavily. Several examples have already been mentioned. Large amounts of state work have been moved out of the state as agencies are re-made as arm's length, self-funding organisations run by chief executives (Next Steps, http://www.archive.official-documents. co.uk/document/cm42/4273/4273.htm) (see the example that follows). Again here the public/private divide is virtually indiscernible. The policy strategies of collaboration and competition, partnership and privatisation interweave, and the result is new kinds of hybrid organisations and new kinds of relationships within the public sector and across the public and private sectors.

Let us look at one example. In 2005 the DfES Standards Unit contracted for a national programme of subject learning coaching in FE colleges at a cost of £100 million.

> To which LSDA, as a lead partner in a consortium of other partners bid successfully to deliver ... The other members of the consortium were CEL, the Centre for Excellence in Leadership, that's an organisation that specialises largely in leadership programmes in schools and colleges [CEL was set up by the DfES as a limited company, Inspire Learning Ltd]. Another partner was the Hay Group [website], which is a fully private sector organisation but which does a lot of work with schools and colleges of various kinds. The other partner was Oxford Brookes University, and they were responsible for validating the accreditation of the programme, where participants wanted to go for accreditation. And another associate partner was CfBT. The consortium had obviously been established much earlier in the year in order to be able to write the document. And although LSDA led on it, and there was a lot of internal discussion about who the members of the consortium should be, and the view was taken that the bid might have a greater credibility if there was a partner like Hay involved.
>
> (DS)

Here then is a non-departmental agency, a DfES-established limited company, a major international management consultancy, a not-for-profit company and a public university working together under contract to deliver a government-funded programme for FE colleges, with credibility accruing to the bid by private sector involvement. In the background to this project further structural and policy changes in the status of the major partner are in train in this part of the education services market.

> On April 1st, LSDA is going to split into two organisations. One is the Quality Improvement Agency [QIA], which will have a strategic commissioning role for quality improvement across the post-16 sector. The other organisation will be the Learning Skills Network [LSN], which will be a

delivery organisation purely. And the QIA will go to Coventry for its headquarters; and the role of the Standards Unit will become, I think, slightly downsized and distanced. Now, why that is interesting is that, although at the moment you could say that CEL and Hay, and LSDA to some extent, are direct competitors in the sense that they could all bid potentially for the same grant funding, for the same projects, after April that competition will become even more acute, because LSN will be on its own and it'll have to gain the totality of its income from successfully bidding for projects and activities.

(DS)

Public sector organisations are positioned sometimes as clients, sometimes as partners and sometimes as competitors of private sector organisations. While Prospects or Tribal may at times have direct client relationships with schools in providing CPD or school improvement services, they also act as inspectors and as agents of the state in other ways at other times (although not with the same schools). With LEAs they may replace 'failing' services or act as partners in joint ventures. In some cases, like that of Atkins in Southwark, a company may run LEA services and sell its improvement and support 'products' to LEA schools – as LEAs do themselves. Accountancy companies are awarded contracts by central government to write contracts for and review LEA services, and are commissioned to provide 'independent' evaluations of government programmes. Again the infrastructure of the state and the meanings of the state and public sector are being re-worked, boundaries are shifted and relationships are reconstituted.

To add to this, voluntary sector organisations and think tanks (IPPR, SMF, ASI) and some professional associations also tender for contracts and other services. There are also intermediary or linkage organisations which animate and facilitate such relationships (see Box 3.13). But relationships within the ESI between the different types of players are not always amicable. The private providers talked about "unfair competition" (BH, Mouchel) and "influence and cross-subsidy".

Now we came across this first, before these UK markets were developed at all and we found ourselves in the early 90s competing with the British Council, and the British Council was an extremely dishonest competitor, in those days . . . and I recall there were three bidders typically for ODA contracts, CEC, which is the overseas bit of CEA, and ourselves, and sometimes we're talking about countries where the British Council representative was actually an embassy official, where they would try and get the ambassador or high commissioner to pitch in on their behalf, where they would use their overheads which were taxpayer-funded overheads, to steal a march on independent organisations.

(NM, CfBT)

Box 3.13 Partnerships and lead organisations

Partnership for Schools is a non-departmental public body (NDPB), wholly owned by the Department for Education and Skills, but jointly managed by the DfES and Partnerships UK (PUK) under the terms of a joint venture agreement.

PUK was formed in 2000 as a joint venture between the Treasury and the private sector and works to provide 'strategic support to public bodies, sharing responsibility for delivering successful PFI/PPP solutions, from the appointment and management of advisers to the scoping, development, troubleshooting and negotiation of value for money project'. It also shares risk by investing its own capital in projects (PUK website). PUK is no longer listed on the government's register of its agencies.

Another respondent explained that:

> the BSF framework run by Partnerships for Schools [PfS], nothing comes out of that; it's a complete and utter waste of time; it's completely stitched up and we're challenging them quite strongly on this. They put us through a process, and there's no work that comes out of it.

These diverse relationships and activities and the various hybridities involved do discursive work within the public sector in a variety of ways, de-stabilising and shifting identities and purposes and requiring the development of new kinds of skills and capabilities and roles, and materially they create new incentives and demands.

The profit role

The largely unspoken rationale which underlies political arguments for the superiority of private sector provision over the public sector is the incentives and disciplines of profit, and clearly private providers are drawn into public services delivery by the lure of profit. However, not all public sector work is profitable. In some areas of work the profit margins are small, not all public services businesses are profitable, and nor do all the generic management services companies that have entered the education business come with strong histories of profitability. Construction and consultancy do deliver considerable profits but several construction companies have run into financial difficulties.

As noted already, Nord Anglia and Tribal issued profits warnings in 2004–5. Jarvis has undergone radical financial surgery after taking on PFI commitments which they were unable to finance and deliver properly, causing delays and other problems for their clients (see Chapter 7). During 2002

Amey's share price fell from 400p to 25p owing to concerns over its PFI contracts. In 2003 the company was acquired by Ferrovial Group, a Spanish company, for £81 million (http://www.clicknewbury.com/zones/news/story/20050130.1236.1.html). However, Amey made pre-tax profits of £21.3 million in 2004 compared with a loss of £225 million in 2003, and by 2005 had £104 million invested in public sector projects running 11 projects in education, health and defence (http://society.guardian.co.uk/privatefinance/story/0,,670708,00.html). HBS has experienced consistent pre-tax losses ranging from £28.8 million in 2000–1 to £23.6 million on a turnover of £120.7 million in 2003–4 (http://www.unison.org.uk/acrobat/B985.pdf).

In other examples, online recruitment firm Eteach 'lost nearly £1m after a year in which it was criticised by teachers for failing to find them work' (*TES Cymru*, 19 September 2005). A £125 million cut-back to New Deal programmes in 2005 hit both colleges and training companies; 'Raj Doshi director and founder of 5E said his £2m funding for running New Deal programmes mostly for refugees and asylum-seekers, is being reduced to a trickle' (*TES FE Focus*, 16 September 2005, p. 3). There are opportunities and uncertainties in policy-based funding and variations in the financial and managerial competences of private firms.

Conclusion

This then is a schematic cross-sectional account of the education services industry in the UK. Some initial generalisations can be attempted on the basis of this, but more detailed analytical work is done on the various sectors identified here in the chapters that follow. 'Stories' signalled here will be filled out later. What we see here is a number of very different privatisations involving very different kinds of relationships with the public sector. Very much at the centre of all this there is 'the omnipresence of the state' (Leys 2001: 107) and the work of 'smart government' (Brown *et al.* 2001: 241): the state as a market-maker, as initiator of opportunities, as re-modeller and moderniser. This is not the end of the state or of state education but the beginnings, real and symbolic, of the emergence of a different kind of state and state education and a different kind of relation between education and the state (this is an issue I return to in Chapter 5). Here privatisation is a policy tool in a number of ways, with a variety of ends and purposes, not a giving up of capacity to manage social problems and respond to social needs but part of an ensemble for innovations, recalibrations and new relationships and social partnerships. There is a dramatic re-marking of institutional and discursive boundaries. There is both a 're-scaling' and a 'destatalisation' of public services and a re-allocation of tasks across the public/private divide (Jessop 2002: 199). Indeed the nation state is no longer the appropriate scale for conceptualising and researching education policy or the delivery of national educational services – education is a global business. These developments reconstitute public service delivery and the ownership of public sector assets as separate from the role of the state as commissioner, contractor, target setter and performance monitor (see Whitfield 2001) and re-work new aspects of the public sector as commodities, as legitimate objects of profit-making, and recognise profit as a major incentive for improving public service efficiency.

The entrepreneurial discourse is also disseminated through public sector organisations in the process of modernisation and privatisation. As several writers have noted, 'partnerships' play an important part in this dissemination. Public sector bodies are drawn into financial relationships with the private sector but also required to act within the framework of market proxies or must maintain their existence from earnings in the education market.

It is important not to over-state the degree of order and thought which goes into market-making. There are many contradictions within and between policies, and gaps between rhetoric and practice. Within the enthusiasm for privatisation there are also many inconsistencies and experiments – 'chance discourse, search processes, policy transfers and social struggles' (Jessop 2002: 135). Much of what we see here is pragmatic solutions to economic problems and funding problems which draw upon a coincidence of interests but which are fostered and informed by heavy lobbying and other forms of influence. New and established private players are eager to push the boundaries of commodification further forward – the resourcefulness of capital (Leys 2001: 91)! These solutions and influences play their part in the re-working of education as a legitimate object of profit and into a form which is contractable and saleable as local authorities 'learn' to 'package work appropriate to the market' (http://www.dft.gov.uk/stellent/groups/dft_control/documents/contentservertemplate/dft_index.hcst?n=16367&l=4). Clearly business is enthusiastic about opportunities arising from and within policies but is not equally enthusiastic about every aspect of reform. The opportunities for profit, the predictabilities and risks differ. But increasingly the private sector is inside policy and inside the state bringing its interests and its discourse to bear and earning money from consultancies which recommend a greater role for the private sector in the delivery of public services – a closed circle of the obviousness within policy. There is also considerable movement of personnel between the state and private sector which facilitates the flow of discourse as well as involving in some cases 'buying insider knowledge', as Allyson Pollack (2004) puts it. This is another dimension of the blurring of public/private boundaries and identities. It is a side-stepping of established procedures and methods, in particular local authority democracy and civil service bureaucracy and their replacement with a different set of relationships and a different ethos, and at the same time this is a means of achieving a reform of local authorities and a reconfiguration of their roles in and relationships to service delivery. This is what Leys (2001: 63) calls the 'interconnectedness of change'.

A further inter-connected item on the agenda of educational modernisation is a re-working of labour relations and conditions of employment, and a side-lining or constraining of the role of trade unions – a process of flexibili-sation and the introduction of new post-Fordist production norms. In a more general sense this constitutes part of a break-up of 'collectivist systems' and the flexibilisation of the state, a move away from structures and bureaucracies to contracts and more malleable and temporary relationships driven by per-formance and output monitoring and benchmarking, and towards greater diversity and a 'mixed economy of welfare'.

The main areas of the market within state education are markedly regulated but there are a considerable number of 'ethical slippages' and private sector inefficacies. More and more areas of education, public and private, are now subject to business practices and financial logics, de-socialised and bought and sold as assets and made part of investment portfolios or generic services empires. The possibilities of privatisation continually change and expand, and the ratcheting up of policy over time opens up more state education services for profit.

4 Economics and actors

The social relations of the ESI

In this chapter I look inside the ESI by focusing on the careers and per-spectives of a group of key players, senior industry executives – the new entrepreneurs. The account starts by looking at the movement of these actors from the public to the private sector and the emergence of an ESI market. This leads on to consideration of values and the distinction, if there is one, between public and private sector values in the ESI. I take very seriously the failures of the public sector and the contributions of the private sector to social justice and argue for the need to avoid ethical simplicities. All of these illustrate blurrings of different kinds between the public and private sectors. The chapter concludes by looking at the relationships of these key actors to and in policy, as part of a 'policy creation community', and the complexities involved. Part of this participation in policy involves the search for new market opportunities within public sector provision.

Market relations

Markets are not just about the economics of profit and loss; they are also about social relations, about 'sociability, approval, status and power' (Granovetter 1985: 506). They work in part by virtue of trust and shared values – they are embedded in social institutions and framed by economic policy. As John Kay explains: 'The complex institutions of the market econ-omy developed largely without central direction and are constantly evolving. Government is an agent in that evolution, not a bystander, but government cannot control the process' (2004: 240).

However, the ESI is less embedded than many markets and more controlled than most. It was to a great extent created and is sustained by deliberation and planning by the state – supply and demand have been encouraged and facilitated by various policy moves and the efforts of particular policy actors. On the other hand, the design and growth of the ES market is also the outcome of the ongoing efforts of 'sellers' in and around various contexts of policy to make their case and influence policy in their interests. The actors within this market, buyers and sellers, constitute a social network of policy and economic activity (see Figures 5.1 and 5.2), although as we have seen this simple binary of market relations is totally inadequate as a way of thinking about the structure of the ESI. There is an interplay of and flows between the various sides of the market – blurrings and boundary reconstitutions – and interpersonal histories and relationships are important to how the market works and how it is evolving. Such histories and relationships play their part inside the complex anonymity of the state in most arenas of economic policy but for various reasons they are relatively more visible in relation to the ESI, and my interviews throw further light on aspects of them.

This chapter looks at the careers of one very specific group of actors within the ESI, 'new entrepreneurs', most of whom spent long periods in but have moved from the public sector, at their entry into the industry, at their motivations and values, and at their actions in relation to one another and to the state. They are mostly men, they are white and they moved from senior positions within the public sector. Their values reflect their positioning within the public sector. I am aiming for a relatively 'thick' account of these actors in terms of their diverse and complex motivations, rather than caricature them as rapacious capitalists. In a sense they inhabit new and virtuous subject positions produced within the discourses of public sector reform and governmentality but they are also individually very active in seizing or forging new career opportunities. I focus specifically here on the contract and services sectors of the industry and mainly a group of companies that are 'in the business of education' rather than in the business of 'selling services into the education sector' as one respondent put it. For simplicity here I refer to them as education businesses. I look, through the perspectives of these players, at the risks, difficulties and opportunities of the ESI and the way in which business follows policy and some of the particular ways of working and buyer/seller relations that pertain.

The new entrepreneurs

The striking and very important point about the 'education businesses' at this point in time is that most are run and managed and in several cases were created by ex-public sector workers who held senior positions in local authority educational bureaucracies (see Table 4.1), most of whom had worked for several local authorities and had long public sector careers. Furthermore, the overwhelming majority of the work done by these businesses is carried out by other ex-public sector workers. "We are recycling the same people in different roles", as one person put it (see Table 4.2). This is privatisation of a very particular kind. In three senses the movement of this body of expertise and of values from the public to the private sector is the result or effect of policy. First, to varying degrees these senior figures were increasingly alienated from their work in the public sector in part as a result of the impact of reform and 'modernisation' and in part because of some of the practices to which reforms were addressed. They spoke about being "stuck in the treacle" (RG), getting "free from an inflexible bureaucracy" (PL) and "banging against the sides of the cage" (DM). (See Newman 2005 for an account of some of the frustrations and possibilities and excitements of public sector reform.) Second, a few saw their careers directly threatened or disrupted by reform. "Mrs Thatcher abolished my old organisation. I treated it as a sign" (DF). Their jobs were privatised or devolved from under them. Also they were experiencing a public sector in which established values were being displaced (Pollack 2004: ix) and in which forms of new public management were already in place, although some of them were agents of this displacement. Third, several also spoke about the ways in which their experiences of reform while in the public sector had stimulated or required them to take an interest in relationships with the private sector or in working in new, more entrepreneurial ways. Policies provide contexts and possibilities which can be 'taken up' entrepreneurially, and as we shall see these actors see no inherent incompatibility between the logic of business and the logic of education.

So by 1992, confronted with making 87 staff redundant, we were approached by one of the members from the council and said "Look, you could run it as a business." And so we did, for a couple of years with the support of the LEA, and then became completely nil net and cash generative.

(Calvin Pike)

Baker [Conservative Secretary of State for Education] got behind the LMS [Local Management of Schools] movement in Cambridgeshire, where it did have party support and was going great guns, except that Cambridgeshire got somewhat bored with being the magnet for everybody from all over the country, and indeed internationally . . . Brian Smith was pretty passionate about it as was I and took early retirement and set up CEA with a view to propagating LMS.

(DF)

I spent a fair amount of time throughout my career working at education–business partnerships with local training enterprise councils and that sort of thing. And in the area of school support services and local education authority support services, during the latter part of the 90s, things really began to happen. A number of companies set themselves up, focused in that area.

(DM)

. . . at that stage when I was working in a local authority I had an opportunity to take the service that I was running so that it operated at arm's length from the local authority. And that gave me a little bit of a taste for getting involved in running a business . . . I'd always had small business side-lines myself anyway, so when the opportunity came with the privatisation of the careers services in the early 90s I moved out of local authorities at that point and started up Prospects.

(RA)

A paradox that is evident running through these personal histories is that a number of initiatives that were later taken up centrally and nationally as part of the modernisation of education had their origins within specific local authorities. Indeed, these initiatives were concentrated in a small number of authorities, some of which also provided key personnel in the 'education businesses' (e.g. Essex, Surrey, Cambridgeshire and Bedfordshire – see Chapter 5 on partnerships). The shift in 1992 away from HMI and local authority inspection systems to contracted-out Ofsted inspections was also a key push–pull factor as existing local authority posts were extinguished and new commercial opportunities created. Several LEA ITC support and educational software development units were also 'levered' out of the public sector at this point (e.g. Inclusive Technology, a company with an annual turnover of almost £5 million, evolved a regional Special Education Media Resource Centre). In effect the new private providers enact a version of New Labour's 'enterprise heroism': they take up a visionary, risky and enterprising position within educational reform and transformation in relation to but outside of the public sector.

Thus, some of these key actors were 'self-starters'. Others were headhunted or having 'exhausted' their careers in a contracting public sector were looking for new challenges or in some cases an escape from what they saw as the frustrations of local authority politics. Several talked about the move from public to private as a liberation:

it's part of a whole life decision. People moving from headship to consultancies, saying "You'll be liberated. It's a hell of a step. You'll feel liberated." I had an offer of a job from Tribal Education. And I know John Simpson well and, if I was going to make the move and it was into the private sector, I would have to work for a company whose ethics I admired.

(RG)

I saw it from the kind of politics, public policy, professional angle, and got to the point where my career had taken me to the Deputy Chief Executive of West London Tech in early 2000, and I was really confronted with a career challenge, in that I could continue doing the job that I was going to do, and I was in my early forties at this point, but I couldn't really see my career progressing much further.

(VF)

I could see more opportunity for making a difference for kids at school level than I could in my previous role, which was too much caught up in the politics and bureaucracy of education.

(PL)

Existing social and professional networks and working relationships were often crucial in providing opportunities or enticements for the move between sectors.

Having been around the place for a bit, having done a fair amount of stuff nationally, one or two of them talked to me about going and working for them. And I joined one company, Amey, three or so years ago now.

(DM)

And everybody, all of us, have been headhunted lots of times over the recent period.

(ES)

We worked together looking at failing schools and he moved into Capita and he gave me a tug basically and said do you fancy coming along?

(PD)

The two exceptions in Table 4.1 are Nick Blackwell of Cocentra and Graham Walker of Edunova, whose backgrounds are in banking and accountancy respectively. But both account for their 'investment' in the business of education as much in terms of commitments to education as in terms of financial opportunity.

There have also been a number of high-profile defectors from the public to the private sector (see Table 4.3).

The leadership of and use of staff with significant public sector expertise is of considerable importance to the education businesses. This expertise in many cases was accrued through the implementation of reforms: "we've got 2,000 years of school-facing educational support; all of our staff are ex-LEA with huge longevity" (PD). These are public sector actors who survived and thrived through the process of reform. This plays a part in the way in which they present and market themselves to potential clients.

The recruitment of staff, 'consultants' they are usually called, is also overwhelming from the public sector. Most companies have a core staff of full-time employees and contract workers, who may work for more than one company. Many of the latter are senior figures who have retired from public sector positions.

(DF)

We take largely people who've been there and done it – not at the end of

Table 4.1 Key actors in the ESI

	Company	Previous employment
Ian Harrison	Capita	Director of Education, Newham
David McGahey*	VT Education and Skills	Director of Education, Buckinghamshire; 'moved in 2005 to become a Political Consultant with Politics International headed by former Conservative political adviser Andrew Dunlop' (http://www.politicsint.com/PI_ourreach_london.htm) and replaced by Simon Whitey who 'has spent the past three years in the central Business Development function and will also be able to apply his previous experience heading up Flagship Training to the important education business' (*VT Staff Magazine*, http://www.vtplc.com/store/VTiwinter0506.pdf)
Derek Foreman*	CEA/Mott MacDonald	Deputy Director, ILEA
Brian Smith	CEA/Mott MacDonald	Deputy Director of Education, Cambridgeshire
John Simpson*	Tribal	Director of Education, Brent and North-East Somerset
Bob Hogg*	Mouchel Parkman	Head of special school; Inspector, ILEA; Executive Director, Education Southampton
Peter Dunne*	HBS	School deputy, Head of Bedfordshire Teaching Media Resource Service
John Tizard	Capita	CEO, Bedfordshire
Elaine Simpson*	Serco	Director of Education, Sefton
Neil McIntosh*	CfBT	Director of Shelter
Ray Auvray*	Prospects	Education Directorate, Haringey
Paul Lincoln*	Edison Schools UK	CEO, Essex
John Jasper	Capita/HBS	Deputy Chief Executive, Warwickshire
Nick Blackwell*	Cocentra (Jarvis)	HSBC Bank
Graham McAvoy*	Alligan Consulting	LEAs; DES; BTEC; FE colleges
Graham Walker*	Edunova	Accountant and management consultant, Cap Gemini

* indicates interviewee

their careers, usually mid-career, very successful – we pay them a lot of money, and we expect them to do a really good job for our clients. And we've now got about 50 people. I think the consultancy business will turn over about 5 or 6 million this year.

(BH)

Table 4.2 Other actors – examples

	Company	Previous employment
Robin Gildersleeve*	Tribal	Head of Nailsea School
Calvin Pike	PRK	Inspector, Bromley
Sally Withington	Mouchel Parkman	ADSI, Slough and Audit Commission
Ken Ball	Mouchel Parkman	Chief Executive, National Association of Gifted Children
Sylvia Richardson	Tribal	Headteacher; Adviser; Chief Inspector, Cambridge
Peter Dougill*	Capita	Ofsted; DfES (now Chief Inspector for Wandsworth)
John Turner	Mouchel Parkman	DfES; SEU Adviser
Peter Sharp	Mouchel Parkman	Principal Educational Psychologist, Southampton
Bob Hart and Carole Fletcher	Directors of Intuitive Media	Respectively IT Adviser for Sheffield and primary Headteacher
Vic Fairlie*	Capital	Deputy Chief Executive, West London Tech
Paul Brett	Serco	Strategic Director of Education, Bedfordshire
Steve Clarke	VT4S	Deputy Director of Education, Surrey
Martin Cribb	Capita	Deputy Director of Education, Tower Hamlets
John Haslett	Tribal (KPMG, CfBT, PPI)	Deputy Director, LEA
Paul Roberts	IdeA Strategic Adviser (Director of Capita Educational Services)	Director of Education, Nottingham City; teacher
Jim Hudson	Chief Education Officer, Cognita	Headteacher, Two Mile Ash Middle School
Gary Williams	Tribal	Chief Executive, Sherwood and Weston FE Colleges; Executive Director, LSC, Wiltshire

* indicates interviewee

In our company we've been, between us, directors of education of probably ten local authorities – in Tribal Education, between some of our senior staff. We've got a group of college principals who've been at the centre of the college principal market. We've got loads of headteachers who've served in SHA [Secondary Headteachers' Association].

(JS)

Table 4.3 Public-to-private sector moves

	Company	*Previous employment*
Michael Barber	McKinsey's	Cabinet Office Standards and Effectiveness Unit/Treasury Delivery Unit
Mike Tomlinson	GEMS	Chief Inspector of Schools
Chris Woodhead	Cognita	Chief Inspector of Schools
Elizabeth Passmore	GEMS (stepped down from Board, May 2005) (and Government Schools' Adjudicator)	Director of Inspection at Ofsted
Alan Milburn	Bridgepoint	Secretary of State for Health
Sir Patrick Brown	Amey; Northumbrian Water Group; Go-Ahead Group (buses and trains)	Permanent Secretary, Department of Transport (1991–7), closely involved in privatising of transport and water and the development of PFI
Sir Peter Gershon	Symbian Limited; Premier Farnell plc	Chief Executive Office of Government Commerce

> . . . it was very much working with and alongside people who were pretty much of the same outlook as I had, because they had been brought out of local authorities.
>
> (PD)

It is worth reiterating that these actors are overwhelmingly public sector managers rather than front-line professionals. Their identities, values and perspectives as public sector workers were constructed within the particular positions they held and they have particular ways of 'telling themselves' and their careers and of accounting for their public-to-private move.

The value of values

Such people provide a kind of credibility and a kind of professional or moral capital[1] and come with forms of expertise and experience that can be re-packaged and sold back in the education services marketplace to public sector clients who are under various kinds of pressure to outsource or seek external support. At the same time preparation and training costs are minimised. Skills and knowledge built up in the public sector are 'cashed in' in the private. It is common practice to hire staff in from the public sector to fulfil specific contracts:

> the London Borough of Haringey which contracted with Capita to, essentially, provide it with a senior management team of good-quality people

who came out of a successful LEA, many of them from Nottingham, and over the last three years have turned Haringey from a really very weak LEA into one that's actually doing really quite well now.

(DM)

By recruiting from authorities which have undertaken outsourcing, the education businesses are able to draw on the insider knowledge and skills involved in the authority perspective in such negotiations, as well as acquiring a 'believer' who may convert others. Some, but not all, of what these companies sell is not new ideas or new ways of working which are drawn from outside the public sector, but the re-deployment of effective working practices already evident in the public sector, although the origins of these practices may lie elsewhere and the language of change through which they are expressed and legitimated is based on recent developments in business change management (see Chapter 6). Elaine Simpson, Director of Children Services for Serco and an ex-CEO, explained that Serco "had people to help with the change management processes . . . you'd got all your sort of experts in how to make change management work". What is offered by the education businesses is ways of doing things differently but, in terms of credibility and history, not that differently.

A part of the credibility, as seen by public sector clients and by government, that is acquired from a history of public service is values talk – an espousal of public service values. In their promotional materials, their presentations of self, and engagements with clients, these values are given considerable prominence: "You can establish your credentials in the first four seconds" (PD). The deployment and commitment to public service values serves to place the companies as not totally outside of the public sector, that is to position them as *public service companies*. The point about these education businesses is that they should display and deliver some of the qualities and characteristics of the private sector but not others – to be just different enough. We 'combine public sector values with high quality organisational and financial discipline' (Prospects website). However, the elusiveness and instability of such values and their susceptibility to erosion and drift have to be reiterated. Haydon (2004) makes the point that 'moral environments' are inevitably diverse and quotes Blackburn's (2001) comment that they are also 'strangely invisible'. Claims to public sector values are thus difficult to pin down, wherever they are made.

Nonetheless, the public sector ex-pats are able to talk a language that public sector clients recognise and understand and feel comfortable with. Indeed for particular tasks specialists are 'bought in' to stand for and speak for credibility in their areas of expertise. This is part of the work of promoting the business.

We brought Jim in as one of our consultants and all of a sudden we started to pick up work. It all had to be tendered for but Jim can talk their language and delivers well, and is highly respected by them. We've built a little team around him.

But all the interviewees made the point that their companies had to translate language into practice. They have to 'deliver', to be as good as they claim:

> one of the things that I always talk about is organisations like ours are really good at talking the talk; they employ people like me to do it. But more and more our future clients, when they're doing due diligence, want to see that talk being walked. They want to talk to people who you're working with; they want to get inside not just how well you're doing but how you're doing it, and what the nature of the partnership is.
>
> (BH)

The networks of social relations between the businesses also serve to reinforce and sustain a values orientation (Granovetter 1985: 496) and to distinguish these public services companies from 'outsiders' (see Box 4.2). The Bannock *Evaluation of News Ways of Working in Local Education Authorities* (2003) noted that 'maintaining the public sector ethos was adduced as a key argument against outsourcing to private providers in many of our discussions' (p. 23). To the extent to which these companies can foreground their values commitments they may be able to assuage the fears and concerns of the public sector. An emphasis on values is also important in attracting the 'right' people away from the public sector to work in the education businesses. These people see themselves as being able to carry their values with them across the public/private boundary. The preponderance of ex-public sector workers creates and maintains a particular values vocabulary and, arguably, a particular 'ethical environment' (Haydon 2004), although a proper understanding of ethical practice and the interplay of business imperatives with 'public sector' values or the recontextualisation of public sector values within businesses would require further, more focused research.[2] Clearly though, the leading actors within these companies are able to establish and maintain a language of principles which makes recruits from the public sector feel 'comfortable' although as the public sector itself becomes more 'business-like' the potential for discrepancies may be reducing as public sector values themselves shift. Maesschalk (2004: 465) argues that research shows that NPM (New Public Management) brought about 'a significant shift in public service ethical standards' and a new kind of 'moral mindset' (p. 466). Perhaps there is a kind of convergence.

> The only way I thought I could do the job is if I worked for an organisation that shared public sector values, principles and had similar ways of working. And in fairness they do, largely because their, 95 per cent of

their, work was with the public sector. And I think I'd really struggle if those values and principles and ways of working weren't there.

(BH)

And since then we've grown from nothing. Now just our education business has got the best part of nearly 500 staff in it and a turnover of 45 millionish. And, you know, I think we've created an organisation which people seem to like to join and work for.

(JS)

Even in the larger management services companies the education divisions appear to have their own culture: "Capita SES was a kind of island . . . they'd sort of talk about your targets . . . then went away again." One respondent talked about creating in his company "a setting in which public sector professionals feel comfortable . . . So our ethos is actually very, very important to us. In that aspect it does govern the calibre of the people that we get in" (RA).

Virtually, well, certainly, all our consultant staff are from the public sector. It's something that we think attracts people to come and work for us and potentially seems to be attractive to our clients if you look at our growth.[3]

(JS)

It was tied in very much with our values, that we are not simply about maximising profit but we also felt we wanted to do some interesting things in education using the freedom of our position to do so. And our company ethos has always been that we achieve more by working with rather than simply decrying and saying only the private sector can deliver this efficiently, because it's just manifestly not true.

(RA)

These then are not people or companies that are antagonistic towards the public sector – and indeed such a stance would be commercially untenable. They do not see themselves as turning their backs on public sector values but rather are adamant that they are able to maintain and pursue their values within the private sector context. But this is not simply a matter of personal commitments; it is also a matter of business sense. As *public service companies*, their business is predominantly working with public sector clients. There is a constant flow of information around the marketplace, and reputation is a key resource and selling point in renewing or obtaining new contracts. Repeat business is absolutely vital to financial viability:

at the end of the day, I can never afford to clash with my client. There'll be arguments about performance indicators and so on, but at the end of the day all that Ofsted or Surrey or the LSC has to do is say, "Go away.

Box 4.1 Values in practice

One of the problems with research of the kind reported here is timing. The ESI may be entering a more 'mature' phase but the business is still developing. There is scepticism and at times resistance to overcome in the media, among politicians and in the public sector itself. Part of the work of these businesses at this stage in their development is building trust and furthering 'institutional thickness' (Admin and Thrift (1995) in Jessop 2002: 241). This is a kind of social capital building, developing social relationships which can be used as a basis for further involvements, a social framework for market relations. There are a number of tactics involved here in establishing good will and assuaging doubts and fears.

> Now, we spent a lot – when I first came we spent a lot of meetings sitting round with the councillors discussing the targets and what size they were. And actually you were expending a lot of energy on something that wasn't actually improving things. Target setting is a waste of time; it's target getting that's where you're really working. So David and I had a chat about it. And he said, "Well, look, I'll get a commitment from the council that if we're paying you any bonuses we'll throw them back into education." And I said, "Well, I'll give the same commitment for Serco then." And we sat there in a meeting and announced that to the scrutiny and overview group and they fell over. And suddenly, where there had been a distrust I think of the private sector, that was reduced hugely by that agreement. And we had to pay a small penalty last year, which we used to buy laptops for all the looked-after children.
>
> (ES)

> We can take a cynical or positive view of such behaviour – let's take a cynical view for a moment. This is a phase, part of market-building, establishing inroads for more work, then they could use that as a sort of platform for learning how to do other things in other schools.
>
> (ESt)

The companies seek to establish and maintain credibility with departments and officials in others ways, through such 'positional investments' for example: "It was quite clear to me that we wouldn't make any money out of it but equally if we could do a reasonable job there then we'd earn a fair number of smarty points with the DfES" (DF).

One of the things that has become apparent to me with these local authorities contracts is that most of the account contractors – Atkins is an exception – regard them as kind of loss leaders, that they actually didn't expect to make money, or much money, out of them, that they saw it as a step towards what might be a much bigger market and now they're all a bit upset that there isn't one.

(PDg)

GEMS is likely to sponsor two of the government's city Academies. Though it says that its interest is philanthropic, the company's schools director has admitted that running Academies will help to establish the company's brand.

(http://www.gemseducation.com/
server.php?show=ConWebDoc.958&viewPage=1)

Hall and Lubina (2004: 269) make the point that contract negotiation is a dynamic process and in their research on the privatisation of public utilities found companies 'submitting loss leaders or unrealistic bids, in the expectation of later upwards revision'.

Edunova's work in South Africa is not-for-profit.

Education Leeds is run as a not-for profit company by Capita.

There may be elements here of what Leys (2001: 83–4) calls 'walk-in ethics'. Loss leaders can 'be represented as a "success story" and serve as an argument for a wider opening-up to market forces' and once the new markets are thoroughly penetrated then the credibility behaviours will disappear. Less cynically we may see these instances as examples of a new kind of Third Way, hybrid capitalism, as already outlined. Certainly some of these education businesses operate financially, and in terms of working practices and working conditions, in ways which are atypical.

We don't want to contract with you any more." I'm not in a position, as Atkins arguably did in Southwark, that I can conclude this is too difficult, I don't want to do it any more, and in effect walk away from it. At the end of the day, in terms of relative power in a relationship, the client has got the greater power than the contractor.

(DM)

In terms of credibility and what they can offer to public sector organisations, these companies were also keen to distinguish between service improvements and cost-cutting, that is between a substantive approach to educational issues and effectiveness and a business or budgetary approach in terms of simple efficiencies. "All of those things help in terms of credibility. Because, you know, that's what people really want. Most LEAs, they don't want cost-cutting. They want to deliver" (PD). This is also reflected in the shift of emphasis from 'cost' in CCT to 'quality' in Best Value assessments. Thus, reputational risks are avoided: "our most precious thing, especially as a growing company, is our reputation. So we don't want to do anything that messes up our reputation" (JS). Derek Foreman explained: "what we want to do is to demonstrate that you don't have to be public sector to deliver a public sector ethos and that's what we try to remain true to". He went on to say: "then you earn respect, professional respect, and people use you again. It's not that big a market. You couldn't come in and raid, even if you wanted to, and expect then to have a continuing business." We "need to be cleaner than clean to get and keep business. Anything else would be 'just business suicide' "(JS).

Box 4.2 Glossing differences

I am not wanting to suggest that all these actors take up exactly similar values positions within the private sector. Their roles and responsibilities differ, as do the particular cultures of their organisations. For example, one respondent was adamant: "I don't give a bugger about selling; I can't get enthused or excited or interested." In contrast another explained: "I mean that's what I do for a living, basically. I market-make. And part of that is about fronting the relationship with central and local government, not just around education but around all the softer people's services." There are different roles and responsibilities and kinds of expertise involved here. Someone has to write the contract bids, make the presentations to clients and 'talk up' the company's services. Financial viability depends on a continuing flow of new business and new business ideas. While profit remains 'the bottom line' for the survival of these companies, the relationship between profit and values here is not straightforward. Values are not an add-on or an afterthought. There is a particular kind of *embeddedness* (Granovetter 1985) that pertains here. Economic transactions take place within a framework of personal relations which values a variety of goals and purposes – not just profit. This is also a self-sustaining community in the sense that people carry values back and forward across the sectors, and 'social relations between firms' (Granovetter 1985: 497) maintain the values community. However, I am not suggesting either that these key actors are unaffected by economic demands and motives, or that these other motives are not carried into their engagements with the public sector. Nonetheless, there was a strong sense of a 'community of practice' across the interviews, that is a clear sense among themselves of the boundaries and differences between insiders and outsiders, and the members are 'informally bound by what they do together' (Wenger 1998: 3) and use a common linguistic repertoire. There was a distinction drawn between the 'slick' newcomers and the public service companies. One respondent referred back to his LEA days to exemplify this contrast:

> I did a group schools contract out when I was there. [The contractor] came in, and they were dreadful. And it was a bunch of slick people who just picked something off the shelf and said, "Look, you know, we're the biggest provider and we do it for everybody. Why do you possibly want to go somewhere else?"

Like other 'communities of practice' this one works 'across company boundaries' (Wenger 1998: 4) and 'it defines itself in the doing, as members develop among themselves their own understanding of what their practice is about' (p. 5). It is a 'home for identities' (p. 9), it 'stewards competencies' (p. 8) and it is a network through which to 'exchange and interpret information' and 'share learning and interest' (p. 8). One respondent explained that: "there's a very clear distinction between selling services into the education sector and calling yourself an education business, and being in the education business. You know, our business is education." As against this, the processes of expansion, acquisition and merger are likely to dilute this specificity over time and may mean a greater reliance on generic 'solutions'. These are businesses; they work within the disciplines of competition and profit. Public sector values may be carried across but new values and a new culture do have to be learned by those who cross the public–private boundary, even if in a number of cases the scale of the enterprise they are joining is more modest than that of their previous employment.

> Culture shock – I personally moved from a £250 million budget, 10,000 staff, incredibly multidisciplinary, largely relating to a political body, to something that was turning over then about £70 million, had about 1,000 staff, was largely engineering. I had no soulmate, and was not politically driven but looked for quick results. And I got sucked into things like flotation and merger and acquisitions and things that I knew about from having been a business studies student, but had no idea what they felt like on the inside. So I needed crampons for the learning curve.
>
> (BH)

We could perhaps then think of these as Third Way companies and Third actors, hybrid or composite social subjects who represent a mix of entrepreneurism and public services values. These actors embody a blurring of positions, languages and perhaps ethics. The language of the public sector is appropriated but also recontextualised and merged with the register of the private sector. There are dual commitments in play, to improving education and social justice and to the interests of their business. Brereton and Temple (1999: 455) refer to this as 'a synthesis of public and private sector ethics' – a two-way process – and the emergence of a 'new public service ethos', which for them rests on 'a move from seeing the public as a client/supplicant to one of seeing them as a consumer/purchaser' (p. 471) and an 'outcome-oriented service ethos'. Both aspects were significant in the way the private providers talked about their work, although the client was in some cases 'the public' and in other cases the public sector itself.

Some respondents distinguished between the public and the public sector and viewed their purpose as being to address the needs of learners who had been failed by the public sector. One talked about "staying focused on what you're actually doing, which is about providing for the kids" (DF); and another said: "my position is kids deserve much better than this" (BH). Again this may be a form of moral accounting but also points to the need to separate off individual from corporate motives. The profit-seeking of companies as financial entities does not translate directly into the values of individual employees but the more senior the employee the more immediate are the financial pressures. The moral and ethical complexities here have to be taken seriously. The public sector does not have an automatic monopoly of positive values commitments.

In relation to the education businesses, what we see here perhaps is a version of what Sellers (2003) calls 'publicization' wherein 'companies are increasingly forced to modify their procedures and processes in order to attract, obtain and especially retain their contracts' (p. 607). Here this is not so much a matter of being forced; it is an anticipation of and 'willing' accommodation to aspects of public service culture and procedures – what Woods *et al.* (forthcoming) call 'an adaptive public service model' – while nonetheless being clear about what is being offered by way of expertise and 'managed change'. However, Sellers, writing about private prisons in the

---

Box 4.3 Social justice

Public pleasure over private regret
And will companies rush to take on difficult schools, when the possibility of high-profile failure is considerable? As John Simpson, director of education at Tribal, said: "Running schools in potentially the most challenging circumstances seems to me to be about the best thing any organisation can do in terms of social justice . . . But there are risks associated with such contracts."

(Warwick Mansell, *TES*, 21 September 2001)

US, sees 'publicization' as having 'a dampening impact upon the expected benefits of privatization" (2003: 618). Again all of this assumes that there is something clear and stable that is public sector values and, as noted already, in practice it is becoming increasingly difficult to determine what we might mean by 'public service values'; such values are increasingly difficult to specify and are being shifted and re-worked by endogenous and exogenous 'market' influences.

Box 4.4 Private sector labour markets

As the ESI evolves and settles, so does its labour market. As well as movements between the public and private sectors, and back again, there is an increasingly fluid 'economy of expertise' within the education business sector. For example, Mark Patterson, Serco's senior manager in Bradford LEA, moved to work for Capita national strategies.

The public–private boundary itself is increasingly porous.

> Paul Brett, who was the strategic director for education, took Bedfordshire into partnership; as soon as the first part of the contract was signed he then left and went to Serco. And moved from Serco. He went there; he was there for about a year, heading up their education division. And then moved to a company engaged in, as I understand it, you know, providing schools overseas.

Susan Shoesmith, an LEA chief officer employed by Capita to run Haringey LEA, stayed on when the services returned to the LEA.

John Jasper – Chief Executive of Supporta plc
John spent five years in local Government as Deputy Chief Executive of Warwickshire County Council before joining Capita plc in 1987 establishing and managing Capita Managed Services. He was a member of the Group board for six years. He subsequently joined Hyder Group, establishing Hyder Business Services as a start up providing outsourcing services to the public sector in 1999. At the time of his retirement as Group Chief Executive of HBS (formerly Hyder Business Services) earlier this year, HBS had grown into a business with a turnover of more than £150 million. John is a member of the CBI Public Services Strategy Board and is a fellow of the British Computer Society.
  (http://www.supporta.co.uk/about/board-of-directors/)

Given the youth of the ESI, there are relatively few actors with a proven track record of success, particularly in the management of projects and contracts. This creates a movement of such people around the industry.

There is also mobility produced by the winning and losing of particular contracts of bodies of work.

> In recent weeks we've recruited key people from KPMG, HBS, Capita. So we're recruiting their director-level people now. And, you know, some people might say, well, are you getting the people who are most marginalised? Other people might say they're leaving because they think it's a better place to be here.
>
> (JS)

Gary Narunsky, Chief Financial Officer of GEMS, moved to the same position in Cognita.

Blurred visions

Following from the previous chapter, one of the things I want to convey here, which is developed further below, is that the forms of marketisation and privatisation which are manifest in public sector education are very diverse. A simple binary of market (private sector) and bureaucratic-professional (public sector) forms (with networks lying somewhere between the two) is of limited analytic value. Nor, as Clarke (2004: 108) points out, is there any straightforward historical sequence of the replacement of bureaucracy by markets.

Here blurring can refer to a variety of levels of analysis. I have tried to demonstrate already that the ESI businesses differ among themselves and indeed that the agencies of the state, if we can call them that for convenience, are differently positioned, sometimes for different purposes, in relation to the market and the state. To treat the private sector here as of a piece, separate and different from a uniform public sector, is unhelpful and untenable. Let me suggest, again heuristically, that the binary of market and bureaucracy can be re-thought as a continuum and that different organisations can be positioned differently along it. Nonetheless, in some cases this positioning is unstable. The organisations are sometimes more market-like and sometimes less, some act sometimes very much like state agencies and sometimes less so and the systems of funding within which they work also change. Sometimes the different players work together with shared goals, as in some partnerships. Figure 4.1 is an attempt to capture some of the messy positioning and inter-play of bureaucracies and markets on a continuum of marketisation.

All of these different sorts of organisations engage at times in market activities and act as though they were businesses and derive profit. Schools (like Ash Green Junior, Greensward, Dixons CTC, Varndean, etc.) sell services and products to others. Colleges (like Richmond Tertiary and Manchester) tender for and have run prison education and Jobcentre Plus programmes.

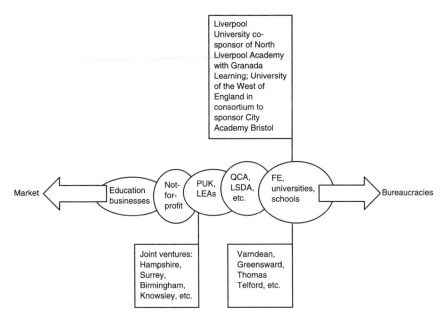

Figure 4.1 A continuum of marketisation.

QCA, LSDA and NCSL, as noted already, compete for government contracts in collaboration with private companies. PUK is a joint venture between the Treasury and private companies. LEAs like Knowsley (with Mouchel Parkman), Hampshire and Surrey (with VTES), Birmingham (with Arthur Andersen) and Essex (with Windsor and Co.) have engaged in commercial joint venture activities. Universities like the IOE work with CEA and in partnerships like Teachers' TV and like other HE institutions market their services abroad as consultants; Brunel, Liverpool and the University of the West of England are Academy sponsors with the private sector. On the other hand, as noted already, education businesses undertake pro bono and charitable work, take on loss-making contracts, and enter into partnerships with public sector bodies and state agencies. Here even the distinction between exogenous and endogenous privatisation is too crude; there is an inter-weaving of values, motives, relationships, methods and forms of exchange across what was once a more discernible public–private divide.

An economy of policy

As well as buying experience and expertise from the public sector, these education businesses are buying into or making use of established social relationships. Through their appointments they acquire access to and build social networks of influence and information. In effect they 'buy' personal relationships, and insider knowledge and trust. The senior personnel in particular who run or work for these companies often have long-standing relationships with government departments and agencies and established personal credibility with civil servants and policy-makers.

> So we've got these links, so we know the people in DfES, so it's not like we're unknown to them as individuals . . . You know, I know people in the industry. You know, I know people in the ITA, I know people in Ofsted, just because I've always known them, not because I know them now, because I've always known them.
>
> (Interviewee)

Within and around these relationships, new kinds of policy networks are being formed (see Chapter 5).

Box 4.5 School firms' forte 'is lobbying for work'

> Private companies brought in by the government to run education owe their success to their skill at lobbying ministers and civil servants rather than any evidence they can deliver services better, a think tank affiliated to the Labour Party argues today.
>
> (*Guardian*, 5 May 2003)

> The common feature of the companies involved in the emerging education 'market' is their prior experience of winning government contracts of various kinds even if the substantive business is new to them.
>
> (Crouch 2003)

These relationships provide opportunities to 'cash in' credibility and 'talk up' the education business, to present ideas and lobby for work, and argue for extensions of the areas of engagement of the private sector in education services and delivery. To some extent at least policies are mutable and malleable. The experimental status of privatisation policies lends itself to extension or elaboration of new initiatives stemming from various sources and thus to new market opportunities. Sometimes what is talk, what is lobbying and what is advice become blurred.

> That's exactly my job. I'm working way ahead, trying to get government policy to be more open than it currently is, to work with policy-makers in terms of saying there are different ways of doing things, to develop contestability as a more universally applied concept and to ensure that we're well positioned to benefit from that.
>
> (BH)

So all the time I'm saying to different people in government, "By the way, we can do this; are you interested? We can do this; are you interested?"

(JS)

I am very active in the CBI private sector education group. And through that we've met Stephen Twigg [Education Junior Minister and Minister of State 2002–5] to talk about the market and we've met others.

(ES)

We're aligned with the CBI public services group, with the Business Support Association, Business Services Association. I chair their education and training panel. And we're a recognised consultee [inaudible] of the department. So we have regular meetings with civil servants and ministers and so on, as do chief education officers, as do builders and so on.

(DM)

These ongoing engagements in and with the state also offer the possibility of seeing new policies early and being able to prepare for the work of selling policy mediation or relevant support services or training to schools (see Chapter 6) before the policy is launched. As I have already noted, and will do again, new policies are new business opportunities.

You go along with the initiatives, so if behaviour is an issue then you target it a) because people care about it but also there's likely to be funding for it either by our government or by the schools themselves, so the marketing is not exactly random.

(DF)

Mr Simpson talked excitedly about the opportunities created by the extra Government investment in computers, buildings and teachers' professional development, which were all predicted in the paper ['Schools achieving success']. He welcomed the encouragement for schools to seek management support. But none of these are new areas for private involvement.

(*TES*, 17 October 2003)

Through ongoing work and established contacts these companies also have relationships or partnerships with non-governmental agencies and associations and organisations involved in public sector education – NAGM, TTA, NCSL, NAHT, SHA, etc. – as well as universities. Income generation is increasingly important to public sector and non-departmental organisations and associations. "So we founded a school in pedagogic research with De Montfort University, who are a teacher training university, and found that extremely useful, because we brought academics in to sit alongside ourselves as resource producers" (PD). Furthermore, involvements in the state can be more or less intimate or formal – in terms of giving advice, paid consultancies, doing evaluations of policies or programme or reviews of departments or functions, or running programmes and services on contract. In some of these capacities there can be very fine or barely discernible lines between advice, paid work and business advantage – more blurring. One respondent who worked as a consultant for the DfES while a bidder for contracts found the ethical dilemmas involved difficult to manage and gave up his consultancy role:

> I was looking at progress and risks across all of the projects, including those of our competitors. But I just decided early on that I'd share a lot of information, I'd just share all the information I was picking up from all the different projects, so that the other companies were actually getting a benefit from these sessions. And it just got silly in the sense it's such a huge conflict of interests that when it came to changing arrangements it wasn't sustainable . . . it was extremely helpful in knowing how things worked, in a variety of circumstances, with the whole range of attainable sponsors. And it helped a lot in risk identification because the sources of risk are very varied.

Again these multiple roles and relationships firm up social relations, establish credibility and reinforce the legitimacy of the private sector and disseminate their language and concepts – as long as services or outputs are delivered 'successfully'. However, the social relations and networks and influence work both ways. To be able to make use of the private sector as a policy device in the reform and modernisation of the public sector the DfES and other departments need to encourage participation in the education services market and to encourage the development of capacity within the businesses (see also Selwyn and Fitz 2001: 140). "You four people across the table are responsible for a very high proportion of government policy delivery in this particular area" (government minister to respondent). There is an increasingly sophisticated procurement process for public sector services. Frameworks are one means of doing this, that is approved-provider lists for particular kinds of business or services.

Box 4.6 A framework example

A separate list includes the six companies approved to go into struggling local authorities and analyse their needs. They are charged with writing the job description for the service contractors – a vital role. On the list are KPMG, Lorien, Capita, The Office of Public Management, PricewaterhouseCoopers and the partnership of Arthur Andersen and Birmingham LEA.

(*TES*, 28 January 2000)

In setting conditions for approval and through a vetting process the state is able to influence the structure and capacity of the education businesses. The framework presentations done by aspirant companies are also further moments of interaction and communication. The requirements of such frameworks are one of the drivers of the consolidation process (mergers and acquisitions) and a way of 'encouraging' new participants. This increases and reduces the number of participants at the same time. One respondent explained:

> Last week we did a presentation to the Cabinet Office, as a group, so this wasn't just education. And the feedback we got from the Cabinet Office was we were unsuccessful because we weren't able to convince them that we were a sufficiently integrated organisation to meet their complex requirements.

The awarding of large contracts is also in some cases dependent on education companies being able to give financial guarantees which are only possible with the backing of large transnational companies: "there is no way that CEA would have got the contract if it had been on the stand without Mott MacDonald" and "QAA would bid for small things and would do things in partnership. But the resources of SERCO suddenly gave them multi, multi million contracts" (quoted in Mahony *et al.* 2004). This is one dimension of what Jessop (2002: 240) calls 'meta-governance' or the conditions for governance and, specifically, 'meta-exchange', that is 'the reflexive redesign of individual markets' or here the creation or invention of markets 'by modifying their operation and articulation' (p. 241). This is done formally, as above, and informally. Here the ESI is literally a policy lever for the state, a means of achieving its ends, a form of governance.

> One of the things that the private sector's involvement has been able to do is leverage capacity from the system and make it available more generally to the system. So the LEA intervention projects that the DfES initiated, beginning way back in the late 90s, had a number of entirely beneficial consequences, but one of them was to re-deploy good-quality people from a) where they were already into b) where they probably would never, ever have thought of going.
>
> (DM)

> [The] people down there in Westminster, one of the reasons they have chosen to engage with the private sector over the last decade or so is because you pull a lever, you, you get the effect you want, perhaps more directly sometimes than if you do it through the old bureaucratic systems that I spent 20-odd years of my career working in.
>
> (DM)

> Quite clearly the government are committed to public services as much as

the public sector. They're trying to create a market, so they've got to talk to us, collectively and individually. Because if we don't present, take up those opportunities, they can't achieve their objectives. So there's got to be that interaction, because it's in both people's interests. So we've got formal organisations, like that one you've come into contact with, the CBI one, which we set up much more informally about four years ago.

(DM)

"Oh, we're going to 10 Downing Street." Well, I tell you what, it's the easiest place to get to if you've got good ideas, you know. Because we've got our own Cabinet Office connections and talk to the Home Secretary, Foreign Secretary, all sorts of stuff, around activities, because the government are desperate to see their ideas, as distinct from visions, reflected in a mirror of achievement.

(PD)

In other words the representatives of the private sector are in regular conversation with government and part of the 'policy creation community' (Mahony *et al.* 2004) in much the same way as the teacher trade unions and LEAs were in the 1950s and 1960s. The state is *primus inter pares* in these conversations and acts as 'mediator of collective intelligence' (Jessop 2002: 243) as well as major funder and client and animateur of the market. These relationships and interactions are examples of what Rhodes calls 'policy networks', and he sees 'the policy of marketizing public services' as accelerating their multiplication and differentiation. In his version of governance such networks are a new alternative to 'the stark choice between hierarchy and market' (Rhodes 1999: xix) (see Chapter 5). It is arguable whether Leys's starker view of these changes as 'mediating a basic shift in the balance of power between market forces and political forces' (2001: 63) is appropriate here, but clearly there are ongoing changes in power relations and there is a mix of the 'structural power' and 'corporate agency' of business at work here (a distinction used by Farnsworth 2004).

However, it appears that in some respects policy and policy pronouncements have outrun the capacity of private sector organisations to participate in the education business. The Bannock *Evaluation of New Ways of Working in Local Education Authorities* (2003) noted that 'The development of the [education services] market has been less than was hoped by policymakers and remains patchy in terms of the range of services available and in terms of geographical distribution' (para. 27, p. 37). Further, the market is not the only current policy lever in the work of metagovernance. As noted previously, outsourcing was only one of a number of 'new ways' experiments fostered by the DfES in the reform of LEAs. Metaorganisation is another mode and another lever, the 'reflexive redesign of organizations' and the 'creation of intermediating organizations' (Jessop 2002: 241). At the level of local government and in educational institutions this translates into endogenous projects of public sector reform and 'continuous improvement' – tactics like mentoring, twinning, secondment and the use of boards and trusts as not-for-profit or insider solutions were sponsored or encouraged and were judged to have been successful in relation to a number of 'weak' authorities. Privatisation may have a high profile but in some areas of public sector reform it is a marginal, or temporary, device or one among several policy devices being used and one of many experiments in the process of reform. The significance of privatisation should be neither over- nor under-estimated. The outcome of reform is not a total transformation but rather a version of 'welfare mix' or 'welfare pluralism' and a mix of endogenous and exogenous privatisations, as well as some new forms of state activity.

Nonetheless, the state is a very active market-maker. One respondent noted that his company "started life saying we would not do it [intervention contracts] . . . it's only because we got kind of bullied into it by the DfES that we feel there's a kind of moral obligation to kind of continue to do it". Indeed some of the respondents made the point that some of the intervention contracts awarded had gone to market newcomers as a way of encouraging their participation in the market; Atkins in Southwark and Mouchel Parkman in NE Lincolnshire were mentioned.

> When the government were looking to grow the market, and they did it fairly crudely, they went to a number of organisations and said, you know those big government contracts you did on X, would you like to carry on winning them? Yes, please. Fine, go into education; you need some people.

The limits of the current market were also noted by other respondents: "it's still, from many, many areas of education services, a limited marketplace, or very much a developing one" (RA).

Box 4.7 Pushing back the boundaries

Stubborn refusal to privatise
Consultants tell ministers to work harder to sell benefits of private services to suspicious LEAs and schools. William Stewart reports.

Ministers need to encourage schools and councils to take more risks if they want the market for private-sector education services to grow, a government-commissioned report says.

Policy-makers have been disappointed by the 'patchy' development of the market in supplying services to education authorities and schools, according to the study by Bannock Consulting and Independent Business Consultants.

The report, which examines new ways of working in LEAs, says growth of privatised services has been held back by inertia and reluctance by schools and LEAs to enter the unfamiliar commercial world.

'For people unused to commercial negotiation, dealing with private providers can introduce risks and, in some cases, lead to an unwillingness to participate,' it said.

The consultants found legitimate fears among LEAs and schools that there was not enough competition in the schools' services market. The small number of firms competing for business might mean one-sided contracts as well as high prices and delivery problems.

Moves to encourage partnerships within the public sector may deter LEAs from working with the private sector in future – and firms may be less willing to invest.

'If it remains government policy to stimulate private provision, procurers will need more encouragement to take the necessary risks and support in how to do this effectively,' the study says.

As the *TES* revealed last week, Serco is in negotiations with a group of headteachers in Essex to provide advice services.

A Department for Education and Skills spokeswoman said there was evidence that the education services market was still developing. East Sussex and Lincolnshire had given contracts to CfBT for school improvement and Surrey was finalising a strategic partnership with Vosper Thorneycroft Education.

(*TES*, 6 June 2003)

There is an apparent contradiction here. On the one hand, the government is 'growing' the education business, making a market, but, on the other, has limits to its enthusiasm to privatise; "it's dependent on the whims of government" (RA). Selwyn and Fitz (2001: 140) remind us that 'government is not a homogenous actor'. The LEA 'intervention' business is a case in point. The initial flurry of such interventions has almost stopped, the Isles of Scilly and North East Lincolnshire (2005) being the only recent examples. One respondent reported being told by a DfES official that "intervention is dead" but went on to say:

Actually we're now being told, "No, it isn't", and there will be more of the North East Lincolnshire kind of project. The more we get into joint area reviews and the next round of CPA, and annual performance assessments, all that kind of stuff, is going to shake out more and more and more.

A 2005 report published by the CBI (2005) is very much a response to what the ESI sees as the failure of government to develop and expand the education services market:

> Despite the initial success of the intervention policy and the use of the private sector in improving educational attainment, the market has failed to develop beyond the initial intervention process. The market is set to decline when contracts end during the next four to six years, primarily because the government had no strategy in place for sustaining the market beyond the initial intervention process.
>
> (p. 23)

The report aims to show that 'outsourced' authorities produce greater achievement improvements in examination results than do equivalent publicly run authorities (cf. Farnsworth 2004). However, the work of private companies in outsourced LEAs has attracted a very mixed press. The *TES* reported:

> *Private sector fails to deliver*
> PRIVATISATION has failed to improve weak council education services, according to a *TES* analysis of inspectors' findings. Local education authorities forced to surrender services to the private sector have improved less than those who failed an inspection but were allowed to retain control ... The lack of progress in Hackney, east London, led to contractors Nord Anglia being replaced by a not-for-profit trust.
>
> (Jon Slater, 4 April 2003)

> *Rare bonus for Bradford firm*
> Ian Harrison, managing director of Capita SES, agrees the market for outsourcing has changed. "The DfES has backed away from the compulsory outsourcing model partly because the contracts were too inflexible and punitive.
>
> "Increasingly, LEAs are going to the private sector for consultancy and strategic planning for interim management and specific projects. Potentially this is still a massive business because lots of LEAs are struggling on their own."
>
> (Michael Shaw, Jon Slater and Stephen Lucas report
> on the progress of private companies running
> education services, *TES*, 30 January 2004)

Nonetheless, as part of the follow-up to *Every Child Matters* (2003) the DfES commissioned a report from, yes, PWC on the future of children's services, which identified 21 areas of work which could be privatised or outsourced and "the majority of those areas had little in terms of non-local authority or non-health service involvement" (RA). Several of the respondents mentioned children's services reorganisations (the creation of integrated education and child welfare services) as a new market opportunity of considerable promise. Bob Hogg of Mouchel Parkman commented of the DfES that:

> interestingly, in the children's services market they're being much more open. They called about five or six of us in to talk with them about how they made the market and how they would expose their thinking about children's services to the market, so we jointly planned a whole series of seminars around the country.

Perhaps we can draw on Jessop (2002) again here to make some sense of what is going on. What is evident is a form of 'rearticulation and collibrating', that is weighing in comparison of 'different modes of governance' and the management of 'the complex plurality' of 'tangled hierarchies found in prevailing modes of coordination' (p. 242). Indeed, we have a good example of what Jessop describes as 'the judicious mixing of market, hierarchy and networks to achieve the best possible outcomes' (p. 242). This is not a set of contradictions or simple incoherence but rather a 'strategic selectivity' – coherent incoherence, that is the use of different policy levers alongside each other and off-set against one another as experiments, possibilities or ways of 'unblocking' bureaucratic systems or weakening professional influence or control, or dismantling entrenched structures, but without any guarantees of success. Within the 'competition state', single model reform strategies like neo-liberalism are passé and dangerous.

Alongside this, potential education services clients, like local authorities, also vary in their enthusiasm or willingness to outsource or use education services offered by education businesses. As Ray Auvray of Prospects commented, "the main competition is not so much another private company; it's the possibility of a service being run in-house". While a number of the active 'outsourcing authorities' are Conservative run, there is no simple relationship between the politics of authorities and their willingness to engage with the private sector (see Chapter 6): "I met the other week with the Tory's front bench spokesman and they were talking about their national policy line, but that isn't necessarily carried through by Tory local authorities" (RA). Best Value and CPA reviews however do continue to work to generate new business and push more local services into outsourcing, but some local authorities are already moving quite quickly towards a 'commissioning' rather than 'delivery' role. Some local authorities, like Bedfordshire, did go down the path of broad SSP (Strategic Service Partnerships) encompassing a range of services outsourced to one provider, while others make limited use of outsourcing.

> It's hard work and it's risky work. So our choice is normally we want to work with people that want to be good to great, but it has to be funded by them. So on the asset side, there's a continuing focus on continuation of

improvement. And you've got the restatement in the next round of CPAs on Best Value.

(BH)

In this chapter I have both described some features of the new education businesses involved in the privatisations of education services and introduced some of the key actors within the evolving ESI and indicated the relationships they and their businesses have with the public sector and the state and their role within governance. I address some aspects of their 'product' in Chapter 6. Running through the account is an attempt to demonstrate the complexity – structural, political, personal and ethical – of the ESI and therefore the need to avoid crude generalisations. I have characterised them as hybrid or Third Way businesses. The importance of social relations, trust and credibility in the embedding of these businesses has been emphasised. The role of the state as market-maker is a crucial aspect of the way the ESI works and how it is evolving. Privatisation has to be seen, in part, as a tool of policy, a means of reform and modernisation of the public sector. More generally, as in the previous chapter, the possibility of continuing to use a simple public sector/private sector binary has been called into question. On the other hand, I have sought to stress the ways in which ESI actors, and others from business, are now 'talking' directly to and about policy and are part of the construction and dissemination of policy ideas.

The following chapter follows on directly to focus more specifically on the 'work' partnerships do in blurring boundaries and disseminating private practices and providing points of entry for new market opportunities and to address more directly the issue of governance. It also explores some other aspects of the relationships in and with the state of the education businesses, business philanthropists and other representatives of and 'heroes' of business as new 'policy communities'.

5 New governance, new communities, new philanthropy

Picking up themes introduced in Chapters 1 and 2, in this chapter I look more closely at the work of the education businesses as part of *governance* or what is sometimes confusingly called '*new governance*' (Rhodes 1995) and more broadly trace the participation of business and the 'new philanthropists' in new forms of governance through partnerships and social networks and identify some 'policy communities' which are evident within and around current education policies. I use the idea of networks here in a descriptive and analytic way, rather than in any normative sense, to refer to a form of governance that inter-weaves and inter-relates markets and hierarchies – a kind of messy hinterland which supplements and sometimes subverts these other forms. 'Governance' is one of those fashionable terms which by virtue of loose and promiscuous use is in danger of being rendered meaningless but it is also productively malleable. Here I use or try it out for size rather than debate this and related concepts (see Newman 2001 and Clarke 2004 for debate). I deploy the term in a fairly simple and straightforward way to mean the use of 'socio-political interactions, to encourage many and varied arrangements for coping with problems and to distribute services among several actors' (Rhodes 1995: 5), that is a 'catalyzing [of] all sectors – public, private and voluntary – into action to solve their community's problems' (Osborne and Gaebler 1992: 20). In general terms this is the move towards a 'polycentric state' or 'new localism' and 'a shift in the centre of gravity around which policy cycles move' (Jessop 1998b: 32).

New governance

As signalled already, I do not intend to suggest a kind of once-and-for-all shift from old government to new governance here, but rather the creation of an unstable hybridity which involves 'different forms of coordination and control' (Newman 2001: 31) which interact and are often in tension. So we need to bear in mind that alongside polycentrism there has also been 'an intensification of a "command and control" style of governing' (Newman 2001: 163), a concentration of power at the centre as well as a movement to localities (in some cases outside of democratic local government). In education, for example, the Prime Minister's Policy Unit is now a key site of policy initiation.[1] Finally, to be clear, I certainly want to divest the concept, as used here, of its normative connotations – that is, the argument that governance is better than government (see Rhodes 1995).

Central to governance is the subsidiary concept of *network*. In much of the literature a contrast is drawn wherein governance is accomplished through networks, while government is done through hierarchies. Rhodes (1995: 9) uses 'the term network to describe the several interdependent actors involved in delivering services . . . these networks are made up of organizations which need to exchange resources (money, information, expertise) to achieve their objectives'. He adds that 'governance also suggests that networks are self-organizing' (p. 10). Newman (2001: 108) elaborates, pointing out that the governance literature views networks 'in terms of plural actors engaged in a reflexive process of dialogue and information exchange'. Again there is a degree of misleading clarity about the concept of networks, as used in the governance literature. It is either used very abstractly or deployed to refer to a very wide variety of real and practical social relationships. Here I want to avoid that vaguery as best I can and explore two sorts of networks which 'catalyse' business in the delivery of education services and the reconfiguration and dissemination of policy discourses. The first is *partnerships* and the second is a set of *social networks* I shall call 'policy communities' – a particular version of networks. 'Policy community' is yet another tricky and slippery term which covers a lot of ground. One way of tidying it up is to think of a continuum of social and ideological cohesion. 'At one end of this continuum are policy communities, as integrated, stable and exclusive policy networks; at the other end are issue networks of loosely connected, multiple, and often conflict-ridden members' (Skogstad 2005 p. 5). My examples are closer to the former than the latter but are not as integrated, stable and exclusive as all that and they are institutionalised via the work of various linkages devices (including key persons) and lead organisations. Helpfully Newman (2001: 163) also distinguishes networks and partnerships quite carefully and asserts that 'partnerships as a policy approach must be distinguished from network forms of governance'. 'Networks are informal and fluid, with shifting membership and ambiguous relationships and accountabilities' (p. 108), whereas partnerships 'are more stable groupings with defined structures and protocols' (p. 108).[2] These latter definitions fit the cases I present fairly well. In the first case the focus is almost entirely on the education businesses and some of their work practices and arrangements in and with the private sector. In the second the focus is broader and explores the participation of a variety of social actors and organisations from business and 'new philanthropy' as an emerging 'policy community'.

Partnerships – working with and in and on and for the public sector

In terms of the analysis of current regulatory processes, governance partnerships are a key device in as much as they provide 'linkages, coupling and congruence between actors and spaces' (MacKenzie and Lucio 2005: 500) and are a way of delivering policy outcomes through collaborative networks and diverse allegiances and commitments. They are fundamental to the architecture of governance and to the fostering and management of public/private relationships and are a key feature of Third Way political rhetoric.

> We will encourage partnerships between the education service and all those who have an interest in its success . . . parents, communities, the cultural sector and business.
>
> (DfES 2001: 17)

4Ps (Public Private Partnerships Programme) is 'the local government procurement expert' (4Ps website) providing procurement support for local authorities.

> Partnerships for Schools (PfS) is responsible for delivering the government's secondary school renewal programme, Building Schools for the Future (BSF). We work with local authorities and the private sector to rebuild or renew every one of England's 3,500 state secondary schools.
>
> (www.p4s.org.uk)

> . . . partnership working based on mutual trust . . . successful workable solutions . . . Cambridge Education's contribution to each partnership is to provide leading professional advice and practical solutions.
>
> (www.cea.co.uk)

Again the proviso has to be entered here that 'partnership' is a buzzword, 'a favourite word in the lexicon of New Labour' (Falconer and Mclaughlin 2000: 121), and it crosses over from rhetoric to analysis and carries dangers of being made meaningless by over-use; 'it is largely a rhetorical invocation of a vague ideal' (Powell and Glendinning 2002: 3). As Fairclough (2000: 11) puts it, the rhetoric of partnerships is part of New Labour's denial of binaries which makes possible the treatment of radically different terms as equivalent. Partnerships constantly recur in New Labour discourse and policies; almost any relationship between organisations or social agents is a partnership. They are a classic Third Way trope which dissolve important differences between public sector, private sector and voluntary sector modes of working and obscure the role of financial relationships and power imbalances between 'partners'. Partnerships are everywhere: 'partnershipitis' Huxham and Vangen (2000: 303) call it. There are a number of agencies and animateurs, both

public and private, which foster, support and facilitate public/private partnerships (see page 81). The term encompasses a wide range of relationships
stretching from PFIs (which were re-conceptualised as a form of partnership
by New Labour) at one end to commercial joint ventures between public and
private at the other.[3] However, the former are perhaps better described as
'relational contracting' (Powell and Glendinning 2002: 7). Ruane (2002: 205)
contrasts the lack of experience of NHS negotiators with the hard bargaining
skills of the private sector in the making of PFI deals and the lack of direct
discussions between hospital managers and private sector design teams, as
well as a fundamental 'clash of philosophy and values' (p. 209), none of
which suggests anything much like a partnership. Grimshaw and Hebson
(2004: 124) report a similar finding and NHS managers' 'lack of expertise'
which 'hindered their capacity to win a good deal for the Trust'. The idea of
partnerships, especially as deployed by New Labour politicians, carries a
sense of a benign and purposeful relationship between equals, 'giving a
favourable gloss to a relationship which some would describe in more negative terms' (Fairclough 2000: 129). The possibilities of 'negative synergy' are
usually ignored. Partnerships may also be thought of as yet another form of
policy 'experiment'.

> The controversial record of some of these [LEA intervention] contracts
> in the past year has cast doubt on their future both politically and finan-
> cially. But an analysis by the *TES* reveals the Government has learned
> lessons from the failures, and a more co-operative relationship between
> the public and private sector is being developed.
>
> (*TES* archive, 30 January 2004)

Here the focus is on the more substantive aspects of such relationships.
Indeed, the language of partnerships is one of the key ways that education
businesses operate and present themselves (see also Chapter 4). This is also a
mode of access to the public sector and an adaptation to the limitations of
the public sector market but not always the preferred way of working of the
education businesses.

In practice a great deal of the work done by the education businesses is
not done by taking services out of public sector control but rather through
collaborations of various kinds with the public sector, although again some
are more meaningfully collaborative than others and not all rest on shared
objectives. These partnerships open up various kinds of flows between the
sectors, of people, ideas, language, methods, values and culture: 'states have
a key role in promoting innovative capacities, technical competence and
technology transfer . . . often involving extensive collaboration' (Jessop 2002:
121). They are a further aspect of the blurrings between sectors. While within
these relationships there may be ambiguities and 'differences in language,
culture and perceptions of strategic interests' (Newman 2001: 121), partnerships can work to colonise local government and public bodies and

re-interpolate public sector actors as entrepreneurs. In some versions they involve 'dangerous liaisons' (Taylor 1998) 'implying a process of incorporation into the values of the dominant partner' (Newman 2001: 125–6). 'The recontextualisation of discursive practices has the capacity to "set in motion" other practices under its own order' (Chouliaraki and Fairclough 1999: 110). Partnerships can also be what Jessop calls a 'linkage device'. They encourage 'a relative coherence among diverse objectives' (2002: 242). They bring about a form of values and organisational convergence and they re-shape the context in which public sector organisations work. Davies and Hentschke (2005: 11) describe partnerships as 'a third form of organizational activity' that have 'elements of both hierarchies and markets as well as unique features'. Some forms of partnership bring 'the private' into the public sector in the form of joint ventures and profit-sharing without wresting 'ownership' entirely from public sector hands (several examples have been noted already and there are more below). Nonetheless, the relations of power within partnerships vary quickly markedly.

As Newman (2001: 166) points out, the language of partnerships is often a 're-labelling' of contractual or outsourcing arrangements. Some partnerships are defensive moves by local authorities which within the current policy regime they see as being in their best interests (Reed Recruitment, Lancashire LEA and Edge Hill College). At the same time for the private sector these may be 'ways in' to new markets that may not be immediately amenable to private sector participation – a kind of Trojan horse.[4]

> Hampshire and VT together took the former Hampshire careers services into the private sector as a joint venture arrangement. Once that had happened with Hampshire, West Sussex also wanted to do the same thing; so this was a bit of the public sector saying, "Will you partner us, please, to secure the future of our careers services?"
>
> (DM)

> The private sector is looking for business opportunities, a steady funding stream and a good return on its investment.
>
> (DfES Public Private Partnership website, May 2004)

> It's always been a matter of during that period of time being able to develop other services. We've ended up being a kind of partnership, you know, often quite an informal one, with the local authority concerned, that's built up in terms of some kind of mutual relationship.
>
> (RA)

> The other acquisition of the group this year was an organisation called 'Career Finder', and that had been an offshoot of Connexions Somerset. They had a series of training and adult guidance contracts in the West Country. And it was sitting increasingly ill at ease with the Connexions

service there, for a variety of reasons. And we basically took that on, set it up as a joint venture, with the Connexions partnership for Somerset still maintaining a minority interest in it. It's a majority Prospects-owned company, and we're now bidding for additional work from Jobcentre Plus and so on. It's about enterprise, training and a whole range of different sorts of training and support for adults, and activities.

(RA)

Of course partnerships also exist among public sector organisations, sometimes as an alternative to privatisation.

Go-Teaching a consortium of 12 LEAs across the south west that provides supply teachers and also helps schools find teachers for permanent positions. Established by Devon in 1999 and involving a private partner (Teaching Associates) from 2002 as a stand alone venture.

(http://www.britgo.org/teaching/teaching.html)

As we have seen some partnerships are forced upon authorities in the form of interventions (see Bannock 2003) and begin at least with suspicion and reluctant interaction (see Chapter 7 on Atkins and Southwark). But in other circumstances they work to foster trust and consolidate network relations between public and private. As Derek Foreman describes in the case of CEA's work with Islington LEA:

We were forced down their throats [but] they trusted me. They certainly gave us the opportunity [and] we moved from genuinely a very fierce and confrontational suspicion through to partnerships. That didn't mean we didn't fall out from time to time . . . now we're in the process initiated by the Borough and by the DfES about staying with them.

. . . we certainly find that, if we're involved in a particular local authority area, and take on one contract, so far in nine years of operation, we've never found a situation where they've – we've come to the end of a contract and they've said, "Right, thanks very much", you know, "Cheerio." It's always been a matter of during that period of time being able to develop other services too. We've ended up being a kind of partnership, you know, often quite an informal one, with the local authority concerned, that's built up in terms of some kind of mutual relationship.

(Ray Auvray, Prospects)

It is also important not to lose sight of the 'opportunities' and excitements that reform technologies can engender among some public services managers, as the 'agents and objects of cultural change' (Newman 2005: 730). Enthusiasm or initiation is not limited to the private sector (see Chapter 6 on

Blackburn with Darwen). Newman (2005: 726) quotes one local authority assistant chief executive:

> We are using public/private partnerships to drive down costs – we can't achieve this with the culture of this organisation. We are using Best Value reviews as a tool or a reason or an excuse for moving services out to the social economy.

Such local authority actors are what Leys (2001: 63) calls 'a new public sector social type' who display 'new personality traits', with a concomitant shuffling off of older 'operating codes'. Some of the education business actors may fall into this category themselves and there are other high-profile examples in education of public sector entrepreneurs like Stanley Goodchild, co-founder of 3Es (ex-headteacher and chief education officer) (3Es like VT works with Surrey CC), and Sir Kevin Satchwell, Headteacher of Telford CTC. "The government have lubricated the mechanism. If people or organisations are up for it you can get on and do things" (Kevin Satchwell, quoted in *TES*, 'Businessman who would rescue schools', 13 November 1998).

As noted already, some authorities are willing to outsource or to partner with the private sector as ways of preserving and disseminating and benefiting from their in-house expertise and, as explored above, the private sector has much to gain from the experience, expertise, credibility and social networks of public sector actors.

> We are just about to enter into a joint venture with Surrey County Council to create a joint venture business, called VT4S, 4S standing for Surrey School Support Services . . . Surrey's rationale for this is to create a means of attracting and retaining good-quality people to work in Surrey for Surrey schools and for the LEA and then to form a business jointly with the private sector partner to make those services available outside Surrey to other LEAs and schools. So it'll sell services to Surrey schools and schools elsewhere, and LEAs elsewhere, on a consultancy basis. It'll compete with HE consultancy in schools and LEA-related contracts.
>
> (DM)

Again in all of this it is important to temper any picture of rampant and enforced privatisation as an ideological state strategy. Rather this is a state which recognises the value of mutual learning and negotiated coordination to enhance efficiency and develop competitive capacity. The private sector is one of several devices deployed to reorganise the local state and reform public sector organisations, sometimes replacing them, but also very often working as a partner. There is no simple, uni-directional move to privatise, although the scope of privatisation is expanding as the obvious 'solution' to public sector difficulties, and the role of local authorities is moving more towards commissioning and monitoring rather than delivery. Both points need to be registered.

Mouchel Parkman is a company which makes particular use of partnership arrangements with the public sector.

> So in Liverpool 2020 and Knowsley 2020 the council owns 20 per cent of the company. It's set up as a stand-alone, but they actually physically and legally own 20 per cent of it. So whatever profit tumbles out of that they get 20 per cent. And that's a model that we're finding local government is really interested in.
>
> (BH)

In limited ways such relationships are aspects of 'entrepreneurial localities' at work (Jessop 2002: 189) (see Chapter 6), which in some cases, like Liverpool, fit into a mosaic of other initiatives in public services provision and economic regeneration. Other partnerships, depending on the 'problem' at hand, can involve a variety of different participations and different forms of working relationships and relations of power.

> Nottingham, we, in two years, helped them to raise their GCSE five A star to Cs by 5 per cent, against a national benchmark of 0.5 per cent. And we wouldn't claim credit for doing it. We'd claim the credit for adding the capacity, the capability and, much more importantly, getting them to believe that they could do it. And we did that with a huge partnership: Tim Brighouse came in as an independent chair of it.
>
> (BH)

Here the company see themselves working alongside the public sector, 'adding capacity' as they put it, rather than working 'with' or developing capacity. In other circumstances the involvement of a private sector contractor can actually mean the 'brokering' of a variety of resources rather than direct involvement, and again this is in part about the credibility and acceptability of 'services'.

> So although we had our teams of people in there we also had some advisers and some heads from Birmingham. We created a buddying system for all of the secondary school headteachers as a starting point; but we said, "That shouldn't be our people. That needs to be a current, serving, successful secondary head who understands working in challenging urban environments and have cut their teeth in terms of continuous improvement", and that just worked like a dream. People said, "Well, actually this isn't about the private sector coming in. This is about the private sector brokering all kinds of stuff for us, which actually is what we would have liked our local education authority to do."
>
> (BH)

Partnerships are a major part of the project of the reform and 'modernising' of local government and public bodies by 'cultural re-engineering'. This is the smiling face of intervention, change without pain. The discourses of business and business management and entrepreneurism are relocated and recontextualised through the medium of partnerships as 'imaginary practices involving imaginary subjects' (Chouliaraki and Fairclough 1999: 110) making and realising relationships in new ways which suppress or select out key aspects of private practice. Partnerships are part of a new landscape of public sector provision. They are also one of the ways that privatisation works as a policy device, on and in the public sector, addressing social problems in new ways, establishing new relationships and re-distributing decision-making (see Chapter 6). Locally and within institutions through partnerships of many kinds the private sector becomes part of the policy process.

I now want to take up this final point in a more general way and at the national level (extending the analysis of private sector participation in policy begun in Chapter 4) and will return to the local and institutional levels in the following chapter.

New philanthropy and new 'policy communities'

'For every epoch and for every social structure, we must work out an answer to the question of the power elite' (Wright-Mills 1959: 23) and 'its composition, its unity, its power' (p. 23).

The education businesses addressed above are not, as indicated previously, the only new participants in the social networks of policy and service delivery. Other social actors with various relationships to business are now 'inside' policy, in a number of senses. New policy communities are developing within education policy which are routes of influence and access for business voices and at the same time new ways of realising, disseminating and enacting policy.[5] These new policy communities both circumvent and incorporate, overlay or extend beyond rather than replace entirely established policy actors. Coleman and Skogstad (1990) use the term 'policy community' to refer to the set of actors, public and private, that coalesce around an issue area and share a common interest in shaping its development. That common interest may be both self-interested and altruistic here. Put another way, these communities consist of 'personal relationships with a shared framework' (Rhodes and Marsh 1992: 17). They have their own 'internal relationships of trust and deference' (McPherson and Raab 1988: 405) and bring different members of the 'power elite' into a very specific relation to state education and education policy. Increasingly it is in 'these decentralized, and more or less regularized and coordinated, interactions between state and societal actors that policy making unfolds' (Coleman and Skogstad 1990: 4). They also involve the import of American-style corporate philanthropy and the use of 'positional investments' by business organisations and the 'acting out' of corporate social responsibility (CSR) (see also Chapter 6). There is a complex overlapping of philanthropy, influence and business interests.[6] Through these kinds of social relationships, trust is established and 'sociability, approval, status and power' (Granovetter 1985: 506) are achieved.

As we shall see, finance capital is particularly strongly represented in these communities but so too are various entrepreneurial and policy 'heroes'. This is, as Wright-Mills calls it, a new form of 'institutional mechanics' (1959: 20) or again in relation to governance 'by examining networks we are looking at the institutionalization of power relations' (Marsh and Smith 2000: 6). Such influences and relationships are of course not entirely new; it is their specificity, obviousness and directness which are different. Despite the substantive differences this policy community is very similar to that described by McPherson and Raab (1988).

These new networks are also 'discourse communities'. They bring into play new policy narratives, specifically the 'enterprise narrative' (see SIFE, NFTE, and Academy for Enterprise), a new hegemonic vision which inserts competition, entrepreneurialism and enterprise into the heart of the project of state education and modifies the political relations of education and reorients political strategies – both exemplified in the Academies programme (see Chapter 7). These modernising narratives become authorised and sensible and accumulate 'value and worth' (Mills 1997) through their association with and articulation by 'significant' social actors. Concomitantly such narratives serve to re-populate the field of policy, legitimating new actors and re-working the possibilities of public sector delivery by identifying new heroes and villains, and establish new key ideas and new logics. These communities work to change the way policies are thought and produce a closed circle of thinking and articulate 'new modes of calculation and strategic concepts' (Jessop 2002: 9).

There is a complex multi-dimensional inter-penetration of education and business in and through policy which develops and maintains and legitimates particular policy visions well beyond the policy community itself. These are in Jessop's terms the bearers of a new accumulation strategy and he notes their 'increasing participation . . . in shaping education mission statements' (2002: 167). Saltman (2005: 49) describes similar developments in the United States:

> The field of education has been greatly remade through corporate influence as business terms of accountability, performance, efficiency, upward mobility, and economic competition have become omnipresent in educational policy rhetoric and journals displacing traditional discussion of the role of schools in making people who can understand and improve the world or live a full life or participate in civic life.

In this section I want to trace some of the relationships and identify some of the participants (individual and corporate) who make up these new communities but this will have to be a partial and indicative exercise. The involvements and connections traced here are by no means exhaustive (reader: you could try filling them in further yourself). Furthermore, some of the specific links shown may be fairly tenuous in terms of personal interactions but do show the 'joining up' of organisations and actors and the re-spatialisation of policy, that is the 'territory of influence' (MacKenzie and Lucio 2005) is expanded and at the same time dissipated.

I am seeking primarily to describe and register the existence of these communities. (Farnsworth 2004: 132–45 does similar work on 'social policy networks' – and informal personal associations – at the local level, looking at the constitution of welfare service boards in Bristol.) We will see here the inter-linking of business, philanthropy, quangos and non-governmental agencies and public and private sector entrepreneurs and there is a recurrence of particular companies and people, related to particular kinds of policies. These communities also illustrate what is perhaps an increasing interdependence of state, private sector and voluntary sector and the complex interactions between them and again the exporting of 'state work'. They also draw in and upon the 'energies' of social entrepreneurs. One of the interpretive problems involved in thinking about how these networks work is that of deciding, at least in the case of some participants, where business ends and philanthropy begins and what philanthropy is for and what is influence or self-seeking. Perhaps it is pointless to attempt to pin down the motives involved here or to try to separate out different elements, and it must be accepted that motives are contradictory and mixed. Nonetheless, as public sector business becomes more attractive and more lucrative for the private sector, 'giving' is a way of registering a presence and making relationships with contractors and opinion-makers; for example, McKinsey (a consultancy company) crops up several times in what follows: "they've actually got a growing business now at McKinsey in the public sector. So . . . it's another example, in a way, of profitable business moving towards the public sector . . . they're flowing towards where the money is", as one of my respondents explained.

These communities establish productive and potentially profitable relationships within the state and they provide access to valuable insider knowledge, but they are also, in effect, another policy device, another way of trying things out, getting things done, changing things, and avoiding established public sector lobbies and interests – part of New Labour's pragmatism. They are a means of interjecting innovation into areas of social policy that are seen as resistant and risk-averse. They enable social issues and problems to be addressed without recourse to traditional procedures and structures. They bring new ideas and new ways of thinking into play in relation to policy problems and the management of the social (see Box 5.1).

Part of the new philanthropy which is represented in these communities is related to a post-Thatcherite, post-Enron (see www.washingtonpost.com/wp-dyn/business/specials/energy/enron/) resurgence of corporate social responsibility which interplays with the attempts by New Labour to introduce an agenda of moral responsibility into civil society. As noted already, there is also an importation of American-style corporate philanthropy, e.g.

Box 5.1 McKinsey: Jesuits of capitalism

11 June 2005

No. 10 risks row to hire new policy boss from 'Jesuits of capitalism'

The decision to bring David Bennett, a former McKinsey executive with no previous experience of politics or links with the party, into such a senior role was already attracting criticism from Labour backbenchers and trade unions yesterday. They believe that the appointment symbolises the growing ascendancy within Whitehall of private sector consultants, on whom the Government spent more than £1 billion last year. Mr Bennett, who is said to have started work and is being paid a six-figure salary, was recruited as part of a major shake-up of No. 10 after the election. He is previously thought to have advised on the multibillion-pound contract for a new NHS computer system. But Mr Bennett's 20-year connection with McKinsey, a global organisation described as the "Jesuits of capitalism" [see also http://news.agendainc.com/mt-agenda/content/archives/2005/06/post_125.html] that has earned contracts worth tens of millions of pounds from the Government in recent years, is particularly incendiary. Last night Jim Cousins, the Labour MP for Newcastle Central, said: "This is part of a wider problem in which the Government is increasingly run by people who do not understand the political impact of what they propose. These private sector consultants appear to be impatient with the views of the party and they alienate the civil servants who have an ethos and commitment to public service. Too much policy is being made in test tubes."

(Tom Baldwin and Jon Ashworth, http://www.guardian.co.uk/
guardianpolitics/story/0,,1505186,00.html)

Goldman Sachs is well presented in the networks outlined. "In the States in particular charitable giving is part of life: it's much more a way of life over there than it is here" (ESt). On the other hand, there is a re-emergence of the Victorian, colonial philanthropic tradition, 'outsiders behaving as if they were missionaries' (Eagle 2003: 33), represented for instance by the United Learning Trust, and other religious impulses (Vardy, Edmiston, Payne, and the Oasis Trust, which also carry undertones of evangelism), as well as a civic version of this through the interested philanthropy of self-made business millionaires (Kalms, Harris, Petchey, Garrard, Lampl, etc.). At an individual level the New Labour discourse of 'civic responsibility', which is another way of thinking about these philanthropic impulses, may also be articulating a reaction to the Thatcherite values of individualism and self-interest – another aspect of post-neo-liberalism. "And obviously under Blair it's been education, education, education, and it has raised people's awareness of what's going on in the system and how it's everybody's problem not just the government's" (ESt). The latter is another form of business philanthropy manifest in the pro bono work and volunteering of workers in companies like McKinsey's and programmes like Teach America and Teach First (see page 132). For some companies this is now a way of retaining and motivating staff as well as playing its part in making up 'portfolios of philanthropic investments' which may contribute to the promotion or legitimation of corporate brands: "it creates a nice warm feeling amongst their customers, the recognition of their name . . . and team-building" (ESt), and corporate giving is of course 'tax efficient'.

In various ways – Academies, specialist schools, Teach First – philanthropy is increasingly incorporated into state policy and is an avoidance of both bureaucratic and market difficulties. It provides a form of 'fast' and often very personal policy action. Personal 'donations' are solicited through the personal relationships of people like Tony Blair and Andrew Adonis. Some of the participants in this new philanthropy constitute a philanthropic elite which is engaged with government, party and state in a number of ways: through business links, making party donations, in the receipt of awards and honours and positions in and around the state itself. (Three Academy sponsors were also involving in making loans to the Labour Party, and an adviser to the ASST resigned after indicating to an undercover reporter that sponsorship of an Academy would deliver an honour – http://education .Guardian.co.uk/newschools/story/0,,1703426,00.html.) Again I am not suggesting that all of this is totally new. The City of London institutions (stretching back through the livery companies) have a long history of philanthropic engagement (see Green 2005: 43–4). What is different is the direct relation of 'giving' to policy and the more apparent involvement of givers in policy communities and a more 'hands on' approach to the use of donations: "they want to be involved in the way the project is managed, for example" (ESt) (see page 131 on Arpad Busson). This is what Peter Lampl (see Box 5.2) calls 'strategic philanthropy' (http://www.philanthropyuk.org/guidetogiving/personal4_main.asp).

What is emerging here is a new 'architecture of regulation' based on interlocking relationships between disparate sites in and beyond the state. Policy is being 'done' in a multiplicity of new sites 'tied together on the basis of alliance and the pursuit of economic and social outcomes' (MacKenzie and Lucio 2005: 500), although the strength of such an alliance should not be over-stated. These communities contain some 'strange bedfellows' and contain actors whose continuing allegiance is to the Conservative Party, as well as others who have made political donations to both Labour and the Conservatives. Some of the people in Network 1 (Figure 5.1) are 'survivors' or carry-overs from the policy networks of the Conservative governments: Paul Judge,[7] Stanley Kalms and Cyril Taylor.

Box 5.2 Peter Lampl

Peter Lampl is the prime example of a new and influential beast: the multi-millionaire education philanthropist. Donations to schools have multiplied since the late Eighties when Margaret Thatcher's government introduced city technology colleges – giving business the chance to fund new schools and influence the way they operated. There are now 365 specialist schools, which are the successors of the original CTCs, and funding the state system seems to be increasingly popular among the very rich. Sir Stanley Kalms, chairman of the Dixons Group, Peter Vardy, chairman of Reg Vardy plc, Lord Harris, chairman of CarpetRight plc, publisher Lord Hamlyn, and retailer Lord Sainsbury are all prominent givers. But Mr Lampl, who made his fortune in investment, has set the pace in recent years. His summer camps giving under-privileged youngsters a taste of top universities have provided the model for copy-cat government schemes and a flagship scheme to fund poor pupils at a private school, which is putting a sledgehammer through traditional independent–state divisions. Mr Lampl will be paying up to £850,000 a year to ensure that The Belvedere School in Liverpool has a 100 per cent 'needs-blind' admissions policy. All pupils in the school will be selected on merit (unlike the Assisted Places Scheme and the old direct-grant schools programme) with those unable to pay the fees getting Lampl money.

(*TES*, 28 January 2000)

As these new sites within the contexts of influence and text production proliferate there is a concomitant increase in the opacity of policy-making. It becomes even less clear as to what may have been said to whom, where, with what effect and in exchange for what (see Cohen 2004). The focus or starting points of the networks (Figures 5.1 and 5.2) are fairly arbitrary (the AST in the case of Network 1 and GEMS in the case of Network 2) and, as will become apparent, the different examples are also inter-linked. As well as being based around inter-personal relationships, and personal commitments to public service in some cases and access to positions of some influence, these communities are important as discourse networks, and I want to reiterate that importance; discourse flows through them, gains credibility and becomes natural (see Chapter 1). They structure and constrain and enable the circulation of ideas and give 'institutional force' to policy utterances, ensuring what can count as policy and limiting the possibilities of policy.

Some members of these policy communities have multiple roles (within

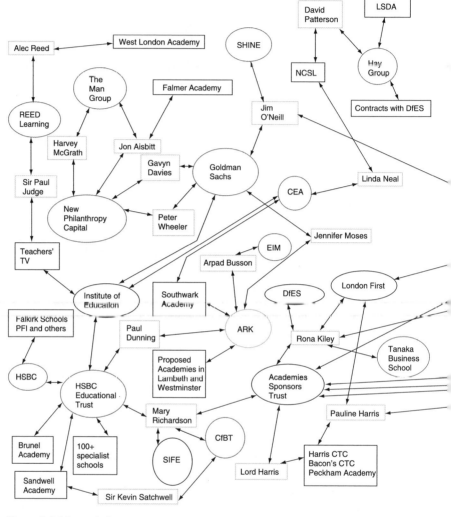

Figure 5.1 Network 1.

agencies, public service and philanthropy) and, as noted already, multiple purposes and loyalties. They are at different times, or sometimes simultaneously, representatives of business, advisers to the state, philanthropists, moral entrepreneurs or doing public service – and these ambiguities do their own work and are yet another kind of blurring of public and private. Some may even be thought of as 'transactors' having both 'shared' and 'additional goals' (Wedel 2001: 130) – that is public and personal motives together. Others are obviously occasional participants and have no positions or roles as

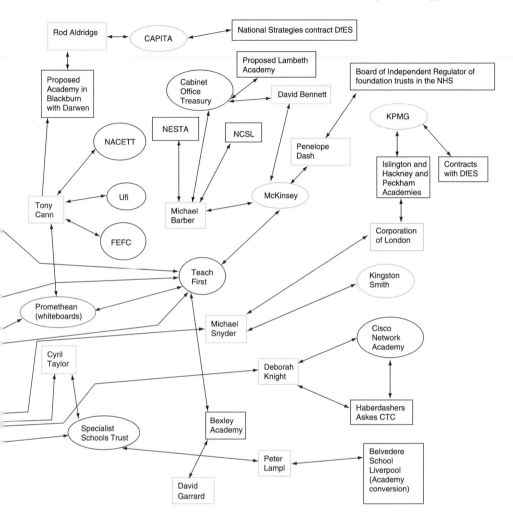

such. People move across and within such networks and as we have seen between the private and public sectors, and there are new kinds of careers which can be constructed within them. Some people who occupy multiple positions join things up. They are catalysts or synergisers (for example, Mary Richardson, Director of the HSBC Education Trust, an ex-state school head and education dame; Sir Cyril Taylor, Chairman of the Specialist Schools and Academies Trust; and Valerie Bragg, Headteacher of Kingshurst CTC, co-founder of 3Es and Chief Executive of the Bexley Academy). Women are much more in evidence here than was the case in the senior positions of the education businesses. The networks also contain flows of influence as well as flows of people and, as we have seen, influence is carried back and forth across the boundaries between the old public and private sectors. Resources

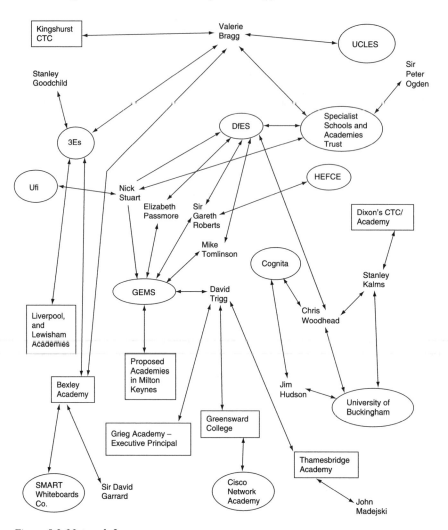

Figure 5.2 Network 2.

are exchanged, interests are served and rewards are achieved. Tony Cann CBE (600th on the *Sunday Times* Rich List in 1999) is an interesting example: founder and now Vice-Chairman of Promethean Technologies Group (a whiteboard company with turnover in 2003 in excess of £38 million – company website), he is Chairman of the Ufi (University for Industry) board, member of NACETT and former member of FEFC, and also sits on FE college and university boards. Promethean is also a 'partner' of Teach First and the Specialist Schools Trust.[8] Tony Cann has also raised the possibility of sponsoring an Academy in Blackburn where his company is based and was a sponsor of the Blackburn EAZ. Some Academies, like Sandwell and Bexley, through their sponsors, supporters and project managers, re-occur and are the focus of several linkages in the networks.

In Network 1 what is particularly noticeable is the participation of representatives of finance capital: Goldman Sachs in particular, and the Man Group and HSBC (HSBC is a member of the PPP Forum and active in the PFI market with equity interests in a number of schools projects). Paul Dunning of HSBC is a director and trustee of ARK, as is Stanley Fink of the Man Group and Jennifer Moses of Goldman Sachs. ARK founder Arpad Busson is senior partner of EIM fund management company (with assets reported as ranging from £5 billion to £10 billion). He describes education as "in crisis" and "the biggest issue government face today" and argues that "Charities must treat donors as if they were shareholders" (*Observer*, 29 May 2005). Jon Aisbitt, once of Goldman Sachs, now of the Man Group, is the proposed sponsor of an Academy in Brighton (in 2003 he was 406th on the *Sunday Times* Rich List with a personal fortune of £80 million and he donated £250,000 to the Labour Party election campaign of 2001); with Harvey McGrath of the Man Group (351st on the 2004 *Sunday Times* Rich List with £112 million) and Gavyn Davies (ex-Chairman of the BBC) of Goldman Sachs he is a trustee of New Philanthropy Capital, which advises companies on philanthropic investments, including advice on participation in the Academies programme.

As well as trusts, other kinds of public sector organisations are integrated into these networks; the Institute of Education, University of London now has an HSBC iNet[9] Chair in International Education Leadership, held by David Hopkins, previously Director of the DfES Standards and Effectiveness Unit, and in 2004 Goldman Sachs sponsored a UK/US Urban Education Conference at the Institute. The IOE is also a shareholder in Education Digital which runs Teachers' TV, teaches Teach First students and has had collaborations with CEA. Brunel University is a co-sponsor with HSBC of a 16–19 Academy, and the Universities of Liverpool and the West of England are also Academy sponsors.

In Network 2 there are also cross-over actors represented – Mike Tomlinson, ex-Chief Inspector of Schools, Chair of the Hackney Learning Trust, Vice-Chairman and sometime Chair of the Advisory Board of GEMS, Elizabeth Passmore, ex-Director of Inspection of Ofsted, and Schools' Adjudicator, who was also a member of the GEMS Advisory Board, as are Sir Gareth Roberts, ex-Vice Chancellor, Director of HEFCE and DfES adviser, and Nick Stuart, ex-DfES senior official. Such people bridge between public sector education policy and private schooling and bring their credibility and contacts to bear. Also there are various 'heroes' of reform from the public sector, models of good practice of 'what works', or traders in 'good advice' – ex-headteachers Dame Mary Richardson and Dame Sharon Hallows (member of the Standards Task Force – see Box 5.3) and serving heads Sir Kevin Satchwell and Dexter Hutt. Deborah Knight, a governor of Haberdashers Askes CTC, moved to become Director of Policy at the AST. These more

---

Box 5.3 Sharon Hallows Consultancy Limited

Sharon Hallows is also a cross-over example in a different sense, re-investing her reputation as an outstanding headteacher and her honour in a consulting company – Sharon Hallows Consultancy Limited. 'We are creative and strategic thinkers with a passion for enabling educational and organizational improvement . . . As well as work in the United Kingdom, she has advised governments of numerous countries including Japan, Canada, New Zealand and France. Other countries have expressed a strong interest in working with the Company' (company website). In 2000 Dame Sharon gave a speech to the Inaugural Garfield Weston Outstanding Principal Awards (the Garfield Weston Foundation are also Academy sponsors). The speech was published on the Fraser Institute website. (The Fraser Institute 'was founded in 1974 to redirect public attention to the role markets can play on providing for the economic and social well being of Canadians'.) Dame Sharon demonstrates again the porosity of the public/private divide.

'ordinary' actors serve an important discursive purpose. They demonstrate that reform is possible, that it works. They show that public sector actors can make a difference and can contribute to policy. In a sense they embody 'what works'. Then there are policy careerists like Sir Cyril Taylor and Rona Kiley, wife of Bob Kiley, London's Commissioner for Transport. Rona Kiley was Director of Education and Business in the Community at London First (which 'works to make London a better city for Business' – website) before becoming founding trustee of Teach First, in which staff from McKinsey's were involved in pro bono activities. She then became Chief Executive of the Academies Sponsors Trust. She had previously worked in the US as Executive Director of the Edison Preservation Foundation (partners in the Young Entrepreneurs Innovation Awards) and was Director of the New York City Office of Nature Conservancy. She is also a member of the Ministerial Advisory Group on the London Challenge (DfES) and on the Advisory Board of Imperial College Business School. Such actors move across and between sites of policy or influence and information. They collect and carry with them fragments of discourse. They join up and fill in bits of the new policy narratives.

Some participants have philanthropic 'careers' of a different kind within personal charities and causes, and through service on boards and committees, and in public service positions – the 'great and the good' as they are sometimes called, like Paul Judge, Lord Harris, David Garrard and Michael Snyder. Again they move between policy 'sites' and accumulate knowledge and credibility and social relations. They are able to bring a form of 'moral capital' to bear upon their pronouncements and participations, ultimately dependent on but separate from the power of their wealth, although as noted already they are also able to speak from the vantage point of their entrepreneurial successes and to speak knowingly about and identify 'problems' and 'blockages' and what needs to be done (see also Chapter 7 on Academies and Alec Reed). They are a new kind of practical intellectual. They play a role in narrating and propping up new compromises within policy and consolidating unstable alliances around policy solutions.

These then are not 'political' networks in the traditional sense. Linkage devices like the AST and NPC bring together businesses and people of different sorts with charity and education policy. They animate, inform and encourage the participation of 'others like us'. These networks and communities are in part at least, as I suggested was the case with the education businesses, a policy device. They are also the product of 'experimentation' and ad hocery by the state; they clearly have a tenuousness and shift and change over time; memberships, purposes, boundaries and relationships change. They have elements of both government and governance but work outside of or around the rational-bureaucratic aspects of government and bring commercial and social entrepreneurship[10] to bear upon policy problems. Once again these individuals represent a new chronotopic of policy, as people who 'get things done' – they bring passion, drive and dynamism to the tackling of social problems.

Network 2 shows a further set of relationships among Academies through the project management work of 3Es, which also runs a CTC and two state schools and is now owned by GEMS (see Chapter 3). GEMS and Cognita, which both own private schools, have indirect links of various sorts with the DfES, and Cognita through Chris Woodhead has relationships with the private University of Buckingham and CTC sponsor Stanley Kalms – these are vestiges of a 'Thatcherite' education policy network. GEMS also has indirect links to the Academies programme and indeed had proposed to fund two Academies itself; this plan was abandoned (see Chapter 3). There are other 'cross-over' actors here. David Trigg, Head of Greensward College, a state school which has taken very seriously the business opportunities opened up by the 2002 Education Act, has had advisory roles with two Academies and with GEMS. Jim Hudson, an ex-primary head, now works with Cognita and the University of Buckingham.

As noted already, these networks 'enlarge the range of actors involved in shaping and delivering policy' (Newman 2001: 125) and constitute 'new kinds of educational alliance' (Jones 2003: 160) which 'New Labour seeks to create' around 'its project of transformation' (p. 160). However, in ways that most governance writers ignore, networks exclude as well as extend. Some potential or previous participants are made pariah – trade unions, for example. And challenges from outside the shared basis of discourse 'may be easily deflected or incorporated' (Newman 2001: 172). These are exclusive networks based partly on prior relationships and special criteria of membership – wealth being one, being 'on-side' ideologically being another (Cyril Taylor,

Stanley Goodchild, Mary Richardson) and personal relationships within government being a third.

Conclusion

This chapter and the previous one have sought to do a number of things: in part to put a social face to privatisation, to populate the dynamics of capital and the blurring of the public/private divide with real social actors; also to illustrate the complexity of motives, rationales and values invested in the education business and in education partnerships and in 'service' to the state which range from forms of 'giving' to forms of 'investment' and forms of influence; further and importantly, to demonstrate the role of the education businesses and the new education policy communities as 'policy devices', as means of governance, as new ways of getting social management and policy work done and public sector institutions re-cultured. New voices are given space within policy talk, and the spaces of policy are diversified and dissociated. New narratives about what counts as a 'good' education are articulated and validated. (This is addressed more directly in Chapter 7.) New linkage devices are being created over and against existing ones, excluding or circumventing but not always obliterating more traditional sites and voices. I have also tried to show how the public sector generally is worked on and in by privatisations of different kinds, from the outside in and the inside out and to make the point that new policy discourses articulate enthusiasm for privatisation from positions inside the public sector not just from the private sector itself. Linkages and alliances around policy concerns and new policy narratives cross between the two. I have indicated the ways in which privatisations rely on the energy, experience and social relations of specific social actors who have had success within the private sector and the work done through and by private/public partnerships of different kinds and new kinds of 'crossover' organisations with characteristics drawn from both sides of the old divide. Altogether, at this point in time, I am arguing that privatisation as a material and discursive process is partial and very diverse, sometimes faltering but of massive and increasing importance within and over and against public sector education. I have also suggested that the work of education businesses and of the new policy communities is indicative of new kinds of state modalities.

6 Selling improvement/selling policy/selling localities

An economy of innovation

> Competitiveness depends on developing the individual and collective capacities to engage in permanent innovation – whether in sourcing, technologies, products, organization or marketing.
>
> (Jessop 2002: 121)

In this chapter I address issues of innovation and change and the involvement of the private sector in public sector education in two different ways: first, by looking at the 'improvement products' which are marketed to educational institutions by education services companies and their role in re-working and surveilling those institutions; second, and rather differently, by considering the role of education as part of the 'place marketing' of and attempt to establish competitive advantage within particular 'entrepreneurial localities' and the ways that this 'joins up' schools to the competitiveness project. Some of the companies mentioned previously re-appear in these localities as participants in 'place-specific development strategies' (Parkinson and Harding 1995: 67). Further aspects of innovation and change, in the form of the Academies policy, are discussed in Chapter 7.

Innovation and change

I argued in the previous chapter that the private education services companies are part of a re-worked system of governance. The selling of their services is linked to the New Labour project of 'transformation' through the re-modelling of schools, colleges and universities, the instilling of new capacities and the management of change. These 'services' and the work they do on and in schools are part of the 'recalibration' of state organisations and their 'organisational ecologies' (Jessop 2002: 241), which also involves the modification of 'the self-understanding of identities, strategic capacities and interest of individual and collective actors' (Jessop 2002: 242–3) – that is the production of new kinds of public sector subjectivities. Innovation is not merely technological but also involves 'changes in the social relations of production … the demand for different types of skills and indeed changes in how we understand innovation' (Brown et al. 2001: 163), for example new ways of organising time and space and their relationships in and to education. In other words, this is part of a process of enabling organisations and their actors to think about themselves, and what they do, differently. I also suggest, and I return to this in the following chapter, that 'improvement', 're-modelling' and 'recalibration' are part of the promotion of economic growth and competitiveness in and through education through 'almost permanent institutional and organizational innovation' (Jessop 2002: 242). This is repre-sented by and intended to achieve what Tony Blair calls 'a modern education system', one that is "open, diverse, flexible, able to adjust and adapt to the changing world" (Speech to parents, 10 Downing Street, 24 October 2005). The re-narration of schooling and learning through innovation and enter-prise is part of an adaptation to a particular version of the economic and social context of globalisation and post-modern society based on what Watson and Hay (2003: 295) call 'the logic of no alternative', through which 'globalisation has itself become a conditioning influence on policy' and competitiveness 'a dangerous obsession' (Krugman 1994), with the effect of making the contingent necessary (this was outlined in Chapter 2). In response to the 'threats' of globalisation, 'Labour has attempted to forward a com-petitiveness strategy that would translate macroeconomic precepts into microeconomic imperatives' (Watson and Hay 2003: 299). In this sense we must see the role of the private sector as strategic to the reform process and not simply substantive to it – not everything happens in the interests of the private sector and neither is privatisation the only method of reform, that is privatisation is a means of reform and of governing rather than an end in itself. Nonetheless, the private sector is increasingly important as a mediator of policy between the central state and local institutions, in the form of technical rather than political solutions to the 'problems' of schools. The chapter also illustrates a second manifestation of innovation as related to entrepreneurism and competition, that is the 'product' innovations of the companies themselves.

Using company brochures and websites and interviews with providers, I explore some aspects of the embedding of the imperatives of competition within schools through the work of 'school improvement'. I focus first on the texts, discourses and practices of innovation and change which 'sell' the private sector to state institutions and are sold *by them* to state institutions, and second on the re-articulation of local schooling within the discourses and techniques of local economic and social regeneration. As argued in Chapter 2, a great deal of the work of improvement involves the deployment of 'the firm' as the model for public sector organisation, a point I shall return to later.

Selling improvement/mediating policy[1]

One aspect of innovation and entrepreneurship displayed here is the response to the processes of 'modernisation' of the public sector by private service providers in search of new markets. For private providers, New Labour education policies and reforms are specific opportunities for profit in two senses. First, policies which announce 'zero tolerance of underperformance' and intervention in underperforming schools (*Excellence in Schools*, Internet summary, 1998) provide opportunities for replacement and/or remediation of 'failing' or 'weak' public sector institutions. The education businesses can sell school improvement – offering schools ways of accommodating themselves to the demands of performativity and producing new organisational identities and 'turnaround services' to those schools and colleges which are 'struggling' to respond to the requirements of performativity. Second, taking up spaces 'vacated' by LEAs and other state organisations, these companies mediate between policy and institutions, making policy manageable and sensible to schools and to teachers. On behalf of the state, in effect, they disseminate the discourses of reform, of improvement and of competition. This is just one part of 'the re-agenting of schooling' (Jones 2003: 159). These services are represented in the company's improvement brands: Cocentra offers 'futureproofing'; Tribal will make you into 'Pupils' Champions'; Edison Schools UK sells the 'Edison Design', which includes coaching and performance management systems; Mouchel Parkman deals in 'enabling improvement' and 'collaborative development'; Edunova has 'Learning Led Design' and stresses that 'Innovation can only be effective as part of a process of school transformation if it arises naturally from a culture that accepts change and continuous improvement as a way of life' (www.ednova.co.uk); Prospects offers Performance Life Coaching; and CEA can provide 'Leading School Improvement Solutions'. The companies present themselves in terms of commitments to the public good and to bringing the public sector into 'the new' – saving it from itself and solving its problems. 'Place Group which is part-owned by Mace, is a specialist education company that works in partnership with its clients to transform education and raise standards in schools' (www.place-group.com). These texts are 'breathlessly enthusiastic' (Parker 2000: 9), energetic and bold; they promise to solve school problems.

> HBS Education has a mission to support all parties engaged in raising standards and transforming the way we learn . . . Introducing a bold change strategy to transform the way we teach and learn in this century, requires new ways of looking at problems and how we solve them . . . HBS is one of a new breed of solution providers in education.

Here again we have the language and imagery of dynamism which was noted in Chapter 2 as a feature of New Labour public sector policy, translated into action programmes for schools, literally a re-articulation of school organisation. Part of this is what Fullan (2001) calls 'reculturing' – which draws its language and methods from business models of change management and which Parker (2000: 11) sees as a shift from bureaucracy and its inefficiencies to 'caring about customers, being innovatory, focusing on quality and so on'.

What is being sold is the urgencies of change, a new language and a kind of self-belief and self-efficacy. This is the retail end of the ESI. There are many small packages of work and one-off events and consultancies: "there's a relatively small amount of profit; the margins are pretty small" (RG).

These companies offer 'solutions', 'holistic change', 'vision', 'customised change', 'values-led approaches', 'creative challenges' and repeatedly 'transformation'. The language and especially the verbs they deploy convey a sense of urgency and speed: they work 'swiftly and efficiently' and are 'focused'; they deliver 'streamlining' and 'manageability'. They trade in professional expertise and trust and work in partnership with the public sector client. 'Edison Schools UK provides school improvement services to schools in Great Britain. The programme is implemented in partnership with schools, and tailored to each school's requirements' (brochure). Edunova 'is focused on working with practitioners, businesses and others intent on helping bring about a step change in the educational achievement of students in our schools and colleges' (website). The Place Group assert that: 'For real education transformation to be achieved, we need to drive authority-wide initiatives and change management programmes, working in partnership with agencies focused on joining-up public services' (website). This is the discourse of the competition state at work within public sector organisations, modernising and re-designing organisational ecologies (and the 'ecologies of learning'), changing workplace relationships and creating flexibility and adaptability, making them more like those in other public and private sector organisations, more like 'the firm'. In effect these programmes disseminate the discourses of reform and modernisation and work to embed them within institutional cultures. They provide authoritative readings and enactments of policy or 'readings of readings' (Ball 1994). The companies also work in partnerships of change with parastatal agencies – LEAs, Ofsted, TDA, NCSL – to 'drive' the 'project of transformation' through 'corporate vision' (Place Group) and as noted above sell their 'assistance' and 'expertise' abroad – 'The UK experience has served as the underlying model for much of the development internationally of SBM' (www.cea.co.uk). All of this narrows and focuses but does not necessarily close down entirely the space of interpretation within policy. Nor are the urgency and enthusiasm for change or the 'products' always shared by the audiences of improvement at the chalk face. Nor is innovation or best practice the prerogative of the private sector; there are plenty of endogenous innovators.

These are generic discourses which at the organisational level have no specificity to education or schools. The company consultants are 'carriers of global institutionalized management concepts' (Hansen and Lairidsen 2004: 515) and these are, as indicated above, framed within the imperatives of inevitability, uncertainty and threat. 'As LEA and school leaders you are faced with tremendous challenges. In a changing world full of new ideas and innovations, we can help you develop transformational learning organisations' (Cocentra advert, *TES*). The transformation discourse imposes new limits on what is recognisable as a 'good school' and what effectivity is, leadership is and professionalism is. 'All of these mechanisms for the structuring, constraining and circulation of information [ideas] have a similar effect: they bring about the production of discourse, but only certain types of discourse' (Mills 1997: 75).

The imperatives of continuous change

These improvement services are produced within a complex of 'required and forbidden enunciations' (Foucault 1980: 100) and 'discursive fragments', what Thrupp and Willmott (2003) call 'eclectic quasi-theoretical soundbites', which make up a new grammar and lexicon of organisation life. They articulate a form of 'scaremongering' which asserts that 'schools have to change and quick' (Thrupp and Willmott 2003: 186). They must learn, adapt and transform. They must respond to a changing economy and to social and economic instability. Perhaps the most significant of the brand names is Cocentra's 'Future Proof', 'a programme of school support *transformation* using state-of-the art systems for self-review and evaluation' (see page 143). What this suggests is a kind of systemic responsiveness and an insurance against the uncertainties and risks of contingent and policy changes.

Through their service offerings these companies re-distribute policy discourses which originate within general economic and social policy in and through institutions. As suggested previously, the discourses of competition and reform move between levels as national, public sector and institutional policies are re-articulated and reoriented toward a common purpose (see Table 6.1).

However, these services are not, in most cases, an imposition or a requirement – they work 'with' rather than 'on' – but neither are they exactly procured freely by the 'client'. Rather they are made necessary in order to accommodate to the disciplines and requirements of policy. Thus the companies stress that they 'work in partnership rather than impose solutions' (CEA) and claim to be bolstering autonomy. They 'emphasize sustainability. We help clients to grow so that they can learn and develop' (Prospects website). Autonomy is a means by which public sector institutions deliver

Table 6.1 Levels of discourse

Economic, social and welfare policy	Competitiveness, knowledge economy, flexibility, responsiveness, modernisation, entrepreneurship, enterprise.
Education policies	Improvement, transformation, reform, diversity and choice, excellence, innovation.
Institutions and persons	Change management, organisational re-culturing, personalised learning, best practice, benchmarks, leadership.

themselves up to policy. Cocentra aims 'to be central to our customers' needs' and, according to HBS, 'Through our existing partnerships we help LEAs and schools to deliver local and national strategies, whilst planning for the future and embracing change.' The 'needs' of the organisation are re-articulated through policy. Edison is 'working with schools in challenging circumstances' and creating 'a framework of collaboration between schools' (brochure). New kinds of organisational subjectivities are produced. Place 'supports' headteachers and governors to become more 'intelligent clients'. These key actors are 'agents and objects of cultural change' (Newman 2005: 730). As in the earlier discussion of partnership, part of what is going on here is a process of induction, a re-modelling of social actors and their language and practices, needs and objectives. 'Edunova is working to pro-mote change by bringing together groups of schools in collective partnerships and federated structures'. These new partnerships and federations replace those previously managed by and through LEAs. But generic solutions are also re-worked to local specificities – a kind of totalising and individualising. Each client is unique within a pre-defined policy framework. 'We can tailor courses to advance your specific school improvement programme' (Prospects). "That particular college is buying 40 days, so that's a lot, that's 320 hours of our time, to address its bespoke needs" (RG).

The work of improvement is done by 'consultants' and 'advisers'. It is a form of what Hardt and Negri (2000: 290) call 'immaterial labour' – 'the exchange of information and knowledges'. As discussed in Chapter 4, public sector expertise is deployed to achieve credibility and trust. Prospects con-sultants 'draw on their own practical experience and listen to their clients' (company brochure). They support schools into 'the new' by 'supporting innovation and research, developing new ways of working, diversifying into new areas' (Prospects website). The advisers and consultants bring to bear 'expertise in change management and education' (Place Group website). Aptly, Rose (1996: 54) describes such expertise as 'modest and omniscient' and 'limited yet apparently limitless in their application to problems'. The services and products on offer in the education services market purvey a set of 'practical truths' – what works! We "model best practice . . . it's about showing the way, demonstrating it . . . we're an intervention strategy" (Tribal consultant). Experience and research combine to provide 'critical insight to deliver successful, workable solutions' (CEA), as in the 'One school176 approach developed from research into effective schools' (Cocentra). The Place Group searches 'for best practice and service excellence' (website). "Like all of my consultants, we go through higher degrees on a regular basis – not as letter collecting: it's a very important intellectual process, and we re-engage at a higher level with our profession" (PD).

Innovation is a recurring theme (see Chapter 7), but in relation to the need for holistic change, to re-make schools differently, to re-engineer them for the new social context of post-modernity – which is fast, complex, compressed and uncertain. 'Innovation can only be effective as part of a process of school transformation if it arises naturally from a culture that accepts change and continuous improvement as a way of life . . . Innovation for whole school transformation must be systemic' (Edunova). 'Raising Achievement through innovative school design' (Edison). Innovation is made a state of mind and an imperative – there is nothing that might not be changed: 'we work with schools who are not content to stand still . . . provide schools with potent educational tools . . . consultancy, professional development and coaching support' (Edison). The websites and brochures of these companies reiterate a set of discursive touchstones – innovation, modernisation, continuous improvement – which destabilise modernist notions of school and of teaching and learning, learners and teachers, organisation and space. 'The Edison Design is based on the findings of extensive educational research from the US, UK and elsewhere . . . This programme remodels and refines the school learning environment.' New kinds of learning are promised, and the traditional classroom and school are positioned as thoroughly out-moded.[2]

Learning is at the centre of the improvement process and is talked about in new ways: as a 'learning skills framework', as about 'learning to learn' and 'schools as organisations for learning', and there is a need to establish 'values and culture for learning' (Edison). Learning is strategically linked to the use of new technologies; 'the full transformational benefits of technology in the classroom have yet to be realised' (Edison). 'Software tools are being developed that will facilitate an open exchange of opinions and provide a channel for the student voice' (Edison). There is 'Learning Led Technology', 'Learning Led Design' and 'Learning Partnerships'. HBS 'recognizes the learning institution as the hub of a learning community'. Edison works at 'creating small schools within the larger school . . . creating an environment which is more conducive to students taking more responsibility for their learning'. HBS will 'address individual needs, including provision for gifted and talented pupils and SEN'. The personalisation (Leadbeater 2004), individualisation (Beck 1992) and responsibilitisation (Rose 1996) of learning are one of the key ecological changes which transformation is delivering. This is a new kind of technology-based child-centredness. "At the heart of school improvement is the child in the classroom" (RG).

Change is arduous and demanding but it is, as noted already, a joint enterprise, a partnership. 'A tribe is a group of families or communities with a common language and culture, and a shared set of values and traditions' (Tribal brochure). Partnership is a way of getting things done, a means of reorientation. 'Our partnership with Edison will ensure that the school continues to improve standards because the emphasis is very much on putting children's learning at the core of everything we do' – Mayflower Primary (press release). Partnerships are based upon 'values' as a 'traded good' and values are also a basis for change. Edison takes a 'value-based approach . . . intentionally and explicitly implemented in every aspect of the school's life'. Cocentra starts with 'people principles'. Difficult distinctions and awkward binaries are avoided. At Tribal 'We place a high value on combining innovation and entrepreneurism with the aims and values of public service delivery' (website). These texts 'are processes in which political work is done' (Fairclough 2000: 158). As Fairclough points out, through the recontextualisation of business and management language the work of governance is achieved. Politics and business get 'into the texture of texts' (p. 158) and change everyday social relations in schools, colleges and universities.

The challenges of specific bits of policy are often used, directly or indirectly, as a selling point for improvement services: 'It is a fundamental part of government policy for schools to become more collaborative and Edunova has developed strategic processes to help schools make a reality of such a vision.' New policy ideas like 'personalised learning' are quickly taken up: 'Edison's practical approach to the challenge of personalised learning' and 'through a learning skills approach to the curriculum at Key Stage 3'. 'Place provides strategies for key curriculum initiatives such as Key Stage 3, ICT, Enterprise, Personalised Learning and 14–19. We were commissioned by the DfES to investigate Personalised Learning from the pupils' perspective' – another kind of claim to practical expertise. Policy documents are incorporated into promotional materials: 'Edison Design and the Five Year Strategy for Children and Learners'; 'A clear synergy exists between Edison's proven approach and the principles set out in the Five Year Strategy'; 'implementation of Workforce Reform Agreement' (Edison). These companies are linkage devices between state and public sector organisations – making change sensible and manageable, by "Offering an educational vision linked to the delivery of the government's five-year agenda" (PD).

> The recent White Paper for schools sets out the Government's vision for education, including an ambitious agenda for high standards throughout the whole sector. Tribal's range of school improvement services is continuing to grow to meet increasing demand for both consultancy and managed services.
>
> (Brochure)

The brochures and websites present the companies as facing both state and schools and as having ready-made or bespoke 'solutions' to the problems of policy – helping schools in 'raising achievement' and 'transforming' themselves and contributing to the raising of national standards. Edison's consultants are called 'Achievement Advisers' who offer 'consultancy, coaching and innovation, to provide a complete package of services and technologies to assist with raising achievement'. This is making operant the discourse and vision of the competition state.

Failure and Ofsted inspections are other policy opportunities. The companies are firmly imbricated in the production of a grid of visibility (Rose 1996: 55) within schools – making them and those who inhabit them accessible and auditable. The state acts upon schools through the language of management and business, among other ways, to shape and utilise their freedoms through new forms of expertise – budget disciplines, audits, management coaching – to generate a regime of critical self-scrutiny. The 'sciences' of numeration, calculation and monitoring which are embedded in and legitimate the work of these companies work to ensure the 'responsibility and fidelity of agents who remain formal[ly] autonomous' (Rose 1996: 55). They construct new diagrams of force and freedom linking measurement to management.

Cocentra provides: a 'distinctive focus on evaluating the schools' organizational culture' and 'an audit process that models best practice in school self-review – primary £1800–2500 and secondary £2800–3500 for first year of full audit' and 'school self review, pre and post Ofsted advice for schools and LEAs'. HBS offers 'effective self-evaluation' and audits of 'subjects, departments and other aspects of provision' and sells 'advice and support' to 'prepare for Ofsted Inspection'.[3] Edison have 'Team culture measurement systems' (see Box 6.1). CEA have a 'performance management consultancy'. All of this draws on the 'disciplines' of business, management and social science and contributes to the production of knowledge about schools and teachers – exams, tests, audits, appraisals, inspections, evaluations, reviews and performance management. These tactics of measurement are techniques for the governing of subjects and the management of the social.

Box 6.1 Edison Design

By combining elements of Edison's school improvement programme with McLaren's range of performance management tools, the partnership provides an all-encompassing and effective environment for building leadership capacity in schools.

Needs are analysed, coaching and mentoring are offered, 'scoping' is undertaken and various forms of 'confession' are elicited, an opening up as a way of recognising weakness and realising the desires produced by policy. The willingness of the organisation to expose and to own and acknowledge its weaknesses is used as a basis for working together to be different and better. The organisation is enabled to achieve, to improve, to better itself and to develop its capacities. These are 'soft' and responsive disciplinary devices, which rest on 'partnership working based on mutual trust' (CEA). They bring about a form of self-subjection (although not in every case). Schools 'bind themselves to expert advice as a matter of their own freedom' (Rose 1996: 58). They are active agents in their own disciplining, recuperation and re-making.

We go in and we have a very detailed scoping meeting which is the needs analysis . . . and we starting talking then about how we might deliver it. You know what the needs are. What we can offer is try to match those up

. . . it may well be its academic mentoring; individual work; it may be help with English as an additional language; it may well be that they want some leadership development . . . and then we say there is a menu of activity days and prices . . . it may well be that the school is using some of its school improvement money, its standards fund money, and it buys us in because they see the way forward.

(RG)

. . . we're saying that that we've got a coherent, holistic design which is research based, which is going to have a real impact in your school. But we're not about selling you bits and pieces. We're not about doing a bit of training and walking away. We're about having a three-year contract with you and putting a team of three advisers with a mix of expertise working with you on a weekly basis . . . that means it's costing a lot more than they're used to spending . . . typically a primary school might be paying £20,000 a year and a secondary school could be spending anywhere between £50,000 and £75,000 a year.

(PL)

Re-culturing instils a new sense of self-worth and esteem in relation to the gaze of standards and achievement. The school is made responsible for policy and the education businesses will supply and support forms of self-organisation, but set within a well-defined framework of educational possibilities.[4] The commitment to continuous improvement 'entails a relation to authority in the very moment it pronounces itself the outcome of free choice' (Rose 1996: 59).

Not all of the work of improvement and self-surveillance is done by the private sector. Partnerships and collaborations between schools bring into play a form of peer discipline, a subservience of equals. A complex logic of disciplines is embedded in processes of transformation.

. . . we had quite an interesting time with the DfES and London Challenge over Battersea and we're quite pleased with the way that's gone. We set up an improvement partnership between Battersea and two other schools and got them out of special measures and now the partnership is actually really very, very interesting indeed as a way forward. And we set it up in, I mean the principle behind it was that we weren't putting jump leads on Battersea but that we were setting it up in a way in which all three schools would be able to learn from the experience of working together. And that's worked surprisingly well.

(PDg)

The DfES facilitates 'excellence clusters' which pair LEAs to enable 'self and peer' review. This is not a system, not a single net of power, but a 'proliferation of little regulatory instances' (Rose 1996: 61).

The discourse(s) of improvement and transformation provide new systems of meaning for school organisation and a new narrative for schools, that is new ways of expressing themselves to themselves and to others, new ways of constructing plausible performances and to be taken seriously and to be seen as succeeding. The improvement and 'turnaround' packages constitute a methodology for schools to 'think' about themselves differently and work on themselves. They can learn to 'say' themselves in ways that are recognisable and 'sensible' to evaluators, 'clients' and 'customers'. Schools are thus reconstituted as generic or isomorphic organisations which 'fit' with (in a variety of ways) and can be 'joined up' to other services and to business. In this sense they are made a meaningful part of the knowledge economy (see Chapter 7 on Academies). However, as the term suggests, there is an interface here, an exchange which is not only one-way. Business is also learning new ways to speak to and within education, to talk about itself and its products in ways that are meaningful to schools and to policy (see pages 155–6 on Fujitsu).

Within the discourse of improvement there is a set of other sub-texts or specificities – management and leadership, 'learning' and inclusion, among others – which again draw upon and activate the lexicons of policy, giving force to semantics. Keywords are brought into a tight and seamless relationship of possibilities and perfections for which schools should strive; 'we help LEAs and schools to deliver local and national strategies, whilst planning for the future and embracing change' (HBS) – schools can become at the same time improved, creative, manageable, inclusive, learner-centred and federated. Here is a multiplicity of discursive fragments with different histories, connotations and effects out of which 'modernisation' and 'recalibration' are constituted. The discourse is all-embracing and unencumbered with tensions and incompatibilities: 'our solutions and services are designed to help those responsible for education and training to improve learner services and management control' (Tribal). Edison will 'foster manageability and creativity in all aspects of school life'; change is 'holistic' and rests upon 'maximising Leadership capacity' (Edison) – in the improved school almost anything is possible.

Inclusion is marginally present. Prospects 'delivers Ofsted training covering key topics such as "How inclusive is your school?" ', and indeed Cocentra brings the two together to offer an approach which 'helps reconcile the tensions that exist between the standards agenda and the drive for inclusion' – an unusually straightforward recognition that not all of the elements of the discourse of transformation fit seamlessly together.

Some companies also see the pressures of policy and of continuous change as another market opportunity – Icp (Prospects) offers 'Stress Management' training and 'motivational and well-being' programmes – '*You can do it!*' Courses on emotional literacy are available.

> This was about children's behaviour, it was about children having a sense of worth and esteem and value, and none of that would happen unless

you could get this right. And emotional literacy gave us an opportunity of having a soft measurement around this, which would drive everything else. And I had an uphill battle with the DfES about it, but in the end they accepted it.

(BH)

The appeal to an emotional register is, as Hartley (1999: 317) suggests, part of the 're-enchantment' of the school workplace, for teachers and students, and a recognition that the 'turbulence, ambiguities and ambivalences which frame and suffuse schools ... cannot be dealt with by mere appeals to hierarchy and authority'.

The private sector are the new experts in school organisation, with expertise to sell (although as we have seen much of this expertise actually comes from the public sector), validated by the truths of research and tested in the crucible of practice, in the form of a new science of improvement. Within their brochures, websites and interviews is a plausible and systematic discourse which works to modify the institutional materiality of schools and within which schooling can be re-narrated as a post-modern enterprise. However, it is important to reiterate that 'The apparently finished discourse is in fact a dense reconstruction of all the bits of other discourses from which it was made' (McGee 1990: 278). It is a composite of rhetorics, claims, allusions, promises, and jargon borrowed from business, educational research and political and policy ideas. The power and meaning of the discourse are accounted for by the fears and desires of the audience which are 'called up' from policy. It is a saviour discourse that promises to save schools, leaders and teachers and students from failure, from the terrors of uncertainty, from the confusions of policy and from themselves – their weaknesses. All of this makes it extremely difficult to resist its claims. It presupposes and recycles a set of imperatives about the urgency and necessity of change which in a variety of subtle and not-so-subtle ways ties educational practices to the needs of the economy and competitiveness. The texts and practices of school improvement only really make sense and take on their more general significance in these terms.

Undoubtedly some things change for the better in all of this. Some schools do become better places to learn, more inclusive, thoughtfully innovative, relevantly and authentically creative and healthily reflexive. Improvement is not simply a rhetorical flourish or ideological fiction (Rose 1996: 61). If I can paraphrase Rose here, I am not making any simple judgements about these new programmes of improvement and transformation but rather I am seeking to disturb the political logics within which they are set and interrogate the discourse of improvement and begin to understand some of the work it does on schools.

Education, transformation and entrepreneurial localities

Now I want to take up some different aspects of innovation and transformation, although latterly some very material realisations of the improvement discourse are apparent, and explore some different kinds and scales of private sector involvement in public sector education. I will also return to several aspects of the analysis of privatisation so far.

One simple point that needs to be repeated is that privatisation initiatives are unevenly spread or to put it another way are concentrated in particular localities – innovation hot spots. This is part of a re-scaling of policy involving denationalisation, regional variation and experimentation[5] and state support for and sponsorship of specific innovative capacities. Jessop (2002: 129) takes this to be central to the economic project of the Schumpeterian state, the 'refocusing of economic strategies around the features of specific economic spaces'. A second issue is the way in which forms of educational privatisation 'join up' with other educational developments and with local regeneration schemes and economic and business development programmes as proactive strategies to achieve dynamic and sustainable competitive advantage. This picks up from Chapter 4 the issue of governance. Again the point is that privatisation is multi-faceted, and private involvements in local educational initiatives inter-penetrate with other agendas and other sorts of economic and political relationships. What we see is an often bewildering combination of policy levers and mechanisms – business, markets, agencies, trusts, partnerships, philanthropy, informal networks, 'local heroes' and other forms of coordination and collaboration – which are mobilised into 'local growth alliances' (Hubbard and Hall 1998: 3) and conceptually reorient (but do not totally displace) the 'discredited' and 'out-moded' political-bureaucratic local state (see for example McFadyean and Rowland 2002 and Newcastle City Council Trade Unions 2002). The local state 'is both a product and agent of regulation' here (Hubbard and Hall 1998: 17). Some 'ordinary cities'[6] (Amin and Graham 1997) are re-imaged and re-imagined as 'entrepreneurial localities' drawing on 'place myths' and a ' "new combination" of economic and/ or extra-economic factors' (Jessop 1997: 31) including education. Others simply remain ordinary. This is a new kind of 'speculative' governance (Jewson and Macgregor 1997: 8), the construction of new urban regimes which have 'the power to act' and through various economic, political and social innovations seek to address the development of structural competitiveness. This involves, as signalled in Chapter 4, but this time at the local level, the legitimation of new policy actors and voices, and these new actors are often both the focus of local or regional network relations and sometimes participants in national policy networks. The local strategies and stances of growth and boosterism bring together 'property interests, rentiers, utility groups, universities, business groups, trade unions and local media' (Hubbard and Hall 1998: 9) and have appeal to local governments of different political persuasions. All of the localities presented below are Labour controlled.

In these entrepreneurial localities, education is drawn into a specific relationship to the economic and to entrepreneurism and competitiveness as part of urban regeneration and local labour market strategies and as part of the marketing of place (see page 149). Education is made part of narratives of local failure and recovery. The narrative of enterprise and entrepreneurism is apparent and relevant in a number of ways, for example the setting up of Academies; the role of Academies and other initiatives in the teaching and promotion of enterprise in schools (see Chapter 7); the fostering of technological innovations in schools; the links between schooling and local economic regeneration; and the role of local entrepreneurs and companies in the transformation and re-culturing of schools.

Within all this, schools are drawn into different policy networks operating on different scales – both local and distant – 'multi-level governance' (Jessop 2004: 6). Academies, as we shall see, are embedded in local partnerships with sponsors and other business interests; in some cases (ULT, Vardy, Oasis) they are part of 'virtual' federations run by sponsors, or local federations of schools, or combinations of these (Education Action Zones). They also have dependence on and responsibilities to the centre (DfES Academies division, Ofsted, ASST). Some specialist schools also have ongoing relationships with other schools via their sponsors (HSBC sponsors 100 schools, Alec Reed 27 schools and Thomas Telford CTC 63 – see Chapter 7). This is a new but fluid socio-spatial fix for school governance.

In this way education is made part of what is called 'new localism', another New Labour condensate which promises 'cost-effective public services . . . equity . . . and greater choice' and to address the 'pressing urgency to reverse the long-term disengagement of people from traditional politics' not by 'greater centralisation – they will only come from decentralisation and devolution of power' (Hazel Blears, MP for Salford and Minister of State at the Home Office, Foreword to the NLGN publication *New Localism in Action*, 2004: 8).

Lastly, the cases presented below are exemplars in another sense. They are working at the leading edge of new policy developments. They are 'Pathfinders', test-beds for new policy ideas, willing innovators, active disseminators of 'good practice' and 'what works', 'centres of excellence' and effective in bidding for new initiatives, often picked out for praise by government ministers and agencies. In this way they are an active facet of the experimental state; they are the recipients of 'targeted' initiatives; they are 'beacons' but also sometimes failures. The important point is that 'entrepreneurial localities' have 'institutional and organisational features that can sustain a flow of innovations, what is involved here is a spatialised complex of institutions, norms, conventions, networks, organisations, procedures and modes of economic and social calculation that encourage entrepreneurship' (Jessop 2002: 189).

I identify below three 'entrepreneurial localities' within which education is a component of the spatialised complex of social and economic regeneration – Sandwell, Blackburn with Darwen, and Middlesbrough – but the exemplars will be necessarily superficial. I will sketch in some of the ways in which these councils are engaged in 'place marketing', re-imagineering themselves as 'new types of place or space for living, working' (Jessop 2002: 188) and highly 'proactive in promoting the competitiveness of their respective economic spaces' (Jessop 2002: 124). These localities are by no means unique but they are not necessarily typical. They are paradigm cases of inter-urban competitiveness in which education has a significant role in their 'space economies'. They may also be 'politically favoured' localities.

Sandwell

Sandwell is in the West Midlands, and the Borough Council is 'Transforming Sandwell'. In place-marketing language, 'The borough is on a journey of transformation with our destination – as set out in the 2020 vision of the Sandwell Plan – "a thriving, sustainable, optimistic and forward-looking community" in which physical, social and economic conditions have been radically improved and remodelled' (all quotations from the SMBC website). Sandwell will be 'better, smarter, healthier, stronger and safer'. The journey is 'powered' by a regeneration company (RegenCo – the 'first in the West Midlands', in which the Council is a partner with English Partnerships and Advantage West Midlands), a housing market renewal Pathfinder area and a New Deal for Communities area – Greets Green.

> Of strategic significance our key relationships with Sandwell MBC and Sandwell Partnership have ensured that NDC policies are written into Borough-wide policies. This has enabled us to develop a housing strategy that will out live the NDC programme, influence future planning of West Bromwich town centre and have a major impact on employment in Greets Green. We are also working with Sandwell College to ensure that their plans fit with the educational needs and aspirations of Greets Green.
>
> (Ally Allerson, Executive Director of Greets
> Green Partnership, ODPM website)

In 2000 Sandwell LEA received interim management support from Nord Anglia in a nine-month contract. Part of the Sandwell journey involves "investing in our young people" – five primary schools have been rebuilt by Total Schools (Vinci/Norwest Holst/Pell Frischmann/Investec) in a £17 million PFI scheme (in which PWC acted as the Borough's adviser) and two CLCs are open as part of the EiC initiative, one specialising in music and digital video and the other language and communication, art and design and digital media. Test performance has been 'boosted by a pioneering £4 million "Teacher of the Future" programme, aimed at transforming teaching and learning . . . in partnership is the University of Wolverhampton'.

The language here represents the themes of change, recovery, innovation, re-design, energy and integration harnessed to achieve social and economic regeneration. A £300 million investment via the government's Building Schools for the Future programme is set to rebuild or refurbish all the Borough's remaining secondary schools, 'equipping them for 21st century learning'.

In a speech in 2002, Tony Blair picked out one Sandwell school for special praise:

> Shireland Language College in Sandwell, under the leadership of Mark Grundy and with strong support from its sponsors HSBC, has virtually doubled the proportion of students gaining five good GCSE passes since becoming a specialist school in 1998, up from 28 per cent to 52 per cent. They teach Chinese and Japanese as well as Panjabi, Arabic and Urdu, and they are now a leading language college.
>
> (Tony Blair's speech to Technology Colleges Trust, 2002)

The Sandwell Academy is scheduled to open in 2006 and is key to the Borough's wholesale regeneration plans – it features as a major plank within the proposed West Bromwich Cultural and Learning Quarter. It is crucial to one of the council's key priorities 'of boosting educational performance and supporting other schools in climbing the nationwide exam league tables' (Sandwell MBC website). The Academy also has a wider brief to make its facilities available to local communities beyond the school day. The Academy is sponsored by a consortium that is led by Sir Kevin Satchwell, Head of the Thomas Telford School in Shropshire (a CTC), and includes the Mercers Company, HSBC Bank, Tarmac plc and West Bromwich Albion FC. Located on the site of the former Thomas Telford school in Halfords Lane on the West Bromwich/Smethwick border, the Academy will cater for over 1,200 pupils. The Council sold the land to the sponsors for £1. The funding contribution from Thomas Telford Online derives from the surplus earned from the Telford Online ICT course. The school is sponsoring two Academies, one in Sandwell and the other in Walsall (an outsourced LEA run by Serco), as well as 63 specialist schools. Not only have these schools been helped with financial support, but they are also receiving advice and support on how to raise their academic standards. Sir Kevin Satchwell is one of New Labour's entrepreneurial, standard-raising, education heroes, and is acting as project manager for the Sandwell scheme. The Academy is in an area of the Borough designated for business activity and is also part of an existing PFI contract. Future plans for the school site include the building of a business centre and swimming pool. It will specialise in sport and business studies and will adopt the Thomas Telford curriculum arrangements whereby teaching takes place in three-hour sessions with an after-school session for learning and cultural, sporting, musical and community activities. The post of headteacher was advertised at a salary of £100,000.

West Bromwich businessman Eric Payne (612th in the 2003 *Sunday Times* Rich List with £65 million) is to sponsor a second Academy, based on Christian principles.

> Jubilant schools and education chiefs in Sandwell are welcoming a Ministerial decision to give the go ahead to further development of plans for a state-of-the-art Design and Enterprise Academy to be built on the Dartmouth High School site in Great Barr. The Minister's decision follows proposals from industrial sponsor, Eric Payne OBE and his wife, Grace, who were both educated in West Bromwich before moving to North Wales when the family business relocated. The Academy, which will have a showcase centre for young designers, will develop a high profile in the creative arts. Sponsor Mr Payne said: "Families deserve the best possible schools for their children and we have a lot of hard work to do to ensure that the students get the best deal possible and achieve high standards. Over the coming months I look forward to the opportunity for dialogue with parents, staff and the community as we forge ahead with building a 'world beater' Academy. The Academy will be a major player in the regeneration of Sandwell and we expect to take our place alongside other local partners in building a positive future for the borough." The Academy also has the backing of the University of Wolverhampton, which has agreed to become its lead education partner and work with the sponsors. Professor Sir Geoff Hampton – Dean of the School of Education and Director of the Midlands Leadership Centre at the university – said: "The University operates on a worldwide basis. We are working with schools in China and Malaysia to develop tomorrow's generation of 'smart' schools."
>
> (http://www.laws.sandwell.gov.uk/ccm/sandwell/news/)

Sandwell's third proposed health and citizenship Academy on the site of Willingsworth High School has been cleared to move to the feasibility stage and is planned to open in the autumn of 2008. This Academy is to be sponsored by the RSA. It is a good example of the ways education is joined up with regeneration and competition strategies involving diverse agencies and partners.

> The Academy already has strong local support from the Council, the Primary Care Trust and the University of Wolverhampton – the lead education partner. The proposed £20 million state-of-the-art Academy will have many innovative features, such as a local health 'one stop shop', a fire safety centre and community access facilities. The Academy will cater for 900 students aged 11–16 and will have a sixth form of 200. It will also provide skills training and development for local people, and will have the potential to offer specialist vocational programmes for health and care professionals. Academy proposals are also being

considered for converting George Salter High, West Bromwich, and Shireland Language College, Smethwick.

(http://www.laws.sandwell.gov.uk/ccm/content/
councilgeneral/pressreleases/pressreleasesmar2006/
new-step-forward-for-academy.en)

Sandwell also received funding for two Education Action Zones (Wednesbury and Blackheath and Rowley). It has an Education Business Partnership, 'the principal agency for brokering education business links across Sandwell' (pdpdirect.co.uk) and is part of Black Country Education Business Links (info@blackcountryebl.co.uk). Other things we might note here are that: both Sandwell and Darwen (see page 153) are among nine Pathfinder areas for a £1.2 billion housing demolition programme;[7] Sandwell with Birmingham made a £62 million bid for market renewal funding; Sandwell 'is now working with CABE and English Partnerships on a housing gap funding mechanism' (*Market Renewal: Birmingham Sandwell Pathfinder*, Audit Commission Scrutiny Report, June 2004); and in 2004 Sandwell agreed a £300,000 contract with Capita to review the authority's central support services – 'Unison believes Capita will simply recommend more services being outsourced to the private sector' (report in *Birmingham Evening Mail*, 18 June 2004).

Blackburn with Darwen

Blackburn with Darwen is referred to by the *Guardian* as a 'progressive council' – in 2004 it was overall winner of the *Guardian* public service award (supported by Hays Public Services) for its 'Charter for Belonging', children's centres and local Strategic Partnership, and in 2002 it was 'council of the year'. It was ranked 'excellent' by the Audit Commission for three years in a row and is involved in pioneering local Public Service Boards. Based upon the reforms in the Green Paper *Every Child Matters*, the Council was among the first wave of 35 'Pathfinder' local authorities to set up children's trusts. It is also a member of the local government 'Innovations Forum' (May 2003). The Forum, which is made up of council leaders and chief executives of the 22 local authorities graded 'excellent' in the CPA plus ministers and civil servants, began with a focus on four themes, one of which was 'school improvement'. Again using the language of place marketing and inter-urban competition, 'Blackburn and Darwen is known throughout the UK as an area that fosters enterprise and job creation' (B&DBC website) and the council 'are working in partnership with its citizens, businesses, and voluntary and statutory agencies to build a sustainable environment in which businesses want to trade and invest'.

In 2002, following a 'scoping' exercise conducted by Capita, the Council signed a £190 million 15-year Strategic Partnership agreement with Capita, the longest such agreement so far and worth £15 million a year to the company, and 450 employees were transferred. As part of the deal, the Capita group has opened one of seven regional 'business centres of excellence' in Blackburn (which deals with TV licence fees, CRB work and Housing Benefit applications, including those from some London boroughs). A target of 500 new jobs was agreed, with white-collar jobs to replace declining manufacturing work; by 2003, 700 had already been created. As part of the £500 million housing market renewal Pathfinder programme (ODPM, February 2004), the Blackburn with Darwen Council has proposed the demolition of 151 houses next to the town centre. The demolitions will make way for an Academy school (see below). 'The valuations of houses in the Red Earth Triangle area were carried out by . . . Capita' (*Corporate Watch Newsletter*, 23, April/May 2005, p. 6).

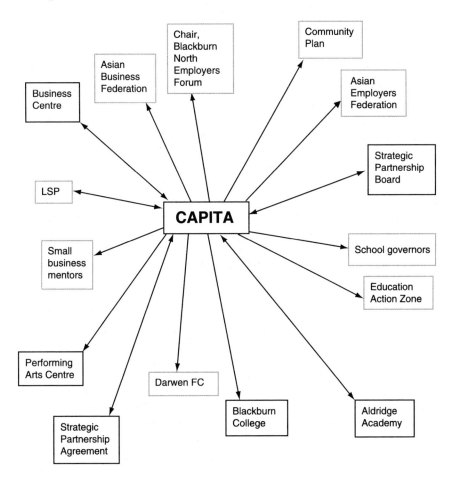

Here Capita is a linkage device and policy participant integrated into the sub-governance networks of business, education and local economic planning. It has representatives on and/or supports a variety of local groups and agencies.

Figure 6.1 Capita in Blackburn.

Four of the nine Blackburn with Darwen secondary schools are specialist schools (2006) and Rod Aldridge, Chief Executive of Capita, is sponsoring a £27 million Academy in a personal capacity, through his charitable trust, but the Head of the DfES Academies division noted that "there were difficulties in his sponsoring an academy in the area because of his relationship with the council" (*TES*, 18 March 2005). Tony Cann, founder and Chairman of Promethean, the whiteboard company (see Chapter 5), also proposed to sponsor a maths and science Academy in Blackburn where the TDS group (of which Promethean is a part) is based. "Education is the key to the future for individuals and the country, and unless we improve the level of education we will have a second class nation" (Tony Cann, quoted in *Lancashire Evening Telegraph*, 25 November 2004). Blackburn with Darwen was granted EAZ funding in the first round of awards.

Middlesbrough

Middlesbrough is in the north-east of England and has a high-profile, Independent elected Mayor, Ray Mallon. According to the Council website, Middlesbrough is 'moving forward' and the Council 'is Open for Business'. Again, in an effort to assert a unique identity and stress comparative advantages, the Council says: 'Our role is to make the area as business friendly as possible' and 'to help local people to meet the needs of local employers, supplying a workforce that meets changing business needs . . . We are specifically tasked with revitalising the town economy, helping to create wealth for local businesses.' As part of this, Middlesbrough offers 'superb training and education. The University of Teesside . . . is developing a leading-edge reputation in digital technologies. Further education colleges share a local commitment to developing training and enterprise.' There is an 'Enterprise Academy', a project which 'helps 11–19 year olds across the Tees Valley to learn about the world of business and self employment'.

In 2001 Middlesbrough BC entered into a ten-year, £260 million PPP with HBS to provide front-line and back office services via a new 'one-stop' customer service centre. One thousand staff were transferred to HBS and up to 500 new jobs were anticipated. The Centre for Public Services (2003) describes Middlesbrough as 'Contract Capital of the World'. In 2005 the Audit Commission announced that Middlesbrough Council had been rated as an 'excellent' local authority under the CPA framework (http://www.middlesbrough.gov.uk/ccm/content/news/middlesbrough-council-press-releases/comprehensive-performance-assessment-gives-excellent-result.en).

Middlesbrough LEA 'embraced the Government's City academies initiative' ('Provision of Secondary Education in South Middlesbrough', LEA document) and is home to three Academies, one of which, the Macmillan (sponsored by the Macmillan Trust), a Beacon and Leading Edge school, is transferring from an established City Technology College status. The first new Academy, opened in 2002, has been referred to above, the Unity

Academy (see page 70), and is sponsored by construction and management firm Amey plc, which is very active in the PFI market (see page 49).

The Chief Executive of Amey said this was Amey's "opportunity to contribute to innovation and leadership in learning – and a strong commitment to supporting public services in Middlesbrough and the North East" (NUT website). The Academy, either the building or online, was planned to open 24/7, 365 days a year, and has community facilities including a learning resource centre with an Internet café. The curriculum is work-focused, with strong links to business. The avant-garde building was designed by Hickton Madeley & Partners and built by M J Gleeson (a PFI specialist) and includes internal balconies 'modelled on a Tuscan mountain village'. It has been criticised. Ofsted commented that 'while impressive at first sight . . . some students do not feel safe or secure. The layout of corridors is confusing' (quoted in *Guardian*, 20 March 2006) (and see 'Sunderland Building Schools for the Future: stakeholders visits to schools', Sunderland City Council, 2005). Fujitsu is providing a managed ITC service for the school under a 15-year contract and is responsible for 'identifying needs, providing technical support, managing refreshing and developing innovation'. An account of the school and its relationships with Fujitsu, on the Fujitsu website (www.fujitsu.com/uk/casestudies/fs_unity.htm – see Box 6.2), captures many of the essential

---

Box 6.2 Unity Academy

The Academy identified IT as one of the fundamental tools for change. "IT helps to develop clarity of thinking and the ability to learn both by oneself and in collaboration with others" said Derek Griffiths, Strategic Leader. To mark this change, Unity Academy opened with 18 interactive whiteboards to demonstrate how technology can support learning . . . An icon for the area, the whole of the structure is designed around flexible learning. It is full of audio-visual facilities, including 10 plasma screens. It has a state-of-the-art lecture theatre with surround sound and a digital recording studio. As Derek Griffiths explained: "We are not simply relocating. Our aim is to achieve a mind shift in a deprived community with low expectations and little value for traditional education. We want to engage with the community in order to change ways of thinking. Our long term vision is to create independent young people who can make judgments about their future." The Trust had a clear vision for learning.

Every room has an interactive whiteboard and is a complete digital environment. There are nearly 2000 data points. Each floor has break-out spaces that are technologically rich. Learning rooms are available for collaborative learning sessions. Mobile laptop trolleys are available to each learning area to provide IT access to any learning situation. The school has a mix of desktops, laptops and tablets: 600 devices for 1200 students. There is lots of wireless technology; a key feature of flexible connectivity and access.

"Moving from a traditional school to a highly rich technological environment is a challenge for members of staff and students" reported Derek Griffiths. "It's about flexibility and learning." Students will have 24/7 access to their online learning spaces and so will be able to review lesson materials at their own pace, using the learning method that best suits them. Teachers will be able to utilize various teaching styles. The school plans to introduce peer mentoring and encourage older students to set up projects to help primary school students. "We are trying to establish new models for learning and the delivery of education. We can provide software for mind mapping and online learning. We also intend to develop our own online learning materials." Working in partnership with Cisco and HP-Compaq, Fujitsu is supplying consultancy advice, design, configuration, installation and network services, and user support.

It is part of Unity City Academy's remit to explore commercial possibilities. To sustain its vision in the long term and continue to innovate, it needs to generate revenue streams. The partnership aims to develop a go-to-market model that demonstrates its vision about learning environments. Both parties are thinking of new ways in which to utilize the managed service, one option is to sell support to other schools.

(From the Fujitsu website)

features of the Academy strategy and various ways in which educationally and substantively schools are enveloped within narratives of competition, business and enterprise which reorient the rhythms and texture of school life. The linking of learning to new technology and to preparation for work is also very evident here. New forms of innovative pedagogy are envisioned using new technologies and new architecture to transform 'learning environments' but also as 'products' which can be sold in collaboration with the ITC partner in the education marketplace. Education is represented here in a new kind of language but may not be experienced as new. Unity is also, as noted above, a 'failure' of sorts. It failed its Ofsted inspection in 2005 (http://www.ofsted.gov.uk/reports/manreports/2661.pdf) and identified a £500,000 year-on-year budget deficit (http://education.guardian.co.uk/ofsted/story/0,,1485081,00.html). Experimentation begets some failures but they are relatively unimportant politically within a more general strategy of transformation.

The third Academy, the King's Academy, has a business and enterprise specialism and is sponsored by the Vardy Foundation, the personal charitable foundation of Sir Peter Vardy, owner of the Reg Vardy car dealership and a devout Christian (http://www.director-magazine.co.uk/December05/vardy.html; http://wiki.cotch.net/index.php/Emmanuel_Schools_Foundation;

http://www.angelfire.com/nb/lt/docs/called43.htm). Vardy has offered to sponsor six Academies in the North-East and so far three are open or planned. These Academies have probably attracted more public and press attention than any others but for their religious values rather than their innovative approaches to teaching and learning.

Middlesbrough was also awarded EAZ funding in the first round, and 22 Teesside schools have specialist school status.

Discussion

Education within these 'entrepreneurial localities' and 'economic spaces' can be thought about in the same terms that Jessop uses to characterise the economy: 'an imaginatively narrated system that is accorded specific boundaries, conditions of existence, typical economic agents, tendencies and counter-tendencies, and a distinctive overall dynamic' (Jessop 2002: 7). Imaginative narration is very evident (see Box 6.2). Within the processes of modernisation and transformation the boundaries and spatial horizons and flows of influence and engagement around education are being stretched and reconfigured in a whole variety of ways – the time and space of education and the school are changed, through extended days, distance and 'virtual' learning, technology transfer, local and national fora, networks, partnerships and federations. This enables a fostering of 'collective intelligence' to service the national competitive interest but also involves competing for advantage with other localities and other institutions. Learning now has no limits in time and space; we are all life-long learners, but new sorts of learning outcomes, particularly those related to business and enterprise and to new technologies, are 'asymmetrically privileged' within the reform process and local hegemonies. There is an emphasis on the 'digital economy' and information and communication technologies and forms of 'immaterial labour' (Hardt and Negri 2000). Creativity, enterprise and entrepreneurism are given priority as new educational specialisms and technological innovations are foregrounded (see also Chapter 7). As belaboured above, the designation of public and private is also shifted on a number of dimensions and tasks are re-allocated. The private is 'in' the schools and in school governance. Education is 'in' business and in the community and joined up with other services as part of strategies of local regeneration linked closely with local business needs and local competitiveness, new local 'social fixes' (Jessop 2004: 6). The 'economic sphere' is redefined to incorporate education in a variety of ways. This is achieved through a discourse of devolution, decentralisation and autonomy – new localism. The conditions of existence of education are also re-set in terms of the new disciplines and demands of competitiveness, innovation and the knowledge economy, together with an inclusive conception of educability and learning – 'autonomy is being exercised in the context of the hegemony of the knowledge-based accumulation strategy' (Jessop 2002: 167) and this is both coercive and empowering. The new economic agents of education range from consumer parents, self-organising learners acquiring the flexible skills required in the changing or imagined local economy, entrepreneurial teachers and managers selling their curricular innovations to others, and private providers eking out profits from running or providing support services for state schools or providing educational services for young people. Local heroes of enterprise (see also Chapters 5 and 7) are making philanthropic contributions, 'giving back' to 'their' locality, but they also stand for and speak for the discourse of entrepreneurism – they are new Victorians! New techniques of governing are inscribed in these visions of education and its future (Dean 1999). These entrepreneurial spaces are material settings in which different multi-scalar influences come together in tangled hierarchies and for diverse ends and purposes. New actors, social patterns, relationships and forms of organisation and communication are being established. New voices are heard and others marginalised. The existing tendencies within the system, as portrayed within policy texts, are to under-achievement, failure and low standards, and the counter-tendencies are excellence, improvement and rising standards. The distinctive overall dynamic is transformation, a change of educational form and an eager responsiveness to the demands of competitiveness. Change – continuous innovation – is the new normal, and *adaptability, flexibility* and *activation* are strategic policy concepts. A set of Schumpeterian political, economic and social narratives coalesce here which give meaning to a set of 'past failures and future possibilities' (Jessop 2002: 92) and constitute 'new economic imaginaries' (Jessop 2004: 4) and new modes of regulation within these distressed localities. The telos of education (Dean 1999) becomes that of an uncertain social and economic future. These new forms of governing and the local economies of innovation become means of reaching or responding to this future and the threat of economic uncompetitiveness. This is a form of governing in the name of uncertainty and of competition.

7 Policy controversies

Failures, ethics and experiments

> The best competition policy is not to restrict monopoly but to promote innovation.
>
> (Leadbeater 2000)

In this chapter, as a complement to the focus in Chapters 4 and 5 on education businesses, attention is directed to the involvement of business 'outsiders' in education services of various kinds – Jarvis and WS Atkins in particular and Academies sponsors in general. Companies like Jarvis and Atkins come from the 'hard' end of the ESI and through expansion and horizontal integration shifted from construction and engineering into managed services and thence have sought or been encouraged to enter the 'soft' services end of the market. Other companies like VTES have made this move more successfully perhaps because their substantive business and expansion trajectory has a cognate relation to the educational services work they have taken on. In the final section of the chapter ('Academies', page 170) other educational 'outsiders' who are now agents of policy (see Chapter 5) through the Academies programme in particular will be discussed. As a vehicle for the discussion I focus on three specific privatisation policies of very different kinds which have given rise to conflicts and controversies over the involvement of the private sector in the delivery of public education services. They are: PFIs, the running and management of LEAs through contracts with private providers, and the Academies programme.

In relation to PFIs, the main issues are profit and responsibility and market failure. Jarvis plc provides a case study. In relation to LEA contracts, profit and responsibility are issues again, and Atkins's involvement with Southwark LEA is the main case in point. More generally these examples underline the importance of recognising the diversity among private sector education service suppliers, the strategic behaviour of the companies involved and the need to attend to the broader financial context and longer-term business prospects which relate to specific privatisations. The ad hoc and experimental nature of these privatisation policies is again evident.

The discussion of the Academies programme brings together many of the main themes and issues identified in the rest of the book. More specifically it will be used to enable a further examination of experimentation and innovation as key aspects of and goals of education reform and as the bases of new language and practices – a systematicity – in terms of which the public sector is being reformed. The Academies programme is a *condensate* of state competition policy with all its tensions and contradictions represented in microcosm. Central to the programme is a concern with 'mobilizing social as well as economic sources of flexibility and entrepreneurism' (Jessop 2001: 295–6). The Academies programme is made up of a complex of policy impulses and influences and exemplifies some of the new kinds of 'private' participation within policy addressed in Chapter 5. This participation is illustrated by examples of some 'heroes of enterprise'.

PFIs

'According to the Treasury, PFI transactions with a total capital value of £35.5bn have been signed since April 2003' (Unison 2004). PFI schemes, as outlined in Chapter 3, have produced a much needed injection of cash into the public sector capital building programme and have the dual attraction to government of delivering new infrastructure apparently risk-free and 'off the books' of government debt. That in itself raises interesting questions about the ethics of state accounting during a period when the private sector, especially in the US, but also to a lesser extent in the UK, has been beset with accounting scandals.

However, the various interested parties in the field of government accounting seem to have agreed to disagree about the efficacy and integrity of the government's position on PFIs. The Treasury on the whole seems to take a much rosier view of PFIs than the NAO (http://www.nao.org.uk), local authorities, unions, ACCA, ASB (Sir David Tweedie), PAC or the House of Commons Select Committee on Education and Skills, but the technical debates involved here obscure some more basic political issues. Ironically in 2000 Arthur Andersen (which had been banned from public sector work by the Conservatives for their complicity in the DeLorean scandal but reinstated by Labour in 1997 – see Cohen 2004) was commissioned to make a report on the PFI programme and was enthusiastic about its advantages and claimed to have found an average 17 per cent saving for the taxpayer. In 2001 Mott MacDonald, which has a variety of involvements in PFI works, was commissioned by the Treasury to write a report comparing costs and over-runs between PFI and public works projects (*Review of Large Public Procurement in the UK*, June 2002), which found PFIs to be superior (see Unison 2005 for a critique of the study). The whole set of issues around cost, risk transfer, financial transparency and profit-taking from PFIs is beset by confusion. Unison argues that 'systematic examination of the rationale for and costs of PFI policy are long overdue' (2004: 37) and the Public Accounts Committee has twice noted its concern over the paucity of data on the relationship between risk and the cost of private finance. The IPPR (2000: 43) make the point that 'A large number of PFI projects have been agreed, yet how these decisions were made and what effects they have on services offered are unclear.'

Two other aspects of PFI financing need noting here. These have been written about extensively by others and they are also the reason why the *Investors Chronicle* described PFI shareholdings as 'hidden gems'. First, refinancing of completed projects often generates substantial windfall profits (see Box 7.1).

Box 7.1 PFI profits

A select group of City banks and building firms have reaped more than £170 million in windfall profits from building four flagship hospitals under the government's controversial Public Finance Initiative policy . . .

An *Observer* investigation has discovered that while new hospitals struggle with mounting debts and building faults, private contractors reap huge financial rewards using sophisticated methods to 'refinance' the original PFI deals.

A little-known London investment firm run by Labour-supporting South African businessman David Metter has made £50m in just over two years from renegotiating the terms of loans on three hospitals it helped to build for the NHS.

Metter's firm, Innisfree Group, recently clinched a deal to refinance the Princess Royal University Hospital in Bromley, south London, which was built in March 2003. Less than 12 months after the hospital opened its doors, Metter's firm, together with building group Taylor Woodrow, renegotiated the funding of the project and pocketed £43m in clear profit between them . . .

It was intended that hospitals would receive at least 30 per cent of the 'refinancing' spoils, but in reality this can be as little as 10 per cent. Last month, the *Observer* revealed how Innisfree, Laing and Serco split a £100m profit from renegotiating the deal on Labour's flagship Norfolk and Norwich University Hospital. While the companies demanded their profits in a lump sum, the hospital trust was awarded a reduction in its rental costs of £3.5m a year over the next 32 years.

(Antony Barnett, *Observer*, 4 July 2004)

The House of Commons Committee of Public Accounts Report, on which this article draws, *The Refinancing of the Norfolk and Norwich PFI Hospital, Thirty-fifth Report of Session 2005–06*, notes, among other criticisms, that:

> Octagon's investors' internal rate of return more than trebled fol-
> lowing the refinancing. The total cash which investors expect to
> receive from the project reduced from £464 million to £335 million
> following the refinancing, but they have now got a large part of it
> much earlier. As a result, their internal rate of return, reflecting the
> value of getting benefits sooner rather than later, soared from 19%
> when the contract was let to 60% . . . This refinancing produced a
> balance of risks and rewards between the public and private sectors
> which, even for an early PFI deal, is unacceptable.
>
> (http://www.pppforum.com/
> PAC%20N&N%20MAY%202006.htm)

Second, as noted in Chapter 3, there is now a very active and lucrative market
in the 'selling on' of PFI contracts.

> Multi-million pound shareholdings in education, health and transport
> projects now change hands in secretive deals between contractors and
> financiers, releasing some immense cash windfalls for businesses – at the
> taxpayer's expense.
>
> (BBC *File on 4*, July 2004)

> . . . they might be concerned that by selling their investments, it might be
> interpreted that they were about to exit the market and create the wrong
> impression in government for winning future work, so for that reason
> they may well decide, you know, not to publicise such a sale.
>
> (Paul Cleal, PWC, BBC *File on 4*, July 2004)

The government is reluctant to impose windfall taxes or profit-sharing
agreements on PFI contracts; rather a voluntary code has been agreed. This
reluctance has to be seen in relation to the government's role (again) as a
market-maker. It does not want to discourage potential PFI contractors.

> In order to get the rapid growth it wants in PFI, the government
> openly dangled before the city the prospect of huge sums of public
> money guaranteed in long term contracts.
>
> (BBC *File on 4*, 4 July 2004)

> . . . the government has always been very clear with PFI that they would
> never seek to share the gains in disposals of equity in PFI projects.
>
> (David Metter, Chair of the PPPF, BBC *File on 4*, July 2004)

The position here is that the lure of profit works to ensure cost-efficient,
low-risk, timely project delivery. As quoted in Chapter 1, Gordon Brown
sees the private sector generally as better at financial management and

service delivery than the public sector. Let us look at that claim by focusing on Jarvis plc – 'We want to be a leading provider of outsourced services across a range of markets, currently including the rail industry, roads, education and other local government sectors' (Annual Report 2004). Jarvis like other major PFI players, Amey and Mowlem for example, has found the 'business opportunity' of PFIs very attractive but has faced financial difficulties arising from losses on contracts (see http://news.scotsman.com/topics.cfm?tid=571&id=1194522004 and http://education.guardian.co.uk/schools/story/0,,945233,00.html) (see also Box 7.2 – a selection of Jarvis's market activities).

Box 7.2 Jarvis and PFIs

2000: PWC resign as Jarvis's auditors after a clash over accounting policy (http://www.lovells.com/Lovells/MediaCentre/Articles/archive/2005/Caution+required.htm).

5 May 2002: Nottingham Trent University chose Jarvis to manage and operate eight halls of residence for 33 years; the contract is valued at £295 million; 104 employees will TUPE from the university to Jarvis.

6 June 2002: Jarvis shares fall 10 per cent to six-month low following Potters Bar derailment (www.citywire.co.uk/News/Archive-ByMonth.aspx?day=13&month=5&year=2002).

10 November 2002: David Milliband, School Standards Minister, orders an urgent report into the company's activities in Kirklees, Yorkshire, after complaints from heads about delays in refurbishments (www.bbc.co.uk/radio4/news/fileon4/index_20021119.shtml).

10 January 2003: Jarvis reached financial close of £97 million contract for England's first PFI ambulatory care centre.

28 April 2003: Jarvis appointed preferred bidder for room project at Nottingham University.

24 March 2003: Jarvis secures financial close on £54 million special schools project in Salford.

22 April 2003: Jarvis to provide a further 400 rooms at University of Reading. 'Headteacher [Kirklees] tells of Jarvis rebuilding woe and believes things can only get worse . . . another head, Christine Spencer of Salendine Nook high school said "This is a very good school, but this year the results have dropped by 2% – I think because of the amount of disruption" ' (*Guardian*, 29 May 2003).

12 June 2003: Jarvis to provide new learning village in South London.

5 September 2003: New school year, new school look – Richmond, Bridlington, Kirklees, Liverpool, Haringey.

20 October 2003: Jarvis secures the UK's largest-ever student accommodation project.

28 November 2003: Jarvis will secure major special schools PPP project.

3 December 2003: Jarvis wins £263 million schools PFI project.

12 December 2003: Jarvis accused by MP Frank Field of 'not delivering' on its Wirral school PFI which has been delayed by disputes over payments between Jarvis and its sub-contractors. Schools were prevented from re-opening for autumn term (bbc.co.uk, 11 November 2003).

25 April 2004: Jarvis and the Miller-led Emblem schools group are competing for Fife council's £53 million PFI deal. Jarvis issues third profit warning of the year (findarticles.com/p/articles/mi_kmafp/is_200407/ai_n6845264).

28 May 2004: Jarvis announces it has been awarded a PFI contract for two schools in Manchester and two in Rhondda and a deal to build 1,500 student rooms for UEL. These contracts have a whole life value of £516 million.

28 June 2004: Jarvis rising debts levels threaten to breach agreements with its two main lenders, Barclays and the Royal Bank of Scotland (news.bbc.co.uk/1/hi/business/3938661.stm). Goldman Sachs acquires 4 per cent of Jarvis (their holding had risen to 23 per cent by November 2005) (http://investing.reuters.co.uk/stocks/KeyDevelopments.aspx?ticker=JRVS.L). Jarvis is to pay University of Lancaster students £304 each in compensation for delays in hall of residence buildings.

11 July 2004: Treasury advised local authorities with Jarvis contracts to draw up contingency plans.

12 July 2004: 'Schools could be left with refurbishment and building schemes in tatters because of the financial crisis facing PFI contractor Jarvis' (*Times*).

30 July 2004: 'Jarvis will sell off PFI units to stay afloat. It has already stated it intends to sell its stake in Tubelines, the part-privatisation consortium for the London underground' (*Guardian*).

29 August 2004: Jarvis's bankers made £25 million available to company until March 2005. K Capital Partners buy more shares in Jarvis (12.7 per cent in May @ 70p – stake raised to 22.3 per cent @ 23p) (politics.guardian.co.uk/elections2004/story/0,,1222623,00.html). K Capital disposed of its Jarvis shares in November 2004 (http://www.dataexplorers.co.uk/dxl/news.aspx?id=97&service=).

29 August 2004: 'Shares in Jarvis continue to fall by first 50% and then 36% in four days. Jarvis is trying to cover its £230m debt by selling contracts. Wirral council where Jarvis has £55m schools PFI is considering options to ensure the work is finished. Cumbria county council have delayed its decision to out-source ICT services to Agilsys (40 per cent owned by Jarvis)' (www.unison.org.uk/bargaining/doc_view.asp?did=1473&pid=73).

21 October 2004: Jarvis pays bonuses totally £807,000 to directors which had been withheld after fatal Potters Bar rail crash (scotlandon-sunday.scotsman.com/index.cfm?id=735112002). Accommodation services division is put up for sale and sells its University Partnership Programme bidding and administration team to Alma Mater, a joint venture between 3i and Barclays Private Equity Partnership (www. unison.org.uk/bargaining/doc_view.asp?did=1589&pid=752).

29 October 2004: Jarvis loses £200 million contract to maintain roads in Cheshire and is dropped as preferred bidder for Fife schools PFI. Jarvis sells its stake in Ultramast for £10 million (www.ukbusi-nesspark.co.uk/jarvisaa.htm).

30 October 2004: Jarvis loses school PFI Deal: the 'Engineering group lost out on a contract to build schools for a local authority for the second time in 2 months' (*Guardian*).

28 November 2004: Jarvis agrees to sell its PFI activities to French construction group Vinci, including its contract to design and build two schools in Manchester (http://news.scotsman.com/topics.cfm?tid =571&id=1194522004). Norfolk CC is to re-advertise its PFI contract for 37 schools after rejecting the plan put forward by Jarvis and Vinci. The construction will be delayed for two years.

6 December 2004: Twickenham MP asks questions about Jarvis's obligations in the House of Commons (http://www.publications. parliament.uk/pa/cm200405/cmhansrd/vo041206/debtext/41206–34.htm).

12 December 2004: Jarvis shares fall 60 per cent after further warning of losses. Jarvis now agrees to sell its PFI bidding operations to German company Hochtief Projektenwicklung for £1.2 million (www.projectfinancemagazine.com/default.asp?page=7&PubID=4&ISS =14410 &SID=496130).

12 January 2005: Jarvis share price doubles to 37p. A further cut of 300 staff is announced; the workforce has been reduced from 6,000 to 2,700 in one year (www.unison.org.uk/bargaining/doc_view. asp?did=1727). Jarvis will continue to work on 14 PFI construction projects. Jarvis sells its Tubelines stake to Amey for £146.8 million (www.tubelines.com/news/releases/200602/20050131.aspx). Richmond Council takes legal advice over delays to a school which is part of an £80 million contract with Jarvis, and essential works in Haringey schools are stopped (www.unison.org.uk/bargaining/doc_view.asp? did=1727&pid=785).

17 January 2005: 'Huddersfield's MP has attacked former Kirklees school company Jarvis' (*Huddersfield Daily Examiner*).

13 February 2005: Jarvis is valued at £39.2 million, down from £827 million in 2002. Star capital is to buy the equity share on Jarvis's PFI contract with Kirklees Council, worth about £1.6 million.

14 March 2005: Alan Lovell, Jarvis Chief Executive, is to receive a

£450,000 bonus for completing Jarvis's rescue (business.timesonline
.co.uk/article/0,,9073–1750026,00.html). (In 2006 he left Jarvis to join
private equity firm Terra Firma.)

25 April 2005: Jarvis considers a name change for its rail engineering
business (www.skyscrapernews.com/news.php?ref=49).

29 April 2005: 'High school praised but building is inadequate:
inspectors said the buildings were inadequate to meet the needs of
pupils despite the fact they have been refurbished over the past two years
under a private public partnership with Jarvis. In March 2003 Jarvis
sold its 35% share in KSSL, set up to manage the project to investment
company Secondary Market Infrastructure Fund' (*Huddersfield Daily
Examiner*).

12 May 2005: 'Date is set for work at new Kirklees schools – building
will start next month on a new school which has been dogged by cash
problems . . . after months of wrangling, the school – which was scheduled to be finished in September this year will be built by Waites Construction' (*Huddersfield Daily Examiner*).

24 May 2005: 'Dismay at school firm's shake up . . . Jarvis which
employs caretaking staff at 19 Kirklees schools . . . share price stood
at just 7 pence yesterday . . . and has debts estimated at £280m'
(*Huddersfield Daily Examiner*).

(Unless otherwise indicated, the material here comes from the Jarvis
company website and company press releases.)

The full public sector costs, direct and indirect, caused by Jarvis's problems
will never be known and are simply not taken into account in the overall
costing of PFI schemes. The social and educational impact of the delays and
difficulties caused is incalculable. Nonetheless, these are costs that the public
sector has to bear (e.g. see 'Education, disruption, and multiplication', http://
education.guardian.co.uk/schools/story/0,,945581,00.html, and *Huddersfield
Daily Examiner*).[1] On the other hand, Jarvis's difficulties produced new profit
opportunities for other private companies and investment groups (SMIF,
Amey, Vinci, etc.).

One of the other issues here is that PFI clients, local authorities and health
trusts are unlike other sorts of clients in that their powers in relation to
service providers seem very limited – in part because in some cases they are
reluctant participants in PFI arrangements. Ruane (2002: 210) also notes,
echoing my point about 'insider/outsider' values, the particularity of what
she terms the 'construction industry culture' as well as 'major discrepancies
in the values and goals of respective partners'.

Like other engineering and management services companies such as
Amey, VT and Atkins, Jarvis also attempted to expand its business into

education services and, in 2003, soon after the Potters Bar rail crash (www.guardian.co.uk/pottersbar/0,11994,713526,00.html), was awarded a programme contract by the DfES (again a market-making move to encourage a new supplier into the ESI).

> *Fury as Jarvis wins contract*
> Teachers' leaders reacted angrily to the news that Jarvis, which has no record of running schools, will be paid £1.9 million to help raise standards in 700 of the worst performing secondaries in England and Wales.
>
> Jarvis will operate a support network to help local authorities and disseminate good practice to under-performing schools. This will include selecting examples of good practice, running a website and organising conferences.
>
> It is the first contract of this type won by the company, whose education activity has previously centred on private finance initiative building work.
>
> Jarvis is believed to be interested in the contract to run education services in Southwark following the withdrawal of rival WS Atkins from the south London borough. Two of the key personnel in Jarvis Education Services formerly worked for Atkins – including Steve Davies, ex-director of education services in Southwark.
>
> (Jon Slater, *Guardian*, 2 May 2003)

The Jarvis story also points up another generic issue arising from private sector participation and some of the inherent problems or limitations, from the public sector side, of contracting. In particular, shifts in ownership, the 'selling on' of contracts, can give rise to disputes over responsibility, slippage or evasion, and compliance conflicts (which involve further costs to the public sector, e.g. SMIF and Kirklees). It would seem that for companies like Jarvis, despite their flirtation with education services business, the public sector is just another profit opportunity and, when financial necessity dictates, they sell off or disinvest and move on, leaving others to think about and deal with the social consequences.

LEA contracts

In 2001 another engineering and facilities services company, Atkins, moved to enter the education services business by bidding to run Southwark LEA services. The Atkins 2003 Annual Report noted that:

> Education is led by a new Managing Director and key senior staff appointed in March 2002 who are harnessing the Group's IT, design, facilities management and professional services capabilities to provide integrated education support services. The Government's White Paper on Education Reform will be a catalyst for growth within the sector.

The company had established itself in the PFI market and had developed a school design team, and education services seemed like a sensible next move for their Government Services division. The Annual Report goes on:

> Our £100m, five-year education outsourcing contract with the London Borough of Southwark is the largest issued to date, covering more than 100 schools and 35,000 children. According to Ofsted, it has delivered significant improvements during its first year . . . Education has great potential – and the Southwark PPP shows we can meet the challenge. Having established our credentials, we are now seeking new contracts and partnerships in which we can sell additional, value-added services.

Atkins's turnover in 2002–3 was £806.3 million but it posted pre-tax losses of £32.8 million, which put the company under pressure to restructure, and a possible takeover was rumoured (http://www.citywire.co.uk/News/NewsArticle.aspx?VersionID=49546&MenuKey=News.Archive). In February 2003 when it was announced that it was talking to potential buyers, company shares fell 7 per cent to 111p. In April, WS Atkins announced it was pulling out of the Southwark contract two years into a five-year term. Their share price rose. Essentially, the company admitted, the contract had been changed in such a way that not enough profit could be made. Council leader Nick Stanton said: "We were paying everything due under the contract and more on top. This year Atkins was told to pay more to schools."

Firm finds a private hell
Raised eyebrows at the 'Education Partnerships' conference last week when WS Atkins, the private contractor running education in Southwark and the event's sponsor, decided to pull out its speaker. David Monger, the company's director of LEA partnerships, had been due to talk on 'Learning from experience'.

   Why the sudden attack of shyness from the normally voluble privatisation people? All became clear on Tuesday when Atkins announced it had learned from experience . . . and was pulling out of Southwark after negotiations with the local council colleagues.
                                                    (Helen Ward, *TES*, 4 April 2003)

One headteacher, who did not want to be named, was quoted in the *TES* saying: "For two years we have been used as a government experiment which has failed. Atkins should have made the jobs of heads and teachers easier but it made them more difficult" (William Stewart, 6 June 2003). 'The government's refusal to cover the costs of the withdrawal left Southwark with a £1.5m shortfall in its education budget' (William Stewart, *TES*, 6 June 2003). 'Despite the Southwark setback, Atkins has insisted that it will continue to expand in PFI ventures' (*TES* archive, 30 January 2004). 'The contract was handed over into the safer hands of CEA; although some Southwark Headteachers were not pleased to be facing a further period of private sector involvement' (Rosie Waterhouse, *TES*, 30 January 2004).

The Unison Companies Update website makes a crucial point here, that is the WS Atkins story illustrates the importance of:

> Fluctuations in the stock market which characterise and influence private companies' performance and viability. This makes their clients, which now include schools and LEAs, vulnerable. Private companies have no statutory responsibility nor public duty to provide education services nor are they democratically accountable to their communities.

The point is that: 'Corporate goals may or may not coincide with public interests at any moment in time' (Hall and Lubina 2004: 274). One of my respondents described the award of the Southwark contract to Atkins as 'bizarre' and suggested that things had changed 'now there's more providers in the market and they [the DfES and the Treasury] want to see organisations that they feel are low risk'. These market failures and failures in market-making are further examples of the fumblings and experimental uses of privatisation as a policy device but also indicate the financial instability of the ESI.

The withdrawal of Atkins and the implosion of Jarvis were failures in a number of senses. They were policy failures, in the sense of failure to 'grow' the education services market. They were also relationship failures in as much as they pointed up, especially in the case of Atkins, the limits to the 'embeddedness' of values within the ESI. In Ruane's (2002: 210) account of health service PFIs, health service managers she interviewed regarded appeals to 'trust' or 'partnership' as part of their relationship with PFI contractors 'with scornful incredulity' (p. 210). As a PFI contractor Atkins appears to have brought its 'construction industry culture' with it into the Southwark contract. There were also market failures as indicated, and they demonstrate the role of 'bottom-line' issues of profitability in private sector decision-making. One respondent commented that 'they were pretty crude and they were certainly a lot more focused on the bottom line than we are'. This is a further example of the way in which the 'education businesses' differentiate themselves from 'outsiders'. Elaine Simpson, reflecting on Serco's difficulties with the Bradford LEA contract, said "the DfES have been concerned that it would end up like Southwark and we would walk away. And Serco have said, 'No, we're not going to walk away. We're going to stay there and make it work.' " The problems which have emerged also indicate technical failures in the operationalisation of LEA outsourcing contracts. Some at least of the controversy and difficulty that have accompanied some of these contracts derives from the inadequacies or peculiarities of the contracts themselves and the processes of mutual learning, adaptation and negotiation between the parties involved at both local and national level. The companies, the local authorities and the DfES and their advisers were all learning as they went along how this new kind of market might work. One of my interviewees talked of "the blind leading the blind" and another reflected that his company "didn't have the foggiest idea when the contracts were written, what they were taking on". A third commented on the "phenomenal transaction costs". CEA in Islington found themselves agreeing to a list of 415 targets and a monthly reporting schedule. This list was eventually reduced to 60. Nonetheless, the penalties levied were given extensive media coverage. One head of service talked about "an appallingly negotiated contract" and, as noted previously, considerable criticism in some cases was directed to the consultants. "They didn't understand education budgets and budgets streams", one respondent explained. Another reported that "the consultants were permanently camped in the Authority [but] people didn't know what they were doing. This was bonkers stuff." This was a process of 'trying out for size' on both sides, state and capital. Clearly, most of the participant companies, Atkins aside, did not expect to make significant money out of these contracts from the outset. The companies had "to take it on the chin", as one respondent put it, talking about losses made. They were testing the water, making friends, demonstrating good will and building trust with central and local government. The consultants made considerable amounts of money.

The third area of controversy, the Academies programme, is rather different. It addresses a different kind of private sector involvement in state education, partly, as discussed in Chapter 5, through philanthropy. However, it is also a policy experiment and it involves a kind of substantive interface between education and business, as discussed in Chapter 6. Also in this section I look at some of the Academies' actors, more businessmen, and this picks up on the importance noted in Chapter 1 and 2 of the role of 'new intellectuals' and agents of education policy.

Academies

> I want teachers able to communicate the virtues of entrepreneurship and wealth creation. And just as business tycoons have become the pop idols of the business world, I want our local business leaders to become role models for today's young.
>
> (Gordon Brown speech, December 2003)

> The model is, quite deliberately, the independent sector: uniforms, strong independent leadership, a distinctive ethos and freedom from bureaucracy.
>
> (M. Baker, *TES*, 30 September 2005)

> In economic and political institutions the corporate rich now wield enormous power, but they have never had to win the moral consent of those over whom they hold this power.
>
> (Wright-Mills 1959: 344)

Why is the Academies programme interesting? It builds on the CTC programme, which was itself informed by the development and experience of Charter schools in the US (PWC 2005) (and there are notable parallels between the Academies policy and its rhetoric and some of the rhetoric of the Edison School Corporation – see Saltman 2005). It is expensive (the HCESSE, 2005, estimates a cost of £5 billion), an example of the strategic allocation of resources, but not very large; there is a target of 400 such schools by 2010, 60 of these in the London boroughs. It is nonetheless significant and relevant in that it stands as a *condensate* of the education policies of the competition state. Academies are an experiment in and a symbol of education policy beyond the welfare state and an example and indicator of shifts taking place in governance and regulatory structures and they enact a set of metaorganisational changes. The programme signals a discursive-strategic shift towards a new kind of regulatory regime. It also constitutes a new set of potential relations between education and the economy within which schools are required to take much more responsibility for fostering 'knowledge cultures' (Peters and Besley 2006). Innovation, inclusion and regeneration are tied together in relation to the requirements of the digital workplace. Academies indicate a re-articulation and re-scaling of the state; they are part of a new localism and a new centralism; they encompass new kinds of autonomy and new forms of control: controlled decontrol. Furthermore, they involve a self-conscious attempt to promote entrepreneurism and competitiveness – as well as a commitment to address social problems and inequalities. They represent and contain all the uncertainties and tensions created by the unstable duality of empowerment and control and the diverse and competing elements of Labour's reform agenda, but also the real but limited possibilities that are available to subtly re-work the 'order of dominance' (Newman 2005: 729) within this agenda, although not so much in the examples I use here. They drastically blur the welfare state demarcations between state and market, public and private, government and business, and (as argued in Chapter 5) they introduce and validate new agents and new voices within policy itself and in processes of governance and play a key role in bringing schools policy 'much closer to the business agenda than it has been at any time in the past' (Farnsworth 2004: 104).

Let me try to be more specific about the significance of Academies within the analytical framework I have adumbrated by itemising the different policy imperatives which are embedded within the programme (these are summarised in Figure 7.1).

* The keyword which encapsulates the Academies programme, and which is a central tenet of the New Labour competition state, is *innovation*. It is envisaged that their 'independent status allows them the flexibility to be innovative and creative in their curriculum, staffing and governance . . . [and work] in different ways to traditional Local Authority (LEA) schools' and 'leaders in innovation' (DfES 2005a); they have 'the freedom

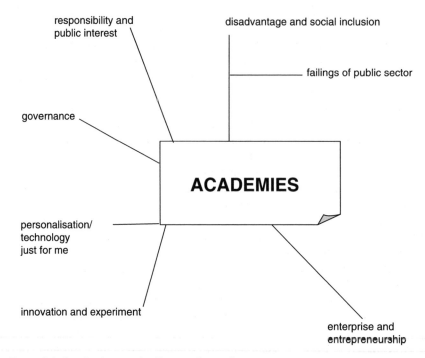

responsibility and
public interest

disadvantage and social inclusion

failings of public sector

governance

ACADEMIES

personalisation/
technology
just for me

innovation and experiment

enterprise and
entrepreneurship

Figure 7.1 Academies as a 'policy condensate'.

to manage and innovate, with minimum interference from the outside' (Thomas Telford school website, 31 May 2005), as Sir Kevin Satchwell described Academies in his AST Annual Lecture, or 'flexibility to succeed' as the AST Prospectus (2005) puts it. An important part of their remit is to think and act 'otherwise' about learning and organisational practice and to escape from the 'limitations' of traditional organisational ecologies. They literally stand for and represent, in their buildings and infrastructure, new, bold and different thinking – more of the dynamic rhetoric of New Labour. The Bexley Business Academy is described by its architects Foster and Partners (website) as 'an icon for the community' and 'hailed as an innovative building that stretches the boundaries of education'. As texts the Academy buildings are enactments of a new 'imaginary' economy. They also embody the enterprise and values of their sponsors. In most cases the Academy buildings are new or major refurbishments. The sponsors can choose the architect, and some leading British architects have been involved. However, the second evaluation report on the Academies programme by PricewaterhouseCoopers (2005) noted that, while the futuristic buildings looked impressive, too much emphasis had been placed on 'creating a bold statement . . . at the expense of some of the more practical requirements of modern teaching and learning'. Innovation is woven into an abstract discursive ensemble which constitutes the programme and its policy context. This incorporates technological advance and skills, the knowledge economy and inter-national economic competitiveness. 'Skills and innovation are critical in the drive to raise productivity, and with it the trend of growth in the economy on which our future prosperity will be based' ('Colleges for excellence and innovation', statement by Secretary of State for Education and Skills on the future of FE in England, p. 6). 'Our secondary strategy is similarly anchored in the achievements of the best schools today and in the requirements of a good secondary education in the knowledge econ-omy and modern society' (DfES 2001: 4). A variety of innovations is being attempted in the Academies (see page 176 on Bexley and page 180 on West London) within and across what Kenway *et al.* (1993: 122) call the 'educa-tion/markets/information technology triad'. Learning and organisational processes are re-articulated in a new hybrid language of staging posts, piping, activity streams, rough cuts, operational imperatives, context-rich learning, technology-enabled learning, stakeholder communications and transitional management. These are rhetorical devices, many of which are imported from business or management-speak, which assert the new and the different and the integration of education into the discourse of the economy or re-word existing practices but they also have semantic force. Many of these schools begin to look and sound like firms. The Unity City Academy Development Team (2003: 28) reports the:

> piloting of incubator activities to improve the use and deployment of ICT [evidenced by the] creation of two learning hubs to simulate and experiment with the new learning technologies and practices that are to be central to the new learning model and new learning environment.[2]

- They are also forms of *partnership*. Academies come into being via 'part-nerships between sponsors and local education partners to enable them and the DfES to assess their individual circumstances and decide if a new Academy is the right solution for their needs' (DfES Standards website). A good deal of this partnership activity is behind the scenes and goes on between the DfES, AST, the Cabinet Office and LEA officers and coun-cillors – another indication of the proliferation of spatial scales of educa-tion policy[3] – but is also part of the day-to-day life of the schools (see Chapter 6 on Unity Academy). New agents and actors are playing a part in the reconstitution of learning and organisation through 'partnerships'. This gives voice to new educationalists. As noted already, partnerships are a key device in the re-making of the architecture of governance in as much as they provide 'linkages, coupling and congruence between actors and spaces' (MacKenzie and Lucio 2005: 500) and are a way of deliver-ing policy outcomes through collaborative networks and diverse allegi-ances and commitments. They are also an opportunity to do business.

In all these senses they are an extension of generic reform models (trust hospitals, fund-holding GPs) and provide exemplars for the further extension of these models, as in the creation of Trust schools: 'self-governing . . . Independent non-fee paying state schools' (DfES 2005b: 8), which will 'control their own assets' (p. 25) and which may be established 'by a wide range of organizations' (p. 27). These are further moves in the break-up of the public sector monopoly of state education, what Pollack (2004: vii) calls the 'dismantling process' and asserts to be 'profoundly anti-democratic and opaque'.

- As another aspect of partnership, Academies are also intended to contribute to local regeneration and are part of an attempt at this level to construct *'joined-up' policies* (see Newman 2001: 161), both to help 'break the cycle of underachievement' and 'acting as a significant focus for learning for pupils, families and other local people and, in time, shar-[ing] their expertise with other schools and the wider community'. They 'serve the local community', 'building partnerships with the local community and businesses', and are 'intended to transform education in areas where the status quo is simply not good enough' (all from AST Prospectus 2005). They are open systems with porous boundaries. Educational problems and educative impulses are 'joined up' to social and economic strategies of regeneration. As noted already, several Academies are located or clustered[4] in proactive 'entrepreneurial localities' and form part of a portfolio of local economic assets and images and a re-focusing of economic strategies 'around the features of specific economic spaces . . . in the face of competitive pressures at home and abroad' (Jessop 2002: 129). They are thoroughly incorporated into 'modes of economic and social calculation that encourage entrepreneurship' (Jessop 2002: 189). More specifically they are to "*challenge the culture of educational under-attainment* and produce improvements in standards" (David Blunkett speech to the Labour Party Annual Conference 2000). The City Academy programme was launched in March 2000 by David Blunkett, then Education Secretary, as 'a radical approach to promote greater diversity and break the cycle of failing schools in inner cities'. (The 'city' has since been dropped, to allow for the creation of Academies outside cities.) 'Academies are now addressing entrenched school failure in our most deprived areas and are starting to transform educational opportunity for thousands of our young people who need it most' (DfES 2005b: 15). Academies are a good example, at least rhetorically, of what Hodgson (1999: 24) calls an 'evotopia', a 'system that can foster learning, enhance human capacities, systematically incorporate growing knowledge, and adapt to changing circumstances', and, as Hodgson also notes, 'the learning economy is necessarily an inclusive economy' (p. 251). Opportunity, meritocracy and inclusion are logical concomitants of policies intended to promote competitiveness. But the Academies also both denote a move beyond the 'failure' of public sector, welfare solutions to educational under-achievement and offer an alternative delivered in the form of the qualities and attributes they seek to instil. They instantiate a novel combination of opportunity and choice, and enterprise and innovation.

- The Academies programme introduces a whole *new set of social and political actors* into education policy – philanthropic entrepreneurs (Garrard, Petchey, Payne, etc.), corporations (e.g. ARK, HSBC), social entrepreneurs (Lampl, Reed), charities (Grieg, etc.) and faith groups (UTL, Oasis and Vardy), a further blurring of the economic and extra-economic. The programme is a vehicle through which the opinions and voices of heroes of enterprise can be heard. Across the programme there is an inter-linking of business, philanthropy, quangos and non-governmental agencies and the recurrence of particular companies and people within new networks of policy. Some of the participants in this new philanthropy constitute a philanthropic elite which is engaged with government, party and state in a numbers of ways.[5] Not all of this is new. What is different is the direct relation of 'giving' to policy and the more apparent involvement of givers in policy networks and a more 'hands on' approach to the use of donations that is evident within the Academies in particular. These networks are a circumvention of established influences on and conduits for new policy. They are also in themselves an experiment in governance and a form of policy ad hocery by the state. 'Enterprise is having energy, creativity and a can-do attitude directed towards achieving purpose' (Academy of Enterprise website).
- The programme gives particular emphasis and prominence to two master narratives of New Labour education policy – *enterprise and responsibility* – which are key tropes of the Third Way. These narratives are represented substantively within the schools themselves and symbolically in their sponsors. In some cases enterprise is to the fore (Garrard, De Haan, Lowe, Reed) and in others responsibility or more broadly 'values' or ethos is prominent (ULT and Oasis, Church of England and RC Church) but in some the two are combined in the image and commitments of the sponsor (Vardy, Edmiston, Payne) or in collaborative sponsorship (the Manchester Academy is co-sponsored by ULT and Manchester Science Park Ltd). Woods, Woods and Gunter (forthcoming) note that, as of autumn 2005, 29 (56 per cent) of the Academies where the specialism is known have or plan a business and enterprise specialism, in 14 cases combined with another specialism. The Academies also demonstrate 'corporate responsibility' and the caring face of capitalism and of 'self-made men' (*sic*) who want to give something back. These hero entrepreneurs embody the values of New Labour: the possibilities of meritocracy, of achieving individual success from modest beginnings, and wealth creation from innovation and knowledge. In this sense the Academies are also a condensate of the Third Way, working within and between the fantasies of neo-liberalism and the social fragmentations

which it caused. There are two versions of individualism mixed in here, the classic liberal competitive individual on the one hand and the active, socially responsible, self-governing citizen on the other, what Giddens calls 'new individualism' and Rawls (1993) 'civic humanism'.[6] This Giddens asserts to be the need for living 'in a more open and reflective manner than previous generations' (Giddens 1998) involving 'a new balance between individual and collective responsibilities' (p. 37).

Box 7.3 Bexley Business Academy

Bexley Business Academy replaced Thamesmead community college, specialising in business and enterprise it opened in September 2002. Sir David Garrard [personal wealth £90 million], chairman of property investors Minerva plc., donated £2m to establish the academy. Mr Garrard is a trustee of the Police Foundation and joint chairman of the international centre for children's studies. The Department for Education and Skills wants the Bexley academy eventually to incorporate a primary school. Mr Garrard said: "I expect to get personal satisfaction from giving something back."

"All children deserve to have the same opportunities, enjoy the same facilities and benefit from the same intellectual stimuli regardless of their social and financial background. Students who come through these doors know that to be ambitious and to aspire to all that the world has to offer is good and that at The Academy they will be supported and nurtured in their aspirations because they deserve the very best. The students at The Business Academy Bexley will learn that no goal is beyond their reach and no prize is unobtainable."

The Academy covers National Curriculum work in four days and Friday is devoted to business-related studies and students can work in a 'trading pit' and build share portfolios in mock trading sessions.

> The school is designed around flexible open areas and 'class-rooms' have clusters of flat-screen display computers and white-boards. The pupils have email accounts through which they can submit homework and registration is done electronically. The 6th Form (16–18 years) will offer the International Baccalaureate.
>
> (Academy website)

- The Academies as 'publicly funded independent schools' are outside of LEA control and relate directly to the DfES Academies Division. They have, as put in the 2005 White Paper, 'freedom to shape their own destiny in the interest of parents and children' (p. 24). Sponsors provide 10 per cent of the costs up to a maximum of £2 million, and restrictions on the running of an Academy are set out in a funding agreement, but sponsors may choose their staff and appoint the majority of governors, with one LEA governor and one elected by parents. 'Issues of ethos, specialism and uniform are entirely for you' (DfES 2005a). They are exempt from the specific requirements of the National Curriculum. In all these respects they represent *a 'break' from roles and structures and relationships of accountability of a state education system.* They replace the democratic processes of local authority control over schools with technical or market solutions. They also have the opportunity to set aside existing national agreements on the pay, conditions and certification of teachers – the flexibilisation of the workforce. This is a radical move in a more general push for the 'modernisation' of the school workforce – 'workforce re-modelling' – which is now the responsibility of the Training and Development Agency for Schools (TDA), one of an increasing number of new 'lead organisations' in the transformation project.

- Over and against this, the Academies are also intended to offer new *'choice' options and greater diversity* of choice for parents. In this sense Academies compete with other local schools to recruit students. (Sandwell LEA sees the establishment of an Academy as a means of raising student achievement, stemming the flow of students out of the Borough and attracting more able students.) They provide models for the Trust schools proposed in the 2005 White Paper which will harness 'external support and a success culture, bringing innovative and stronger leadership to the school, improving standards and extending choice' (pp. 24–5). In this way two dynamics of reform come together, autonomy, flexibility and business-like innovation on the one hand and consumer choice and the freedom to respond and expand on the other. It is less clear how the competitive impetus will sit alongside the emphasis on partnership and knowledge as a common resource.

- They are also one point of articulation of New Labour's project of *'transformational leadership'* – a move beyond and between bureaucracy

Box 7.4 Capital City Academy

Capital City Academy, Brent, specializing in sports. Sponsor: Sir Frank Lowe. Opened September 2003. Approximately 10% of students have been chosen on sporting ability, although the aim is to create a 'culture of success,' improving standards across the entire curriculum. The school is designed by architect Norman Foster.

Sir Frank Lowe is chairman of the Lowe Group, an advertising agency he started in 1981 with five people in two rooms. The agency now spans 80 countries and is ranked fourth in the world. He donated £25,000 to Labour MP Frank Dobson's bid to become London mayor in 2000 and is also a Labour party donor. Downing Street reputedly called him to ask him to fund the school. He said: "I have no knowledge of education in the sense of how to run a school, but I might be able to help. I might be able to inspire a few of the children."

"In order to achieve its goals, I believe very strongly that Brent's new Capital City Academy must be the school the local community wants. Recognising this, the school is committed to being a good neighbour, making its facilities – sporting and academic   widely available to local people, outside school hours."

(Academy website)

and management to instil responsiveness, efficiency and performance improvement into the public sector. 'Here the practitioner is viewed as facing outwards, building partnerships and engaging communities for the purpose of delivering "joined-up" and sustainable policy outcomes' (Newman 2005: 720). These are dynamic, visionary, risk-taking, entre-preneurial individuals (like David Trigg or Valerie Bragg – see Chapter 5) who can 'turn around' histories of 'failure', deploying their personal qualities in so doing, and, as Newman (p. 721) notes, 'this idea is entirely consonant with the style of Blair himself'. 'The driving force at this critical juncture is leadership . . . It is the vocation of leaders to take people where they have never been before and show them a new world from which they do not want to return' (Barber and Phillips 2000: 11 – two of Labour's key education advisers). The model here again is business and the firm. The literature and discourse of school leadership draw explicitly on business writing and business gurus. Leaders, as opposed to managers (see Thrupp and Willmott 2003 on this distinction), are the key agents in the re-culturing and re-engineering of the welfarist school. Davies and Ellison (1997: 5) see leadership as part of the 'second wave' of education reform and as about 'hearts and minds' rather than structures; 'we consider it equally important to reengineer mindsets as well as processes within schools'.

In an attempt to summarise and exemplify the Academy condensate (see Figure 7.1), let us look in a little more detail at one school and one sponsor – the West London Academy and Sir Alec Reed.

Alec Reed CBE – hero of enterprise/Third Way capitalist

'Innovations and innovative people give competitive advantage' (Reed 2002).

Alec Reed is a new kind of policy entrepreneur, a proselytiser for enterprise and creativity – an educationalist and businessman, writer, professor and philanthropist. He demonstrates the complexity of the new form of governance apparent in the overlapping and inter-linking roles of the new policy actors and the complexity of the actors themselves. The Reed Group of companies works with the private and public sector to provide specialist employment services, including to schools. Alec Reed himself runs a charity (the Academy for Enterprise) which sponsors specialist schools and he sponsors an Academy (West London) but has been criticised in the press for charging fees from his companies to the school. He is 606th in the 2004 *Sunday Times* Rich List with family wealth of £67 million. An article in *Creating Wealth* (PWC customer magazine, http://www.bestbusinesswriting.com/interview-Reed.html) describes Alec Reed as 'an innovator, a businessman and an educationalist with a power vision'. He is Professor of Innovation at Royal Holloway and Bedford College (and set up a course there, LIES – Leadership, Innovation and Enterprise Studies – which in itself encompasses many of the themes outlined above), and Visiting Professor of Enterprise at Guildhall University. He has worked with four think tanks: the Adam Smith Institute, Demos, EPRI and the Smith Institute. In his book *Capitalism is Dead – Peoplism Rules* (2002), Reed argues that creative and innovative people have become fundamental sources of value and wealth in business and the economy and that there has been a 'shift in power in the workplace from capitalism to people'. He also argues in the book that 'Business is more than just making money, and it has got to have a social return as well. Social responsibility has replaced institutions like the church' (http://libr.org/isc/articles/18-Reviews.html). Peoplism means valuing employees, or 'co-members' as they are called in Reed companies. Individuals who thrive in the people economy are a new breed of 'skillionaires' benefiting from their talents and creativity. He sees a future in which employees are shared and career is integrated with charitable work, family life and breaks. Many of these ideas are embedded in the West London Academy. He also envisages 'citizen accounts', to which we are charged for services we use and from which payments are taken once we reach the threshold for tax. All of this 'fits' well with the Third Way and New Labour's economic and educational discourses of innovation, meritocracy, talented and gifted, knowledge economics and responsibility – Reed is a kind of Third Way capitalist. We can see in his roles, views and activities an interplay of discursive work, influence, symbolisms and interests.

Reed Executive (Alec Reed started the company with £75 in the 1960s) now has 200 branches worldwide, 1,500 employees and a turnover of £250 million. It includes Reed Graduate and Reed Education Professionals, which 'meets the needs of schools, Colleges and Local Education Authorities by providing a quality, total staffing solution'. The latter is a partner with Lancashire LEA and Edge Hill College in Lancashire Teaching Agency (LTA). Reed Learning, which holds prison education contracts, also runs the Reed Business School and deals in 'knowledge and learning management' and 'corporate, outsourced and bespoke learning solutions'. Reed Re-Start is a prison-based charity project.

In November 2001, Alec Reed pledged a personal donation of £2 million to help transform the Compton High School and Sports College, Northolt into a state-of-the-art City Academy, designed by Millennium Bridge architect Norman Foster. Reed Learning provided initial project management consultancy in setting up the Academy and it opened in September 2003. 'The aim is to give the children of Northolt every opportunity to go to a successful school and achieve their potential' (Reed website).

> I went to school in Ealing myself and I feel privileged to be in a position to give something tangible back to the community ... It's not about creating hundreds of Richard Bransons. I want to improve education so that ordinary children have a better life.
>
> (Alec Reed, quoted in *TES*, 22 February 2002)

In 2002 the Academy appointed the country's highest-paid headteacher, on a £120,000 salary and benefits package. But in 2005:

> He was moved by the school's sponsor, Alec Reed ... to an administrative position in an education foundation. The action 'took effect immediately'. Mr Falk, whose leadership style was criticized by Ofsted this summer, will be director of the Academy of Enterprise ... He has been replaced by Hilary Macaulay, who was previously vice-principal at the ADT City Technology College in Wandsworth, a successful secondary school sponsored by an alarm company ... In July, Ofsted delivered a damning report on the school, which singled out Mr Falk's leadership for criticism. In August the school was forced to admit that its GCSE results had worsened since it became an academy.
>
> (Sarah Cassidy, *Independent*, 5 November 2005; based on 2005 Ofsted report, http://www.ofsted.gov.uk/reports/134/ scc_134369_20050630.pdf – the 2006 report noted considerable improvements in management and performance)

Alec Reed is also the founder of the charity Academy for Enterprise, which runs a 'network of UK secondary schools committed towards creating an enterprising school culture. The 27 schools in the network were given over £300,000 towards their successful bid for specialist schools status' (http://www.academyofenterprise.org/schools.shtml). The aim of the Reed College Enterprise Network is to facilitate ideas and practice sharing between schools. 'We have also organised conferences, competitions, pupil enterprise days and INSET days for schools in the network.' The enterprising schools section of the website contains 'research findings from the Reed Colleges of Enterprise and guidance for embedding enterprise throughout the whole school' (Academy for Enterprise website).[7]

The example of Alec Reed illustrates a number of key themes within new governance (see Chapter 5). He is a new policy agent and a proselytiser for a new kind of capitalism, espousing new values. He is a 'responsible' capitalist. He is partner with and participant in several public sector organisations in a variety of roles and part of a circle of discourse which moves between significant sites of articulation and networks of influence in the state, the public sector and civil society. He 'stands for' Third Way principles and embodies its discourses of innovation and creativity and knowledge economics. His charitable work inter-twines with his business interests and these also cross the private and the public sectors.

He brings together the virtues of enterprise and responsibility, social and cultural entrepreneurship (Woods *et al.* 2007). As a hero of these virtues he is a potent policy symbol – as both public-spirited and a wealth creator, a post-Enron, post-bubble capitalist. Such heroes of enterprise are also a kind of condensate and achieve a discursive gravitas in speaking about personal and national priorities as 'enterprise intellectuals' who, as Jessop (2002: 6) puts it, have a key role in the development of 'economic strategies, state projects and hegemonic visions' and in the consolidation of 'an unstable equilibrium among different social forces'. They offer a new kind of imaginative narrative for education and its relation to the economy.[8]

The Academies programme is then a new educational imaginary and microcosm of political transformation and the establishment of a new mode of regulation – constituted within sets of new identities, social relations and institutional orders, that is part of an experimental move and a policy path-finder towards a new 'fix' and new set of relations between state, market, public sector and civil society organised in relation to global competitiveness. It is also a key rhetorical device that ties the project of New Labour into a single seamless reform trope.

The programme represents and advances the reform project, at different levels, along a number of dimensions:

- *Governance* (local and institutional): new partnerships, networks and agencies.
- *Innovation:* the Academies are what Jessop calls 'innovation milieux' and are part of learning localities and urban 'knowledge fabrics' (Amin and Graham 1997).

- *Icons:* in practical, material and symbolic ways Academies are beacons; they are leading edge; they are texts of difference, models of a Third Way and a knowledge economy. They stand for the doing of state education otherwise.
- *Technology:* these are experiments in a new form or perhaps a new language of learning, that is technology rich (in both senses).
- *Flexibilisation or 'occupational recomposition'* (Clarke 2004): as part of the decomposition of national pay structures for education workers and of their conditions of work and more generally the break-up of 'collectivist systems' (Jessop 2002: 155).
- *Re-agenting* (Jones 2003): the entry and validation of new voices in education policy and meaning.
- *Curriculum discourses:* the teaching of enterprise and entrepreneurism and the development of 'meta-capacities' (Jessop 2002: 128). This is a curriculum of 'performance' and 'competence' (Bernstein 1996), of examination and projects, individual and group work, vocational and esoteric knowledge, technology and tradition.
- *Responsibility:* reconstitution of students as enterprising and responsible subjects. This is a complex of social responsibility and individuation, a form of self-organisation. Students are conceived of as responsible for their own learning and for making a planning office for themselves (Alheit 1999).
- *Urban regeneration:* a local/central policy as part of a process of urban revitalisation and the creation of 'entrepreneurial localities' and 'joined-up' social and economic policy at a local level.
- *Trust:* a move against social fragmentation and towards the building of social capital.
- *Organisational ecologies:* a new form of self-organising school, based on the principles of transformational leadership and modelled on the firm.
- *Opportunity:* an innovative, fresh start in addressing under-attainment and social inequalities in education.
- *Collaboration and competition*: Academies occupy contradictory roles as disseminators of good practice and competitors for parental choices.

The programme is explicitly and implicitly tied to the competitiveness project, addressing a number of the key extra-economic conditions for competitiveness, and works to mobilise and penetrate 'micro-social relations in the interests of valorization' (Jessop 2001: 295–6) both in the formation of new entrepreneurs and in the production of marketable 'learning innovations'. The economic and political changes of post-Fordism are here being mirrored or rather strategically disseminated within the education system through the example of the Academies (and other school reform initiatives). But all this is linked at least rhetorically to social policy and equity (inclusion, responsibility and social disadvantage), although 'Half of city academies [are] among worst-performing schools' (*Guardian*, 19 January 2006).

As systems for or symbols of innovation, Academies 'bring the economic, technological and socio-institutional spheres into an unprecedented alliance' (Bullen *et al.* 2006: 64) and demonstrate in education policy the ascendancy of a particular concatenation of 'interests, actions, lucidity and relative strength' (Perez 1983: 360) among those political and economic agents committed to fostering the 'knowledge economy'. Academies are part of the 'hardware' of the knowledge economy discourse.

The programme is also indicative of the proliferation of spatial scales of policy and regulation which are relatively dissociated 'in complex tangled hierarchies' (Jessop 2001: 297), which in part move 'statework out of the state' (Clarke 2004) and involve the creation of new lead organisations and linkage devices (e.g. ASST). These schools, as many others now do, have functional and accountability relationships with sponsors (multiple in some cases), units and divisions within the DfES, local partners, private service companies and non-government agencies (like PUK). 'This is a complex and contradictory system of governance' (Newman 2001). It is also part of an 'unstable, ongoing and unfinished' (Clarke 2004: 119) process of change (see 2005 White Paper).

8   Not jumping to conclusions

The provision of education is a market opportunity and should be treated as such.

> (European Round Table of Industrialists, 'Job creation and competitiveness through innovation', ERT, Brussels, November 1998)

The public sector and the private sector are different. It is dangerous to introduce private sector practices into the development of the essential public services.

> (Lord Browne, CEO of BP, World Economic Forum, Davos, 2005)

For a number of reasons I wanted to escape the burden of writing a conclusion for this study. Book conclusions are modernist conventions which typically represent knowledge in a particularly authoritative way, and I see what I have attempted here as a set of starting points and methodological possibilities rather than as conclusive, although much of what follows does not exactly sound tentative. There are also practical reasons for my reluctance; privatisation is an ongoing and contested process, not a complete, predictable nor necessarily foregone one. The ESI is adapting and developing and my analytical work captures the processes of privatisation at a particular stage in that development. Thus, in the preceding text there are many unfinished thoughts; I am still thinking about a lot of the issues and may change my mind about some of them. Nonetheless, I will foray into some general statements about or commentaries on what has gone before, avoiding summarising the content of chapters or taking up a set of simple or fixed positions that emerge smoothly or obviously from the research presented. My statements are of three kinds: about totalities or epistemes; about ethics; and about inevitability. These three sections roughly map on to the 'tools' of analysis outlined in Chapter 1, and each rests on a different ontological stance.

Totalities

As I have tried to indicate, privatisation involves a variety of kinds of change in political processes and the role of the state, in organisations, people and their social relationships. It may be that we should see privatisation as part of a much larger canvas of social changes and changes in the social. Leys (2001: 63) emphasises the 'interconnectedness of these changes' and claims that 'the analytical task has become more complex . . . the main causal links no longer converge conveniently' (p. 5). He is absolutely right. There are no straightforward paradigms to be applied nor any simple positions from which 'privatisations' can be viewed. Privatisation is an ongoing but unstable process which encompasses changing relationships between the state, capital, the public sector and civil society and which connects the grand flows of the global economy to the re-working of the textures of everyday life, for students and teachers (and researchers), and families. I want to propose that we can think about the extent and consequences of these changes as being epistemic, as involving the 'continuous reshaping of "deep" social relations' as Leys (2001: 2) puts it, in an emerging Market Society within which 'everything is viewed in terms of quantities; everything is simply a sum of value realised or hoped for' (Slater and Tonkiss 2001) and which becomes embedded in our daily lives through an array of subtle processes that take shape as the flesh and bones of the dominant discourse. What is happening is a profound change[1] in the underlying set of rules governing the production of discourses and the conditions of knowledge, in a single period. This constitutes a cultural totality or multi-dimensional regularity, a new 'order of things', a new set of conditions for the possibility of social relations.[2] This general transformation in the nature of social relations – based on the removal of many of the key boundaries which have underpinned modernist thought and a concomitant collapse of moral spheres and a thorough subordination of moral obligations to economic ones (Walzer 1984) – is what Bernstein (1996) calls a dislocation: a break as significant as, and a break from, the creation of the welfare state. In this dislocation a new kind of citizen is produced in relation to new forms of government and governance. More specifically, new kinds of relations to and within education and learning and parenting are being enacted – 'there is a crisis, and what is at stake is the very concept of education itself' (Bernstein 1996: 75).

Generally speaking, within this new episteme, education is increasingly, indeed perhaps almost exclusively, spoken of within policy in terms of its economic value and its contribution to international market competitiveness. Even policies which are concerned to achieve greater social inclusion are edited, modified and co-opted by the requirements of economic participation and the labour market and 'the values, principles and relationships of trade/exchange' (O'Sullivan 2005: 222). Cowen writes about this as the 'astonishing displacement of "society" within the late modern educational pattern' (Cowen 1996: 167). Education is increasingly subject to 'the normative assumptions and prescriptions' of 'economism', and 'the kind of "culture" the school is and can be' (Lingard *et al.* 1998) is articulated in its terms. Within policy this economism is articulated and enacted very generally in the joining up of schooling to the project of competitiveness and to the 'demands' of globalisation and very specifically through the 'curriculum' of enterprise and entrepreneurship.

I have tried to indicate a broader dimension to these changes in terms, on the one hand, of the commodification of parenting and learning relations within the home (as part of a more general commodification of the life course – Blackburn 2006), the targeting of schools for advertising and commercial selling to children and the transformation of more and more of our social and educational relations into opportunities for profit and, on the other, the dissemination of the disciplines of perfection – school improvement, performance management, leadership, etc. – that is a transposition (and sale) of the sensibilities and positivities of management from the private into the public sector.

Within institutions – colleges, schools and universities – the means/end logic of education for economic competitiveness is transforming what were complex, interpersonal processes of teaching, learning and research into a set of standardised and measurable products. The use of benchmarking, National Curriculum levels of achievement, performance indicators and targets, etc. all contribute to this reification of educational processes or, as Basil Bernstein put it, 'the contemporary dislocation, disconnects inner from outer, as a precondition for constituting the outer and its practice, according to the market principles of the New Right' (Bernstein 1996). Social relations are rendered into tables and grids of representation,[3] emptied of affect, of commitment and of the possibility of reflexivity (see Ball 2005). These new currencies of judgement in education provide an infrastructure of comparisons which value practitioners and institutions solely in terms of their productivity and their performances! Productive individuals, new kinds of subjects, are the central economic resource in the reformed, entrepreneurial public sector.

Within all this, as many other writers have noted, knowledge itself is subject to 'exteriorisation' or alienation. This is summed up in Lyotard's terms in a shift from the questions 'Is it true?' and 'Is it just?' to 'Is it useful, saleable, efficient?' (Lyotard 1984). This is the pre-condition of the knowledge economy, or what Lyotard calls 'the merchantilization of knowledge' (p. 51). Knowledge is no longer legitimated through 'grand narratives of speculation and emancipation' (p. 38) but, rather, in the pragmatics of 'optimization' – the creation of skills or of profit rather than ideals. Again, it is economism which defines the purpose and potential of education.[4]

What I am arguing here is that privatisation is not simply a technical change in the management of the delivery of educational services – it involves changes in the meaning and experience of education, what it means to be a teacher and a learner, but is also part of a broader social dislocation. It changes who we are and our relation to what we do, entering into all aspects of our everyday practices and thinking – into the ways that we think about ourselves and our relations to others, even our most intimate social relations. It is changing the framework of possibilities within which we act. This is not just a process of reform; it is a process of social transformation. Without some recognition of and attention within public debate to the insidious work that is being done, in these respects, by privatisation and commodification, we may find ourselves living and working in a world made up entirely of contingencies, within which the possibilities of authenticity and meaning in teaching, learning and research, as well as other aspects of our social lives, are gradually but inexorably eroded.

Ethics

This has been one of the most perplexing and difficult pieces of research and analysis I have undertaken, difficult because of the scope and complexity of the issues involved and perplexing because many of my preconceptions about privatisation have been challenged and some have had to be abandoned.

Over the course of the research I also found it increasingly difficult to find a solid and comfortable personal position from which to view privatisation, partly because it is not a single phenomenon with uniform characteristics. It also became more and more clear to me that a blanket defence of the public sector, as it is or was, over and against the destructive inroads of privatisation, is untenable. There is no going back to a past in which the public sector as a whole worked well and worked fairly in the interests of all learners. There was no such past. The response to privatisation, as Michael Apple puts it, 'cannot be based on the simple assertion that everything we now have has to be defended' (Apple 2006: 44).[5] Some public sector institutions were and are in significant ways ineffective or racist, sexist and class-biased. Over and against this it is difficult to deny that some education businesses do some things well, and perhaps better than some of the public sector, and do enhance the lives and opportunities of some young and not-so-young people. This is not a defence of the private sector as a whole but it may involve an acceptance that some kinds of private sector participation are more defensible than others and that some public sector 'work' is not as defensible as all that. Some critics of privatisation routinely deploy the unexamined superiority of public services values. However, what these are and whether they are really practised rather than just preached is often unclear. Do we mean a set of practices which typify the sector as a whole? Do we mean a social ideal, something to be aimed for or something which is more or less well and routinely enacted? Or is this another romantic fiction, how we would like things to be but they almost never are? Furthermore, if they are practices, surely they are unstable and changing, shifted by the framework of policies within which they are realised, for example by endogenous privatisation. Maybe there is a kind of convergence, a blurring of values or the emergence of new hybrids. If there is something under threat and worth defending then we need to be a lot clearer about what that something is. On the other hand, I have indicated ways in which some businesses have not worked effectively in the interests of their clients. The bottom line for business is ultimately profit. Concerns about profit (or business failures) have led some firms to renege on or sell off their public sector contracts. Markets are by their nature unstable and not all businesses are socially responsible. Education reform policy trades on what is often a romantic view of the private sector erasing its warts and blemishes. Moreover, the more that the ESI consolidates, the more power the providers accumulate, and the more vulnerabilities there will be in the public sector if any of these businesses fail. Perhaps such failures, if they do happen, will lead to a reassessment of private participation. We also need to ask whether the current moral environment in the ESI will stand the longer-term test of changing financial pressures and shareholder interests. As the ESI evolves and the current incumbents move on, will we see a process of values attrition? Further to this, as I indicated in Chapter 3, parts of the infra-structure and some of the delivery of public sector services in the UK are moving into foreign ownership. Maybe in the era of globalisation this does not matter, although clearly there are other countries which do not tolerate this. But it does raise entirely new issues about responsibility for public services which are simply not being discussed publicly.

Embedded in the blurrings and movements across the public/private divide is a new set of ethical positions. The new policy framework of the competition state, and privatisation in particular, constitutes a *new moral environment* for both consumers and producers of education – a form of 'commercial civilisation' (Benton 1992: 118). Within this new moral environment the 'procedures of motivation' which are being realised elicit and generate the drives, relationships and values which underpin competitive behaviour and the struggle for advantage or what Novak (1982) calls 'virtuous self-interest'. Perhaps what we are witnessing then in the celebration of entrepreneurship and the dissemination of the values of the new paradigm of competitiveness in education is the creation of a new ethical 'hidden curriculum' (see Whitty 2002) in and for schools, within which teachers and students learn new iden-tities. In some schools this curriculum is increasingly explicit and the values and practices of enterprise and entrepreneurship are fostered and taught, what Farnsworth (2004) calls a 'business-centred curriculum'. Put crudely, the education market both de-socialises and re-socialises; it destroys older forms of sociability, while at the same time encouraging competitive indi-vidualism and instrumentality. Prevailing values are changed and the spaces within which reflection upon and dialogue over values were possible are closed down and replaced by the teleological promiscuity of the technical and managerial professional, 'a professional who clearly meets corporate goals, set elsewhere, manages a range of students well and documents their achieve-ments and problems for public accountability purposes' (Brennan 1996: 22). Teachers are thus encouraged by the prevailing policy ensemble to recognise and take responsibility for the relationship between their contribution to the competitiveness of their organisation and their security of employment. 'Marketness' replaces 'embeddedness' (Robertson 1996), what O'Sullivan (2005: 230) calls a 'mercantile solidarity, derived from contractual, partial and calculating association'.

Necessities

The new necessities of education policy and their solutions – privatisation – are probably best captured in the simplest sense through the concept of space and the re-spatialisation and re-scaling of education policy – a simultaneity of many political trajectories and processes. Among many dimensions, there is most obviously the subordination of education to the competitive pressures of the global market and the attempt in the UK, and elsewhere, to facilitate a 'knowledge economy' within which surplus value is generated by new kinds of 'immaterial labourers' – involved in both affective and symbolic practices. This new kind of labour is itself spatially particular, working in and through networks of 'continual interactivity' (Hardt and Negri 2000: 291), and I have tried to give some general indications of a 'new correspondence' (Whitty 2002) between schooling and capital in terms of the ways in which schooling is being re-worked by technology and through new forms of temporal and spatial arrangements for learning. Educational institutions increasingly look like, act like and have social and organisational arrangements like those of firms. Students are also being made up differently and can be 'home schooled' or virtually 'connected' to a digital schooling community, and they can choose among diverse providers and curricular offerings – a borderless education. The spaces of knowledge itself are reorganised as sequences of knowledge gobbets ('Bytesize' as it is on the BBC revision website) which can be transferred as 'credits' and combined in novel ways with no guarantee of internal coherence – a 'cut and paste curriculum', as Robertson (2000) calls it, fluid and non-linear. In such changes, students are rendered as active consumers but passive (and responsible) learners (Fabos and Young 1999; Cloete *et al.* 2001). In the home, learning and recreation are blurred into new forms of 'edutainment' and state education can be supplemented by parents buying in expert services or enrichment activities for their children (Vincent and Ball 2006).

Schools are becoming new kinds of spaces and places as they are rebuilt and re-designed, figuratively and literally. They stand for, are icons of, new policy, new modalities of learning – the products of a re-imagineering. They have new kinds of social and architectural ecologies, which promise new kinds of learning experience, in technologically rich, flexible learning environments. They represent learning in new kinds of ways with flair and dynamism, a break from, policy tells us, both the lumpen commonalities and the class-ridden divisions of the previous education policies regimes. They are also assets, owned by construction companies or private equity funds (national and foreign), providing long-term income flows and built for flexible use, which can be bought and sold in financial markets. They are spaces in which new kinds of policy actors can act out their ideas about education and personal commitments (social, moral and religious). The public sector generally is now thoroughly enmeshed within the 'systemic power of finance and financial engineering' (Blackburn 2006: 39). Finance capital (e.g. HSBC, Goldman Sachs, UBS) is involved in school financing in a wide variety of ways, ranging from PFI project funding to sponsorship and philanthropy. New-generation schools (like Academies) are also joined up with and open to their communities, with facilities (swimming pools and post offices) and services (health and business centres), longer hours and shared spaces (cyber-cafés, conference centres). Variously in these ways education is both more global and more local, and new 'power geometries' (Massey 1994) are emerging, creating new patterns of social access and exclusion – a highly complex social differentiation set alongside new insecurities. Schools are more 'open' in other senses. In the context of competitive and contract funding, there is an individuation of schools *and* of the school workplace involving more and more short-term projects, and freelancers, consultants and agency workers with fixed-term contracts and skill mixes – some of these new kinds of workers are 'with' and 'for' the organisation, rather than 'in' it, as Wittel (2001: 65) puts it. Social ties within educational work become ephemeral, disposable, serial, fleeting – and educational labour is 'flexibilised' and made more amenable to the requirements of competition between institutions and the generation of 'profit'. This further contributes to the dissolution of older moral obligations and the invention of new ones, the dissolution of older professional identities and the invention of new ones.

The spaces of policy have also changed in other ways. Policy itself is being done in new places by different people, locally, nationally and internationally; the creation of a European 'education space' and the competition policies of the World Trade Organization insinuate themselves into, or simply over-ride, 'national' policy-making. The SWS is in important ways a post-national state. The places that matter for policy are more dispersed. There are shifting 'geographies of power' (Robertson and Dale 2003). There are school autonomies (reflexive self-organisation) of a sort. There are new networked federations of schools and colleges and universities and multiple partnerships, both local and dispersed, relating together through digital communication and economies of scale. There are entrepreneurial localities, and their networked 'growth alliances'. There is a proliferation of new non-governmental agencies, lead and link organisations and trusts, most of which are also required to act entrepreneurially. Many of these also act internationally to disseminate, to learn and to sell – through networks. There are new players, individual and corporate, who sit at the tables of policy, seek influence and favour, and 'do' policy by contract and in relation to outcome measures and performance payments. These policy contexts are, again paradoxically, both more transparent and less visible. Think tanks, advisers and entrepreneurial actors are able to speak about and speak to policy, through new social networks which cross between public, private and voluntary and philanthropic spaces. Identities and interests and commitments morph as the new policy actors move between these locations. Policy discourse flows through these new places, gathering pace and support and credibility as it moves – achieving a high level of active consent. Together all of this constitutes a new but unstable 'spatio-temporal fix' as Jessop (2002) calls it, and as I have been at pains to emphasise it is 'made up' out of a mix of different kinds of policy ideas and is only incoherently coherent.

In relation to all of this the state itself is increasingly dispersed (meta-governance) and in some respects smaller, as it moves from public sector provision to a contracting and monitoring role and engages in its own auto-redesign (destatalisation), but also at the same time more intrusive, surveillant and centred. In particular, as already signalled, the sphere of 'economic policy' is greatly expanded and the state is increasingly proactive in promoting competitiveness and scaffolding innovative capacities – collective and individual – in education and elsewhere through focused funding and strategic interventions.

However, in the heat and noise of reform it would be a mistake to neglect the remaining (and new) spaces of dissent and resistance as well as the resilience of 'discredited' discourses and alternative educational narratives. Unions (http://www.publicnotprivate.org.uk/articles.html), parents and local alliances have organised with some success to oppose some aspects of some policies and to assert their roles as citizens rather than as consumers (Whitty 2002: 79–93) and to defend impersonal concerns and keep education 'in' and 'of' place and 'for' local communities.

The questions raised by all of this concern what kind of future we want for education and what role privatisation and the private sector might have in that future, and crucially how justice and ethical behaviour can be balanced against a necessary pragmatism within a modern and democratic system of education.[6] The task at hand is to understand the situation we are currently in with respect to the phenomenon of privatisations and to develop an appropriate and effective language and set of concepts for thinking about what is happening and about possible alternatives. Only once a proper understanding of privatisation is achieved can we begin to think constructively beyond the pressures of the present. We need to struggle to think differently about education policy before it is too late (e.g. see Yarnit 2006). We need to move beyond the tyrannies of improvement, efficiency and standards, to recover a language of and for education articulated in terms of ethics, moral obligations and values.[7]

Appendix
Research interviews

Leisha Fullick (LF) (ex-Chief Executive of Islington, now Institute of Education)

Chris Abbott (CA) (ex-ILEcc, ILEA schools computing centre, now King's College London)

David McGahey (DM) (VTES)

Simon Lapthorne (SL) (Corporate Synergy)

John Simpson (JS) (Tribal)

Bob Hogg (BH) (Mouchel Parkman)

Peter Dunne (PD) (HBS)

Derek Foreman (DF) (CEA)

Robin Gildersleeve (RG) (Tribal)

Nick Blackwell (NB) (Cocentra)

Paul Lincoln (PL) (Edison Schools UK)

Vic Fairlie (VF) (Capital)

Elaine Simpson (ES) (Serco)

Elenor Sturdy (ESt) (AST/ULT)

Graham McAvoy (GM) (Alligan)

Dennis Sargeant (DS) (LSDA consultant)

Neil McIntosh (NM) (CfBT)

Ray Auvray (RA) (Prospects)

Graham Walker (GW) (Edunova)

Peter Dougill (PDg) (Wandsworth LEA, ex-Capita and DfES)

A DfES civil servant

Extracts from interviews and other direct speech are indicated in the body of the text by double quotation marks.

Notes

1 A 'policy sociology' introduction to privatisation(s): tools, meanings and positions

1 Or more precisely England. Many of the policies and developments referred to in this account do not extend to Scotland, Wales or Northern Ireland.

2 This is a 'relatively open-ended empirical investigation and empirical interpretation that involve[s] no commitment to explanations that rely on generalisations associated with reductionist substantive theories' (Sibeon 2004: 14).

3 Discourse rather than discourses or a discourse. The latter are regulated utterances with a coherence; the former constitute a general domain for the production and circulation of possibilities for thought, syntheses of meaning, rules and structures, within a particular context.

4 Resigned as CEO of Capita in 2006 in the wake of the Labour Party loans for honours scandal.

5 In Cox's terms this constitutes 'a framework for action . . . a particular combination of thought patterns, material conditions, and human institutions which has a certain coherence among its elements' (1996: 97).

6 At times things that have been excluded and perhaps destroyed by policies have to be put back, discursively re-invented and re-legitimated.

7 'As history constantly teaches us, discourse is not simply that which translates struggles or systems of domination, but is the thing for which and by which there is struggle' (Foucault 1981: 52–3).

8 I first deployed Jessop's analytic in a 1997 paper.

9 Transformation is a key term in the lexicon of New Labour in relation to the public sector in general and education in particular. For example, the 2001 Education White Paper *Schools Building on Success* (DfES 2001) begins with a chapter on 'Transforming education'; there is another on 'Primary education transformed' and one on 'Transforming secondary education'.

10 '[A] supercomplex series of multicentric, multiscale, multitemporal, multiform and multicausal processes' (Jessop 2002: 113).

11 In one interview the respondent commented "that everyone [ESI colleagues] said you were very, very anti-private sector, everyone who said about seeing you".

12 Boyles (2000) notes that in US schools Six Flags Theme Parks Inc. has a reading programme, 'Colgate-Palmolive Company operates what it calls a "Dental Health Classroom Project" ' (p. 73), Amoco oil runs science enrichment classes in schools, and Chevron and Ford offer an 'inter-disciplinary curriculum for "average" students' (p. 90). In the UK Procter & Gamble, McDonald's and Kellogg's among many others produce and distribute curriculum materials for schools. Barclays Bank produces booklets aimed at contributing to the citizenship curriculum in schools, and a former Schools' Minister rigorously defended this kind of

commercial involvement in schools: 'young people must learn about . . . business realities . . . business and education partnerships can help young people develop as citizens and improve pupils' educational standards . . . it means businesses such as Barclays going into schools – and bringing students out of schools so the pupils gain an understanding of life outside the school gates' ('Everyone has a responsibility', *Independent*, 25 February 2003) (quoted in Centre for Public Services 2003: 33). And between 1992 and 2001 Tesco supermarkets delivered 42,200 computers to state schools through their customer voucher scheme, most of them bearing the Tesco logo.

13 "I worked pretty closely with the Institute of Education at the time. We worked with Pat Gulliver and Peter Mortimer and tried – in looking at the serving heads bid that was being put forward at that stage – really trying to combine leading educational thinking with leading commercial thinking about learning organisations and about how you make things happen" (Graham Walker, Edunova, then of Arthur Andersen, explaining discussions towards a bid for a contract to run an LEA).

2   Privatisation(s) in contexts

1 This trope obliterates the failings of private sector management (like those of Arthur Andersen, Enron, Jarvis, Ballast, etc.), both romanticising and cleansing private sector practices.

3   Scale and scope: education is big business

1 Sodexho and Compass, through its subsidiary Scolarest, are the two world leaders in institutional catering. Scolarest provides catering services to 2,500 schools, colleges and universities.

2 Stagecoach Theatre Arts founded in 1988 now operates from 355 UK schools and in 2001 was floated on the AIM.

3 TUPE or Transfer of Undertakings (Protection of Employment) regulations are an important plank of employment law in Britain and, under different names, in other EU countries. Introduced in 1981, they aim to ensure that employees whose company is taken over have their existing conditions respected by their new employer. The regulations also apply in some cases for work transferred to contractors. This includes hours of work, pay, pension entitlement and so on.

4 From 2005 the payment for these services was switched to a monthly management fee (interview GM).

5 'Currently over 50,000 classrooms worldwide operate their group learning systems. The company has grown rapidly and has seen its turnover double year on year, with turnover for 2002 in excess of £24 million and 2003 exceeding £38 million. Promethean's status as a leading provider of whole group interactive technology to the education sector has been achieved in less than five years' (company website).

6 Comprehensive Performance Reviews are conducted by the Audit Commission and give an overall judgement based on the delivery of core services and corporate strength of each local council (see ODPM website).

7 A small number of US states, led by California, have imposed bans or limits on the selling of fizzy drinks in schools. ('Junk food to be banned in schools: Ruth Kelly and Tony Blair attended a school breakfast club in Brighton. Foods high in fat, salt or sugar are to be banned from meals and vending machines in English schools' (http://news.bbc.co.uk/1/hi/education/4287712.stm).)

8 In 2001 the National Consumer Council and the Incorporated Society of British Advertisers in conjunction with the DfES formulated and published good

practice guidelines for dealing with commercial activities in schools. Anecdotally it would appear that the guidelines are not well known in or commonly used by schools.

4 Economics and actors: the social relations of the ESI

1 Ratnapala (2003: 215) defines individual moral capital in relation to 'Persons who are habitually moral in conduct [and] may gain a reputation for trustworthiness that induces others to deal with them.'

2 Antonsen and Jorgensen (1997) found that organisations where public sector values have a high presence show a low rate of change.

3 However, Maesschalk (2004) identifies as a key public sector value 'a long term perspective, societal goals are more important than the immediate satisfaction of users' (p. 350). New public sector values, borrowing from the private sector, give stress to the short term and priority to user satisfaction.

5 New governance, new communities, new philanthropy

1 Ted Wragg's (*Times Educational Supplement*) character Tony Zoffis is the organising mind behind a great deal of educational change in recent years.

2 I am not sure that the latter is always the case. Again the term is applied to a wide variety of arrangements (see Cardini 2006), and Newman's definition of networks is related to her particular interest in local policy initiatives, but the distinction is a good starting point.

3 IPPR (2001) *Building Better Partnerships: Commission on Public Private Partnerships* identifies seven types of partnership.

4 Partnership is also a necessary aspect of the relations of the companies with one another, for example in Academies work or joint bids for programme contracts (other examples have been quoted).

5 Networks refer to relationships and community to the actors.

6 Selwyn and Fitz (2001: 130) make the important point that policy communities like these are also to a great extent 'state-directed'.

7 Sir Paul Judge is Chairman of the Teachers' TV Board of Governors, is a former Director-General of the Conservative Party and Ministerial Adviser at the Cabinet Office. He is Chairman of the Royal Society of Arts, Manufactures and Commerce and President of the Association of MBAs.

8 The Academies and Specialist Schools Trusts are now merged (as the ASST). For clarity of presentation I have kept them separate here.

9 iNet is the international arm of the Specialist Schools Trust.

10 'The job of a social entrepreneur is to recognize when a part of society is stuck and to provide new ways to get it unstuck ... Nothing is as powerful as a big new idea – if it is in the hands of a first class entrepreneur' (Ashoka website). The UK government has set up an agency called Futurebuilders which has a £215 million fund to make loans to social enterprises.

6 Selling improvement/selling policy/selling localities: an economy of innovation

1 All the quotations used come from company brochures or website documents and these were accessed during 2005. For examples of full documents see: http://www. cocentra.info/gateway/uploads/panda%20leaflet.pdf, http://www.edisonschools. co. uk/ and http://www.prospects.co.uk/data_page.asp? pageID=97& mid=4.

2 This new kind of learning is highly individualised and personalised, undertaken by responsible learners who are self-directing and self-monitoring, who use new

technologies to maximise their learning, whose learning is accelerated, who learn to learn rather than being dependent on fixed bodies of knowledge, who are thus rendered as flexible learners, high-modern learners – the 'basic figures' of the new ecology of learning.
3 Some of these companies are also inspection contractors; they derive income from both sides of the inspection process as in effect working for transparency and opacity.
4 Alternatively, endogenous collaborations can through a mutual strengthening of self-confidence bring a release or loosening of the pressures of reform. I am grateful to Phil Woods for making me think more about such scenarios.
5 This would also describe the English education system of the 1960s and 1970s.
6 The question why some and not others is not addressed here.
7 English Heritage has warned of the 'dislocation and loss of community cohesion' which may occur as a result.

7   Policy controversies: failures, ethics and experiments

1 '*Classrooms languish half-built as £340m PFI project covering 27 schools, collapses.* The biggest privately-financed school building scheme in the South-east was halted this week after a construction company involved in a £340 million PFI project went bust. Ballast plc had been sub-contracted by the Tower Hamlets Schools Partnership to carry out major building and repair work at 27 of its east London schools. Last week Ballast's Dutch parent company Ballast Needham stopped funding its UK subsidiary and it was placed in administration' (Dorothy Lepkowska and Karen Thornton, 'Private finance builder goes bust', *TES*, 24 October 2003).
2 In March 2005 Unity City Academy 'failed' its Ofsted inspection. The inspection report found that 'The weaknesses in provision, low standards and the fact that pupils make insufficient progress as they move through the academy mean that overall, leadership and management are unsatisfactory.'
3 Some respondents reported that some local councillors have been told that if they do not accept an Academy then no other sources of capital funding, for instance through Building Schools for the Future, will be made available to them.
4 This clustering is also produced by a concatenation of local and national political 'willingness' to take New Labour reforms very seriously.
5 Three academy sponsors – Garrard (£2.3 million), Townsley (£1 million) and Aldridge (£1 million) – also made 'loans' to the 2005 Labour election campaign (http://news.bbc.co.uk/1/hi/uk_politics/4836024.stm).
6 In writing about the Third Way, Giddens (1998) argues for finding 'a new balance between individual and collective responsibilities'.
7 There is already a diverse and sophisticated educational and political network supporting and disseminating 'enterprise education' and the 'building of enterprise skills' in schools, a great deal of which is funded by the Treasury and its 'enterprise team' and the agenda for which was set by the Treasury's Davies Review. Regional Development Agencies are involved and most LEAs run Education Business Partnerships. Manchester Metropolitan University runs a Master in Enterprise programme. The *Youth Matters* Green Paper and the *Every Child Matters* targets both address the development of enterprise skills.
8 But they represent only one of several versions of capitalism. There are paradigmatic differences within business different positions in relation to responsibility, and different interpretations of vocationalism (see Ball 1990 on progressive vocationalists).

8 Not jumping to conclusions

1 Or at least marked 'mutation' which involves new ways of representing and constituting 'man in so far as he lives, speaks, and produces' (Foucault 1970) and a collapse of life, labour and language into a single positivity.
2 That is a move beyond existing forms of fetishism and commodification.
3 Without in any way eliminating the paradox of invisibility – given the use of promotion and fabrication to simulate organisational performances.
4 'In the computer age, the question of knowledge is now more than ever a question of government' (Lyotard 1984: 9).
5 And, as Michael Apple suggests, 'we may need to take seriously the possibility that some of the intuitions behind new managerial impulses and audits may also constitute an improvement over previous visions of educational policies and practices' (Apple 2006: 23).
6 'Privatization is likely to provide only part of the solution not the whole solution' (Green 2005: 180).
7 Unions like the NUT, the Public and Commercial Services Union and Unison and groups like Catalyst are already doing important work in this respect, and many individual educators struggle daily in their own practices to hold at bay the pressures of commodification. As I write, Greek and Chilean students are occupying schools and universities and demonstrating on the streets in opposition to public sector reforms which might be moves towards forms of privatisation. In England, groups of parents and educators are mounting legal challenges to the creation of new Academies (http://news.bbc.co.uk/1/hi/education/5075268.stm).

References

Alheit, P. (1999) 'On a contradictory way to the "Learning Society": a critical approach', *Studies in the Education of Adults*, 31(1): 66–82.

Amin, A. and Graham, S. (1997) 'The ordinary city', *Transactions of the Institute of British Geographers*, 22(4): 411–42.

Antonsen, M. and Jorgensen, T. B. (1997) 'The "publicness" of public organizations', *Public Administration*, 75(2): 337–57.

Apple, M. (1986) *Teachers and Texts: A Political Economy of Class and Gender Relations in Education*, New York: Routledge.

Apple, M. (2006) *Educating the Right Way: Markets, Standards, God and Inequality*, 2nd edn, New York: Routledge.

Atkinson, R. and Savage, S. P. (2001) 'New Labour and Blairism', in S. P. Savage and R. Atkinson (eds), *Public Policy under Blair*, Basingstoke: Palgrave.

Ball, S. J. (1990) *Politics and Policymaking in Education*, London: Routledge.

Ball, S. J. (1994) *Education Reform: A Critical and Post-Structural Approach*, Buckingham: Open University Press.

Ball, S. J. (1994) 'Political interviews and the politics of interviewing', in G. Walford (ed.), *Researching the Powerful in Education*, London: UCL Press.

Ball, S. J. (1998) 'Ethics, self interest and the market form in education', in A. Cribb (ed.), *Markets, Managers and Public Service?*, Occasional Paper No. 1, London: Centre for Public Policy Research, King's College London.

Ball, S. J. (2000) *School-Based Management: New Culture and New Subjectivity*, Lisbon: Superior School of Education and Open University of Portugal.

Ball, S. J. (2001) 'Performativities and fabrications in the education economy: towards the performative society', in D. Gleeson and C. Husbands (eds), *The Performing School: Managing Teaching and Learning in a Performance Culture*, London: RoutledgeFalmer.

Ball, S. J. (2002) 'School-based management: new culture and new subjectivity', *Da invetigacao as praticas: Esrudos de Natureza Educacional*, 3(1): 59–67.

Ball, S. J. (2003) 'The teacher's soul and the terrors of performativity', *Journal of Education Policy*, 18(2): 215–28.

Ball, S. J. (2004) 'Education for sale: the commodification of everything!', Annual Education Lecture, King's College London.

Ball, S. J. (2005) 'SERALecture 2005: educational reform as social barbarism: economism and the end of authenticity', *Scottish Educational Review*, 37(1): 4–16.

Bannock, C. (2003) *Evaluation of New Ways of Working in Local Education Authorities*, Vol. 1: *Main Report*, London: DfES.

Barber, M. and Phillips, V. (2000) 'Fusion: how to unleash irreversible change (lessons for the future of system-wide school reform)', Paper to the DfEE Conference on Education Action Zones.

Baudrillard, J. (1998) *The Consumer Society*, London: Sage.

Beck, U. (1992) *Risk Society: Towards a New Modernity*, Newbury Park, CA: Sage.

Bennett, R. and Gabriel, H. (1999) 'Headteacher characteristics, management style and attitudes towards the acceptance of commercial sponsorship by state-funded schools', *Marketing Intelligence and Planning*, 17(1): 41–52.

Benton, T. (1992) 'Adam Ferguson's critique of the "enterprise culture" ', in P. Heelas and P. Morris (eds), *The Values of the Enterprise Culture: The Moral Limits of Markets*, London: Routledge.

Bernstein, B. (1996) *Pedagogy, Symbolic Control, and Identity*, London: Taylor & Francis.

Blackburn, R. (2006) 'Finance and the fourth dimension', *New Left Review*, 39 (May/June): 39–70.

Blackburn, S. (2001) *Being Good*, Oxford: Oxford University Press.

Boyles, D. (2000) *American Education and Corporations: The Free Market Goes to School*, New York: Falmer Press.

Brennan, M. (1996) 'Multiple professionalism for Australian teachers in the information age?', American Educational Research Association Conference, New York.

Brereton, M. and Temple, M. (1999) 'The new public service ethos: an ethical environment for governance', *Public Administration*, 77(3): 455–74.

Brown, P. and Lauder, H. (2001) *Capitalism and Social Progress: The Future of Society in a Global Economy*, Basingstoke: Palgrave.

Brown, P., Green, A. and Lauder, H. (2001) *High Skills: Globalisation, Competitiveness and Skill Formation*, Oxford: Oxford University Press.

Buckingham, D. and Scanlon, M. (2005) 'Selling learning: towards a political economy of edutainment media', *Media Culture Society*, 27(1): 41–58.

Bullen, E., Fahey, J. and Kenway, J. (2006) 'The knowledge economy and innovation: certain uncertainty and the risk economy', *Discourse*, 27(1): 53–68.

Cabinet Office (1999) *Modernising Government*, Cm 4310, London: HMSO.

Campbell, C., Evans, J., Askew, S., Hughes, M. and McCallum, B. (2004) *Evaluation of Education Partnership Boards*, London: Institute of Education, University of London.

Cardini, A. (2006) 'An analysis of the rhetoric and practice of educational complexities, tensions and power', *Journal of Education Policy*, 21(4): 393–415.

CBI (2005) *The Business of Education Improvement*, London: CBI.

Centre for Public Services (2003) *Mortgaging our Children's Future*, Sheffield: University of Sheffield.

Centre for Public Services (2005) *Strategic Partnership in Crisis: An Investigation of the Strategic-Delivery Partnership between HBS Business Services Group and Bedfordshire County Council*, Bedford: Bedfordshire Unison.

Cerny, P. (1990) *The Changing Architecture of Politics: Structure, Agency and the Future of the State*, London: Sage.

Chouliaraki, L. and Fairclough, N. (1999) *Discourse in Late Modernity: Rethinking Critical Discourse Analysis*, Edinburgh: University of Edinburgh Press.

Clarke, J. (2004) *Changing Welfare, Changing States: New Directions in Social Policy*, London: Sage.

Clarke, J. and Newman, J. (1997) *The Managerial State: Power, Politics and Ideology in the Remaking of Welfare*, Bristol: Policy Press.

Clarke, J., Gewirtz, S. and McLaughlin, E. (eds) (2000) *New Managerialism*, London: Sage.

Clarke, J., Langan, M. and Williams, F. (2001) 'Remaking welfare: the British welfare regime in the 1980s and 1990s', in A. Cochrane, J. Clarke and S. Gerwirtz (eds), *Comparing Welfare States*, 2nd edn, London: Sage.

Cloete, N., Fehnel, R., Maasen, P., Moja, T., Perold, H. and Gibbon, T. (eds) (2001) *Transformation of Higher Education: Global Pressures and Local Realities*, Cape Town: CHEPS/Juta.

Cochrane, A., Langan, M. and Gewirtz, S. (eds) (2001) *Comparing Welfare States*, 2nd edn, London: Sage.

Cohen, N. (2004) *Pretty Straight Guys*, London: Faber & Faber.

Coleman, W. D. and Skogstad, G. (1990) *Policy Communities and Public Policy in Canada*, Toronto: Copp Clark Pitman.

Colley, H., James, D., Tedder, M. and Diment, K. (2003) 'Learning as becoming in vocational education and training: class gender and the role of vocational habitus', *Journal of Vocational Education and Training*, 55(4): 471–96.

Convery, A. (1999) 'Listening to teachers' stories', *International Journal of Qualitative Studies in Education*, 12(2): 131–46.

Coopers & Lybrand (1988) *Local Management of Schools: A Report to the Department of Education and Science*, London: Coopers & Lybrand.

Cowen, R. (1996) 'Last past the post: comparative education, modernity and perhaps post-modernity', *Comparative Education*, 32(2): 151–70.

Cox, B. (1996) *Superdistribution: Objects as Property on the Electronic Frontier*, Reading, MA: Addison-Wesley.

Crouch, C. (2003) *Commercialisation or Citizenship*, London: Fabian Society.

Crump, S. and Slee, R. (2005) 'Robbing public to pay private? Two cases of refinancing education infrastructure in Australia', *Journal of Education Policy*, 20(2): 243–58.

Davies, B. and Ellison, L. (eds) (1997) *School Leaderships for the 21st Century*, London: Routledge.

Davies, B. and Hentschke, G. (2005) *Public/Private Partnerships in Education*, Nottingham: National College for School Leadership.

Dean, M. (1999) 'Risk, calculable and incalculable', in D. Lupton (ed.), *Risk and Sociocultural Theory: New Directions and Perspectives*, Cambridge: Cambridge University Press.

DfEE (1997) *Excellence in Schools*, London: DfEE.

DfEE (1998) *The Learning Age: A Renaissance for a New Britain*, London: Stationery Office.

DfES (2001) *Schools Building on Success*, White Paper, London: DfES.

DfES (2005a) *Academies Sponsor Prospectus*, http://www.standards.dfes.gov.uk/academies/pdf/Amended05prospectus.pdf?version=1.

DfES (2005b) *Higher Standards, Better Schools for All: More Choice for Parents and Pupils*, White Paper, London: DfES, http://www.dfes.gov.uk/publications/schoolswhitepaper/.

Driver, S. and Martell, L. (2003) 'New Labour: politics after Thatcherism', in A. Chadwick and R. Heffernan (eds), *The New Labour Reader*, Cambridge: Polity Press.

du Gay, P. (2000) 'Entrepreneurial governance and public management: the anti-bureaucrats', in J. Clarke, S. Gewirtz and E. McLaughlin (eds), *New Managerialism, New Welfare?*, Buckingham: Open University Press/Sage.

Eagle, A. (2003) *A Deeper Democracy: Challenging Market Fundamentalism*, London: Catalyst.

Edwards, P. (2000) 'Late twentieth century workplace relations: class struggle without classes', in R. Crompton, F. Devine, M. Savage and J. Scott (eds), *Renewing Class Analysis*, Oxford: Blackwell/Sociological Review.

Edwards, R. and Nicoll, K. (2001) 'Researching the rhetoric of lifelong learning', *Journal of Education Policy*, 16(2): 103–12.

Esping-Andersen, G. (ed.) (1996) *Welfare States in Transition: National Adaptations in Global Economies*, London: Sage with UNRISD.

Exworthy, M. and Halford, S. (1999) 'Professionals and managers in a changing public sector: conflict, compromise and collaboration?', in M. Exworthy and S. Halford (eds), *Professionals and the New Managerialism in the Public Sector*, Buckingham: Open University Press.

Fabos, B. and Young, M. (1999) 'Telecommunications in the classroom: rhetoric versus reality', *Review of Educational Research*, 69(3): 217–60.

Fairclough, N. (2000) *New Labour, New Language*, London: Routledge.

Falconer, P. and Mclaughlin, K. (2000) 'Public–private partnerships and the "New Labour" Government in Britain', in S. Osborne (ed.), *Public–Private Partnerships: Theory and Practice in International Perspective*, London: Routledge.

Farnsworth, K. (2004) *Corporate Power and Social Policy in a Global Economy: British Welfare under the Influence*, Bristol: Policy Press.

Fergusson, R. (2000) 'Modernizing managerialism in education', in J. Clarke, S. Gewirtz and E. McLaughlin (eds), *New Managerialism, New Welfare?*, Buckingham: Open University Press/Sage.

Fitz, J. and Beers, B. (2002) 'Educational management organisations and the privatisation of education in the US and the UK', *Comparative Education*, 38(2): 137–54.

Foucault, M. (1970) *The Order of Things*, New York: Pantheon.

Foucault, M. (1980) 'Two lectures', in C. Gordon (ed.), *Power/Knowledge*, London: Longman.

Foucault, M. (1981) 'The order of discourse', trans. R. Young, in R. Young (ed.), *Untying the Text: A Poststructuralist Reader*, London: Routledge.

Fullan, M. G. (2001) *Leading in a Culture of Change*, San Francisco: Jossey-Bass.

Gewirtz, S. (1999) 'Education Action Zones: emblems of the Third Way?', in H. Dean and R. Woods (eds), *Social Policy Review*, 11, Social Policy Association, Bristol: Policy Press.

Gewirtz, S., Ball, S. J. and Bowe, R. (1995) *Markets, Choice and Equity in Education*, Buckingham: Open University Press.

Giddens, A. (1996) *Introduction to Sociology*, New York: Norton.

Giddens, A. (1998) *The Third Way: The Renewal of Social Democracy*, Cambridge: Polity Press.

Giroux, H. A. (1992) 'Language, difference and curriculum theory: beyond the politics of clarity', *Theory into Practice*, 31: 221–7.

Granovetter, M. (1985) 'Embeddedness', *American Journal of Sociology*, 91(3): 481–510.

Green, C. (2005) *The Privatization of State Education: Public Partners, Private Dealings*, London: Routledge.

Green, D. (1987) *The New Right*, London: Wheatsheaf.

Grimshaw, D. and Hebson, G. (2004) 'Public–private contracting: performance, power and change at work', in M. Marchington, D. Grimshaw, J. Rubery and H. Wilmott (eds), *Fragmenting Work: Blurring Organizational Boundaries and Disordering Hierarchies*, Oxford: Oxford University Press.

Hall, D. and Lobina, E. (2004) 'Private and public interests in water and energy', *Natural Resources Forum*, 28: 268–77.

Hall, S. (2003) 'New Labour's double-shuffle', *Soundings*, 24(1): 10–24.

Hansen, M. B. and Lairidsen, J. (2004) 'The institutional context of market ideology: a comparative analysis of the values and perceptions of local government CEOs in 14 OECD countries', *Public Administration*, 82(2): 491–524.

Hardt, M. and Negri, A. (2000) *Empire*, Cambridge, MA: Harvard University Press.

Hartley, D. (1999) 'Marketing and the "re-enchantment" of school management', *British Journal of Sociology of Education*, 20(3): 309–23.

Hatcher, R. (2000) 'Profit and power: business and Education Action Zones', *Education Review*, 13(1): 71–7.

Hatcher, R. and Hirtt, N. (1999) 'The business agenda behind Labour's policy', in M. Allen (ed.), *Business, Business, Business: New Labour's Education Policy*, London: Tufnell Press.

Haydon, G. (2004) 'Values education: sustaining the ethical environment', *Journal of Moral Education*, 33(2): 116–29.

Hodgson, G. (1999) *Economics and Utopia: Why the Learning Economy Is Not the End of History*, London: Routledge.

Hoggett, P. (1994) 'The modernisation of the UK welfare state', in R. Burrows and B. Loader (eds), *Towards a Post-Fordist Welfare State?*, London: Routledge.

Hubbard, P. and Hall, T. (1998) 'The entrepreneurial city and the "new urban politics" ', in T. Hall and P. Hubbard (eds), *The Entrepreneurial City: Geographies of Politics, Regime and Representation*, Chichester: John Wiley.

Husbands, C. (2001) 'Managing performance in performing schools', in D. Gleeson and C. Husbands (eds), *The Performing School: Managing, Teaching and Learning in a Performance Culture*, Buckingham: Open University Press.

Hutchings, M. (2006) *Private Teacher Supply Agencies: An Under-Researched Aspect of Private Sector Activity in Education*, London: Institute for Policy Studies in Education, London Metropolitan University.

Huxham, C. and Vangen, S. (2000) 'What makes partnerships work?', in S. Osborne (ed.), *Public–Private Partnerships: Theory and Practice in International Perspective*, London: Routledge.

IPPR (2000) *The Private Finance Initiative: Saviour, Villain or Irrelevance*, London: Institute of Public Policy Research.

IPPR (2001) *Building Better Partnerships: Commission on Public Private Partnerships*, London: Institute of Public Policy Research.

Ireson, J. (2004) 'Private tutoring: how prevalent and effective is it?', *London Review of Education*, 2(2): 109–22.

Jessop, B. (1997) 'The entrepreneurial city: re-imagining localities, redesigning economic governance, or restructuring capital?', in N. Jewson and S. Macgregor (eds), *Transforming Cities: Contested Governance and Spatial Dimensions*, London: Routledge.

Jessop, B. (1998a) 'The narrative of enterprise and the enterprise of narrative: place marketing and the entrepreneurial city', in T. Hall and P. Hubbard (eds), *The*

Entrepreneurial City: Geographies of Politics, Regime and Representation, Chichester: John Wiley.

Jessop, B. (1998b) 'The rise of governance and the risks of failure', *International Social Science Journal*, 50(1): 29–46.

Jessop, B. (2001) 'What follows Fordism? On the periodization of capitalism and its regulation', in R. Albritton, M. Itoh, R. Westra and A. Zuege (eds), *Phases of Capitalist Development: Booms, Crises and Globalisations*, Basingstoke: Palgrave.

Jessop, B. (2002) *The Future of the Capitalist State*, Cambridge: Polity Press.

Jessop, B. (2004) 'From localities via the spatial turn to spatio-temporal fixes: the strategic-relational odyssey', Contribution No. 6, SECONS Discussion Forum, University of Bonn.

Jewson, N. and Macgregor, S. (eds) (1997) *Transforming Cities: Contested Governance and Spatial Dimensions*, London: Routledge.

Johnson, N. (ed.) (1999) *Mixed Economies of Welfare: A Comparative Approach*, London: Prentice-Hall Europe.

Jones, K. (2003) *Education in Britain: 1944 to the Present*, Cambridge: Polity Press.

Joseph, K. (1975) *Reversing the Trend*, London: Centre for Policy Studies.

Kavanagh, D. (1987) *Thatcherism and British Politics: The End of Consensus*, Oxford: Oxford University Press.

Kay, J. (2004) *The Truth about Markets: Why Some Nations Are Rich but Most Remain Poor*, London: Penguin.

Kellner, D. (2000) 'Globalization and new social movements: lessons for critical theory and pedagogy', in N. Burbules and C.-A. Torres (eds), *Globalization and Education: Critical Perspectives*, New York: Routledge.

Kenway, J. (1990) 'Education and the Right's discursive politics', in S. J. Ball (ed.), *Foucault and Education*, London: Routledge.

Kenway, J. and Bullen, E. (2001) *Consuming Children: Education–Entertainment–Advertising*, Buckingham: Open University Press.

Kenway, J., Bigum, C. and Fitzclarence, L. (1993) 'Marketing education in the post-modern age', *Journal of Education Policy*, 8(2): 105–22.

Kirkpatrick, I. (1999) 'The worst of both worlds: public services without markets of bureaucracy', *Public Money and Management*, 19(4): 7–14.

Kirkpatrick, I. and Martinez-Lucio, M. (1995) 'Introduction', in I. Kirkpatrick and M. Martinez-Lucio (eds), *The Politics of Quality in the Public Sector*, London: Routledge.

Krugman, P. (1994) 'Competitiveness: a dangerous obsession', *Foreign Affairs*, 73(2): 28–44.

Leadbeater, C. (2000) *Living on Thin Air: The New Economy*, London: Penguin.

Leadbeater, C. (2004) *Personalisation through Participation: A New Script for Public Services*, London: Demos.

Lewin, K. M. (1997) 'Knowledge matters for development', Unpublished Paper, University of Sussex.

Leys, M. (2001) *Market-Driven Politics*, London: Verso.

Lingard, B., Ladwig, J. and Luke, A. (1998) 'School effects in postmodern conditions', in R. Slee, G. Weiner and S. Tomlinson (eds), *School Effectiveness for Whom? Challenges to the School Effectiveness and School Improvement Movements*, London: Falmer.

Lyotard, J.-F. (1984) *The Postmodern Condition: A Report on Knowledge*, Manchester: Manchester University Press.

McFadyean, M. and Rowland, D. (2002) *PFI vs Democracy*, London: Menard Press.

McGee, M. C. (1990) 'Text, context, and the fragmentation of American culture', *Western Journal of Communication*, 54: 274–89.

MacKenzie, R. and Lucio, M. M. (2005) 'The realities of regulatory change: beyond the fetish of deregulation', *British Journal of Sociology*, 39(3): 499–517.

McPherson, A. and Raab, C. D. (1988) *Governing Education: A Sociology of Policy since 1945*, Edinburgh: University of Edinburgh Press.

Macsschalk, J. (2004) 'The impact of NPM reforms on public servants' ethics: towards a theory', *Public Administration*, 82(2): 465–90.

Mahony, P., Menter, I. and Hextall, I. (2004) 'Building dams in Jordan, assessing teachers in England: a case study in edu-business', *Globalisation, Societies and Education*, 2(2): 277–96.

Marsh, D. and Smith, M. (2000) 'Understanding policy networks: towards a dialectical approach', *Political Studies*, 48(1): 4–21.

Massey, D. (1994) *Space, Place and Gender*, Minneapolis, MN: University of Minnesota Press.

Mills, S. (1997) *Discourse*, London: Routledge.

Molnar, A. (2005) *School Commercialism: From Democratic Ideal to Market Commodity*, New York: Routledge.

Newcastle City Council Trade Unions (2002) *Our City Is Not for Sale: The Impact of National, European and Global Policies*, Sheffield: Centre for Public Services.

New Local Government Network (NLGN) (2004) *New Localism in Action: An NLGN Collection*, London: NLGN.

Newman, J. (2001) *Modernising Governance: New Labour, Policy and Society*, London: Sage.

Newman, J. (2005) 'Enter the transformational leader: network governance and the micro-politics of modernization', *British Journal of Sociology*, 39(4): 717–34.

Novak, M. (1982) *The Spirit of Democratic Capitalism*, New York: American Enterprise Institute/Simon & Schuster.

OECD (1995) *Governance in Transition: Public Management Reforms in OECD Countries*, Paris: Organization for Economic Cooperation and Development.

Osborne, D. and Gaebler, T. (1992) *Re-inventing Government*, Reading, MA: Addison-Wesley.

O'Sullivan, D. (2005) *Cultural Politics and Irish Education since the 1950s: Policy Paradigms and Power*, Dublin: Institute of Public Administration.

Ozga, J. (1987) 'Studying education policy through the lives of policy makers', in S. Walker and L. Barton (eds), *Changing Policies, Changing Teachers*, Milton Keynes: Open University Press.

Parker, M. (2000) *Organisational Culture and Identity: Unity and Division at Work*, London: Sage.

Parkinson, M. and Harding, A. (1995) 'European cities toward 2000: entrepreneurism, competition and social exclusion', in M. Rhodes (ed.), *The Regions and the New Europe: Patterns in Core and Periphery Development*, Manchester: Manchester University Press.

Paterson, L. (2003) 'The three educational ideologies of the British Labour Party, 1997–2001', *Oxford Review of Education*, 29(2): 167–86.

Perez, C. (1983) 'Structural change and the assimilation of new technologies in the economic and social system', *Futures*, 15(5): 357–75.

Peters, M. A. and Besley, A. C. (2006) *Building Knowledge Cultures: Education and*

Development in the Age of Knowledge Capitalism, Lanham, MD: Rowman & Littlefield.

Pollack, A. (2004) *NHS plc: The Privatisation of Our Health Care*, London: Verso.

Powell, M. and Glendinning, C. (2002) 'Introduction', in C. Glendinning, M. Powell and K. Rummery (eds), *Partnerships, New Labour and the Governance of Welfare*, Bristol: Policy Press.

Power, S. and Whitty, G. (1999) 'New Labour's education policy: first, second or third way', *Journal of Education Policy*, 14(5): 535–46.

PricewaterhouseCoopers (2005) *Academies Evaluation: Second annual report*, London: DfES, http://www.standards.dfes.gov.uk/academies/publications/.

Rao, N. (1996) *Towards Welfare Pluralism*, Aldershot: Dartmouth Publishing.

Ratnapala, S. (2003) 'Moral capital and commercial society', *Independent Review*, 8(2): 213–33.

Rawls, J. (1993) *Political Liberalism: The John Dewey Essays in Philosophy*, Vol. 4, New York: Columbia University Press.

Reed, A. (2002) *Capitalism is Dead – Peoplism Rules*, London: McGraw-Hill.

Rhodes, R. (1995) *The New Governance: Governing without Government*, State of Britain ESRC/RSA Seminar Series, Swindon: ESRC.

Rhodes, R. (1999) 'Foreword', in G. Stoker (ed.), *The New Management of British Local Governance*, Basingstoke: Macmillan.

Rhodes, R. A. W. and Marsh, D. (1992) 'Policy networks in British politics: a critique of existing approaches', in D. Marsh and R. A. W. Rhodes (eds), *Policy Networks in British Government*, Oxford: Oxford University Press.

Rikowski, G. (2001) *The Battle for Seattle: Its Significance for Education*, London: Tufnell Press.

Rikowski, G. (2003) 'The business takeover of schools', *Mediactive: Ideas, Knowledge, Culture*, 1(1): 91–108.

Robertson, D. (2000) 'Students as consumers: the individualization of competitive advantage', in P. Scott (ed.), *Higher Education Reformed*, London: Falmer Press.

Robertson, S. (1996) 'Markets and teacher professionalism: a political economy analysis', *Melbourne Studies in Education*, 37(2): 23–39.

Robertson, S. (2006) 'Public–private partnerships, digital firms and the production of a neo-liberal education space at the European scale', in K. Gulson and C. Symes (eds), *Out of Place: Contemporary Theories and the Cartography of Education Policy*, London: Routledge.

Robertson, S. and Dale, R. (2003) 'New geographies of power in education: the politics of rescaling and its contradictions', Globalisation, Culture and Education Conference, University of Bristol, BAICE/BER.

Rosamond, B. (2002) 'Imagining the European economy: "competitiveness" and the social construction of "Europe" as an economic space', *New Political Economy*, 7(1): 157–77.

Rose, N. (1996) 'Governing "advanced" liberal democracies', in A. Barry, T. Osborne and N. Rose (eds), *Foucault and Political Reason: Liberalism, Neo-Liberalism and Rationalities of Government*, London: UCL Press.

Ruane, S. (2002) 'Public–private partnerships: the case of PFI', in C. Glendinning, M. Powell and K. Rummery (eds), *Partnerships, New Labour and the Governance of Welfare*, Bristol: Policy Press.

Rutherford, J. (2003) 'PFI: the only show in town', *Soundings*, 24: 41–54.

Saltman, K. J. (2005) *The Edison Schools: Corporate Schooling and the Assault on Public Education*, New York: Routledge.

Saltman, R. B. and Von Otter, C. (1992) *Planned Markets and Public Competition*, Buckingham: Open University Press.

Sayer, A. (2005) *The Moral Significance of Class*, Cambridge: Cambridge University Press.

Schick, A. (1990) 'Budgeting for results: adaptation to fiscal stress in industrial democracies', *Public Administration Review*, 50(1): 26–34.

Sellers, M. P. (2003) 'Privatization morphs into ' "publicization": businesses look a lot like government', *Public Administration*, 81(3): 607–20.

Selwyn, N. and Fitz, J. (2001) 'The National Grid for Learning: a case study of New Labour education policy-making', *Journal of Education Policy*, 16(2): 127–48.

Sibeon, R. (2004) *Rethinking Social Theory*, London: Sage.

Skogstad, G. (2005) 'Policy networks and policy communities: conceptual evolution and governing realities', Canada's Contribution to Comparative Theorizing, Canadian Political Science Association, University of Western Ontario.

Slater, D. and Tonkiss, F. (2001) *Market Society*, Cambridge: Polity Press.

Somers, M. (1994) 'The narrative constitution of identity: a relational and network approach', *Theory and Society*, 23(4): 605–49.

Stronach, I. (1993) 'Education, vocationalism and economic recovery: the case against witchcraft', *British Journal of Education and Work*, 3(1): 5–31.

Taylor, M. (1998) 'Dangerous liaisons: policy influence through partnership', Paper presented at the Centre for Voluntary Organisations Symposium 'Third sector organisations in a changing policy context', September.

Taylor-Gooby, P. and Lawson, R. (1993) 'Introduction', in P. Taylor-Gooby and R. Lawson (eds), *Markets and Managers*, Buckingham: Open University Press.

Thrupp, M. and Willmott, R. (2003) *Education Management in Managerialist Times: Beyond the Textual Apologists*, Maidenhead: Open University Press.

Torrance, H. (2004) 'Systematic reviewing – the "call centre" version of research synthesis: time for a more flexible approach', Paper presented to the ESRC/RCBN Seminar on Systematic Reviewing, University of Sheffield, 24 June.

Unison (2002) 'A web of private interest: how the Big Five accountancy firms influence and profit from privatisation policy', *Positively Public*, London: Unison.

Unison (2004) *PFI: Against the Public Interest*, http://www.unison.org.uk/acrobat/B1457.pdf.

Unison (2005) *The Private Finance Initiative: A Policy Built on Sand – An Examination of the Treasury's Evidence Base for Cost and Time Overrun Data in Value for Money Policy and Appraisal*, London: Unison.

Unity City Academy Development Team (2003) *The Unity City Academy Transformation Opportunity*, London: UCA/Edunova.

Vincent, C. and Ball, S. J. (2006) *Childcare, Choice and Class Practices: Middle-Class Parents and Their Children*, London: Routledge.

Walzer, M. (1984) *Spheres of Justice: A Defence of Pluralism and Equality*, Oxford: Martin Robertson.

Watson, M. and Hay, C. (2003) 'The discourse of globalisation and the logic of no alternative: rendering the contingent necessary in the political economy of New Labour', *Policy and Politics*, 31(3): 289–305.

Wedel, J. R. (2001) *Collision and Collusion: The Strange Case of Western Aid to Eastern Europe*, New York: Palgrave.

Wenger, E. (1998) 'Communities of practice: learning as a social system', *Systems Thinker*, http://www.co-i-l.com/coil/knowledge-garden/cop/lss.shtm.

White, S. (1998) *Interpreting the 'Third Way': A Tentative Overview*, Cambridge, MA: Department of Political Science, MIT.

Whitfield, D. (2001) *Public Services or Corporate Welfare*, London: Pluto Press.

Whitty, G. (2002) *Making Sense of Education Policy*, London: Paul Chapman.

Wittel, A. (2001) 'Towards a network sociality', *Theory, Culture and Society*, 18(6): 51–76.

Woods, P., Woods, G. and Gunter, H. (2007) 'Academy schools and entrepreneurism in education, *Journal of Education Policy*, 22(2).

Wright-Mills, C. (1959) *The Power Elite*, New York: Oxford University Press.

Yarnit, M. (2006) *A New Model of Schooling*, Thinkpiece 10, London: Compass.

Young, H. (1990) *One of Us*, London: Pan.

Index